D1482101

THE TIME OF MY LIFE

THE TIME OF MY LIFE

AN AUTOBIOGRAPHY

GAY BYRNE

with Deirdre Purcell

Gill and Macmillan

Published in Ireland by
Gill and Macmillan Ltd
Goldenbridge
Dublin 8
with associated companies in
Auckland, Delhi, Gaborone, Hamburg, Harare,
Hong Kong, Johannesburg, Kuala Lumpur, Lagos, London,
Manzini, Melbourne, Mexico City, Nairobi,
New York, Singapore, Tokyo
© Gay Byrne, 1989
0 7171 1615 8

Designed by Design Image, Dublin
Print origination by
Design and Art Facilities, Dublin
Printed by
The Bath Press, Bath

All rights reserved. No part of this publication
may be copied, reproduced or transmitted in any
form or by any means, without permission of the
publishers.

British Library Cataloguing in Publication Data
Byrne, Gay
    The time of my life: an autobiography.
    1. (Republic) Ireland. Radio programmes. Television
    programmes. Radio & television programmes.
    Broadcasting. Biographies
    I. Title II. Purcell, Deirdre
    791.44'092'4

ISBN   0-7171-1615-8

DEDICATION

To Kathleen, Crona, and Suzy, the women in my life,
who must once again suffer the embarrassment
of reading even more gumph about the man in theirs.

CONTENTS

■

	Acknowledgments	(viii)
	Prologue	1
1	Family Ways, Family Days	5
2	Growing Up a Dub	37
3	Synger and All That	59
4	A Foot on the Ladder	72
5	Kathleen	90
6	Private Lives	109
7	The Betrayal	124
8	The 'Late Late'	152
9	These We Have Loved	187
10	New Beginnings–Almost	203
11	Pauses for Thought	221
	Index	246

ACKNOWLEDGMENTS

Michael Gill is a most persuasive man. He published successfully my earlier book about the 'Late Late Show' on its tenth anniversary, *To Whom it Concerns*. When he approached me about an autobiography several years ago, I had neither the time, energy nor inclination to do it; I could not face into all the writing again, and said no. But he persisted, and suggested that the time-consuming task of writing be undertaken by someone else.

Deirdre Purcell took on an impossible task: to write a book in the first person as by Gay Byrne. I think she has done so superbly, and in congratulating her I would also like to record my appreciation of her unfailing courtesy and kindness to me during hours of tape-recorded sessions during which she mined all the information out of me. This was frequently done in difficult situations and at inconvenient times, and often with less than full co-operation from me. I admire greatly how she brought the task to fruition.

My brother Al was, as always, a tower of strength and objectivity in reading the book in typescript, and made many helpful suggestions, as did my sister, Mary Orr, who also helped with old photographs and family history. Maura Connolly, my long-time assistant on the 'Late Late Show', did a lot of work with photographs and research, and I thank her for her efforts. My thanks also to Des Gaffney, our own RTE photographer, for his splendid pictures of the show in action through the years. Bridgín and Declan Bonar of Dungloe, Co. Donegal, were handed the typescript almost on a whim one day; they both read it and came back with most helpful comments. I am very grateful. And to my old friend Patsy Sweeney, also of Dungloe, for many words of helpful advice not only with this undertaking but through the many years.

To all those mentioned, I send my appreciation for their time and interest.

PROLOGUE

'Ecce hospes vester, Gay Byrne!'

For those of you who do not have the Latin, friends, that is how one of us doctors would say: 'Here is your host, Gay Byrne!' And that is how I was introduced, on 3 March 1988, to an audience I had not faced before and never in a million years would have expected to face.

Gaybo was being given an honorary doctorate in letters by Trinity College, Dublin. The public orator, Dr J. V. Luce, introduced me: *'Hospes noster candidus de vita et de moribus nostris multa et salutaria disputanda curavit quae nemo antea palam profere est ausus . . .* [Our candid host has masterminded many salutary debates about our life and attitudes, in the course of which he has dared to bring into the open matters never so discussed before . . .] '

The first part of the process was the receipt of a letter from Mr Gerald Giltrap, the Secretary of Trinity College, informing me that my name had been put forward for the honour and seeking my permission to allow the process to continue. He explained that in ninety-nine cases out of a hundred there was never a hitch and the name was accepted by the advisory committee, which includes the Chancellor, the Vice-Provost, and the Registrar. But there is always the chance that it will be rejected—and, Dublin being the village it is, this fact would get around: Gaybo's name was put forward for an honorary degree from Trinity College and Gaybo was rejected. Mr Giltrap said he could give no guarantees.

I felt that it was no shame to be rejected, and I told Mr Giltrap to let my name go ahead. Then I put the knowledge that I was being considered for a degree in Trinity College, Dublin, into a little box marked 'pleasure', which holds all the nicer things in my life. I also felt it was a little step further beyond the Jacobs Awards and Entertainment Awards, to which, although they are lovely to receive as acknowledgment by one's peers, I do not attach all that much importance.

But when I rang my brother Al to tell him he practically broke down, wishing that Ma and Da and Ernest were alive to savour the moment, saying, 'There will be celebrations in Heaven tonight.' Ms Kathleen Watkins rated the honour rather highly too, as did my other brother, Ray. Between them all they were so thrilled that it was hardly necessary for me to raise my heartbeat by a tremor. Without being ungracious, or downgrading the honour in any way, because I did really appreciate it, they got all excited and I did not.

So there I was, giggling, with Maureen Potter on one side of me and

Hugh Leonard on the other, tassels bobbing on the mortar-boards, gags flying; Maureen saying, 'This is it, lads, the door'll fly open and in'll come the Provost: "Joke over, give us back the frocks!" . . . ' Our irreverent voices echoed like those of schoolchildren sharing secrets in church. (We did have to give back the frocks, a fact that deeply shocked Paddy Moloney, D.Mus., who, after the ceremony, it was alleged, actually sent a runner into the robing room to fetch his personal frock so he could take it home. But that may have been a gag from Ms Potter.)

The robes, glowing with their jewel-colours of reds, greens, blues, and purples, were wheeled in on a mobile tailor's rail, the type you see being shunted all over the garment district in New York. The mortar-boards were laid out on a huge board-room table running down the centre of the imposing panelled room in which we robed, sized so they would not fall down over our noses.

When we were ready, we ten—Bernadette Greevy, Paddy Moloney, James Dooge, Hugh Leonard, Carmencita Hederman, Maureen Potter, Willie Bermingham, Kevin Heffernan, Feargal Quinn, and I — 'processed' as nobly as we could across the ancient stones of Front Square towards the Public Theatre. (As we walked, I was really struck by how many ordinary Dubs had come into the square to watch and applaud us.)

At the stroke of three o'clock we went into the historic room in which generations of students, the notorious as well as the famous, perspired over their examinations, overlooked sternly by the brown portraits of ancient bishops and Jonathan Swift, and the founder of the college, Queen Elizabeth I. The organ pealed as we followed the city councillors in their green-and-blue robes past our sons and daughters, wives, husbands, and friends, who, bursting with pride, craned to see us.

We stepped up onto the raised dais at the end of the theatre and sat on our stuffed leather chairs while the organ, having played 'Dublin in the Rare Oul' Times', subsided into ringing silence. That anthem was chosen because this ceremony was to honour us Dubs, we ten who the college had estimated had brought honour to our native city in its millennium year: a celebrated singer, a traditional musician, a real professor, a playwright, a lady Lord Mayor, a comedienne, a fireman who worked tirelessly for the old and alone, a football manager, a grocer—and the host and producer of the longest-running live television chat show in the world.

I thought it was a great, amusing day out. I found it difficult to take it as other than what I believe it was: a sort of showbiz spectacular for the Dublin millennium. If it had been more serious and heavyweight, with people like T. K. Whitaker and Ivor Kenny and all of those guys, well, then I think I would have been a lot more overawed and impressed.

☐ *Aunt Kathleen, grandmother, grandfather and Aunt Mary (above) at Gilspur Lodge, Kilruddery (below), home of my granny and grandad, my father and all his brothers, which was on the Estate of the Earl of Meath. There's no sign left of it now.*

☐

But at the actual conferring, while the public orator read all those flattering things about me, I stood on the mark appointed and I looked down at them all, seated on the wooden folding chairs in their best clothes—Kathleen, Crona, Suzy, Al and Frances, David and Mary, Kathleen's sister Phil, even my godmother, Cathy—and I realised it was one of the few occasions in my life when I have been truly happy. I wished Éamonn could be there. (There will be a lot about Éamonn Andrews in this book.)

I also wished that I could organise my life in such a way that I could fulfil a long-held ambition to get out of the fish-bowl for a couple of years and for that period to concentrate solely on one narrow-based academic subject on which I could become a specialist instead of the widely read but dilletantish grasshopping person I am now. To work solely in one area and on one subject for an extended period would be bliss.

I realised that the last time our family had been in Trinity College was when Al was receiving his hard-won degree. I wondered what he was thinking as he looked at the array of Catholic Dubs on the platform. I know now that he was thinking and feeling himself in and out of a morass of conflicting emotions: how Dublin had changed since his days at Trinity (which he attended between the hours of a split shift recording numbers on barrels of Guinness), where lunch was ninepence but affordable for him only once a week, where the public orator, now so wittily expounding on my virtues and eminent suitability for my honour, was the man who examined him in his 'vivas' in logic—and where all Catholics who went to Trinity, including, briefly, himself, were excommunicated by the hierarchy as personified by John Charles McQuaid, Archbishop of Dublin.

Later, Al stood high on one of the lovely wooden galleries of the atrium overlooking the very jolly entertainment organised by the professor and poet Brendan Kennelly, and heard the Professor of Spanish singing 'The Spanish Lady' and watched the Provost join in with the students in a chorus of 'Molly Malone', while all his family and we new doctors jostled in the large crowd, singing along and clapping.

To him it was almost surreal. How life for the Byrnes had changed! Dr Gay Byrne. At long last. Actually, it is what I had always intended . . .

CHAPTER 1
FAMILY WAYS, FAMILY DAYS

My father was like Brutus: a plain, blunt man. He was one of nine brothers—Alexander, Richard, Edward, Thomas, William, John, Patrick, Robert, and Dan—eight of whom joined the British army (the only exception was Robert) and seven of whom went off to fight in the Great War of 1914–18. Grandfather Alexander Byrne, who also had a daughter, Mary, was coachman to the Earl of Meath, in charge of all the horses and carriages, and was, like all other retainers, given a lodge on the grounds of the earl's estate near Kilruddery, Co. Wicklow. He called his lodge 'Gilspur', and my brother Al has called his own home 'Gilspur' in his memory.

As each of Alexander's sons became old enough he walked with his brothers every morning for an hour and a half around the Little Sugarloaf mountain to the little school in Kilmacanogue, and then walked for an hour and a half to get home, where he was required to help his father on the estate. Each left school at 13 or 14 and worked full-time on the estate until he became old enough to join the British army.

My father was third-youngest in that family, and joined the Irish Guards in 1912, being transferred to the 19th Hussars, Infantry Division, when war broke out, fighting at the Somme and at Ypres. Uncle Dick served in the Royal Horse Artillery. All the brothers were placed in separate regiments; some were even sent to India. The extraordinary thing is that all seven of them who fought in the big battles of that war to end all wars survived and came home, although one—Dan, the youngest in the family—died from mustard-gas poisoning about a year afterwards. My grandfather's proudest day was when he accepted the 'privy purse' (which meant an annuity of £10) from his employer, the Earl of Meath, on behalf of the King. It was awarded for his having sent so many sons to the front.

We know very little of my mother's family, the Carrolls. Ma's mother and father, who were both from Bray, had died before any of us was born. My maternal grandmother's name was de Courcy, which might suggest that at some stage her family had come down in the world; and Ma had four sisters and a brother: Tessie, Kathleen, Maggie, Lizzie, and Tommy.

My father and mother had met before the war on the Dargle Road near Bray. He and his brothers would come into the seaside town, some in a pony and trap, some walking alongside. They were big, strapping six-footers, handsome men who caught the eye of any girls they met along the road; and since they timed their incursions to coincide with May devotions or the other pious rituals that attracted the town girls, they were quite successful. My mother, Annie, and her four sisters were one group that came to their attention, and a sedate courtship began. As it happened, two of the sisters, Annie and Kathleen, married two of the brothers, Edward—who became my father—and Dick. Annie worked as a clerk in the Dargle and Bray Laundry with two of her sisters, but when war broke out and their young men left for the front they all decided that life would be more adventurous elsewhere than in Bray. They went north and took jobs in the Monarch Laundry in Belfast, where the pay was better.

In 1917 my father came home on two weeks' leave from the trenches to marry his Annie in Belfast, and then he went back to war. She made a private vow to God that if he returned safely from the war she would go to Mass and Communion every day for the rest of her life.

He did, and she did. I remember only one or two days when she was just too ill to drag herself out of the bed; otherwise every single day until she died, even after Da died, she fulfilled her promise. (In fact she regularly attended two daily Masses, both eight o'clock and ten o'clock.) Like ninety-five per cent of the men who served in that appalling war, it never crossed my father's mind when safely at home on leave to do a bunk and stay put, safe and sound, even though they knew that back in the trenches their life expectancy was a matter of weeks—with luck. To desert would have been an act of cowardice and treachery to their comrades. Apart from which, if they'd been caught they would have been shot.

The family connection with Guinness's brewery started right after the war when three of the brothers, including my father, got jobs there. The jobs were known in our neighbourhood around the South Circular Road as 'jobs fit for heroes', because of the policy of the Guinness organisation, which went out of its way to offer jobs to soldiers returning victorious from the fight 'for the freedom of small nations'. They were labouring jobs, six days a week, with a fortnight's annual holiday, but the conditions were very humane for the times that were in it, with a free pint of Guinness thrown in morning and evening.

My father, Edward, worked on the barges—or lighters, as they were sometimes called—that plied the Liffey. These were lovely, sturdy craft, with the 'chuff-chuffing' sound from the big steam engines, a sound that boomed excitingly as the slow craft passed under the archways of the

Dublin bridges of stone. Da's run was from the brewery at James's Gate, where he loaded the heavy wooden casks, down to the ships at the North Wall. His talk at home was always of weather and east winds, driving rain and sunshine. He worked hard, and loved his job.

People in our area who worked in Guinness's always had a special status, and this spanned the era of our family involvement, from the early twenties up until the present day. The company had a long and distinguished connection with the city of Dublin. For instance, in 1865 Benjamin Guinness paid for the restoration of St Patrick's Cathedral. A few years later, Arthur, Lord Ardilaun, presented the city with a tract of land, once a medieval common, which was landscaped and opened to the public as St Stephen's Green in 1880. Edward Cecil Guinness established the Guinness and Iveagh Trusts, to provide housing for the poorer working class of Dublin, and built the Iveagh Market.

There were also unofficial perks for the employees, like the days during the years of the Second World War on which Da managed to secure for us some of the lovely soft white loaves of bread that were brought in from Liverpool on the Guinness cargo ships. During those years, we in Ireland ate chewy, indigestible bread, which as time passed became blacker and blacker and more and more unappetising. The 'Emergency', as it was so cutely called in Ireland for most people who did not have friends or relatives actually involved, meant very little except dietary inconvenience. Only those lucky families with sons who were serving with the RAF in sunny climates like Egypt's ever saw a citrus fruit. We all re-used our tea-leaves, spreading them out to dry again and again until they were like specks of dust; and most children of that era developed a sweet tooth because the biggest treat afforded us was bread dipped in milk and spread with sugar.

When one of the Guinness ships, the *Carrowdore* or the *Clarecastle*, was arriving home from Liverpool, she sounded her siren as she came slowly up the Liffey. Da, alert for the signal, no matter what hour of the night or day it was, got up on his bicycle and cycled down to meet her at the North Wall. The crew gave him this beautiful soft white bread for our mother, who could not, she claimed, digest the awful black stuff. It was the sort of bread, tiny white loaves with the consistency of cotton wool, that today's nutritionists would throw down the nearest septic tank, but how we drooled at the sight and smell of them! Needless to remark, the smell was all we got. This bread was for Ma and that was that.

Eventually Da became a barge skipper, a Paycock captain in charge of his own little domain, and he was endlessly patient with the gurriers who, when he was lowering the funnel for passage under O'Connell Bridge, would line the parapet to amuse themselves by shouting smart-alecky

□

remarks like 'Bring us back a parrot!' It was tidal work, and depending on the tides, he left for work and came home at strange hours. It was just normal to all of us children that he would go to work sometimes at two in the morning, sometimes at four in the afternoon.

He was a man of few words and little education. He left school at the age of 12. I was never very close to him, nor, I believe, were any of his sons. (Our sister, Mary, remembers him differently. To her he was strong, quiet, and loving, whereas to us he was strong, silent, and strict.) Yet I think we all knew that if there were any external threat to any of us he would fight to the death for us. Every Thursday he came home and handed to my mother his unopened pay packet of £3 10s (£3.50 in today's less elegant coinage). She gave him some pocket money out of it for his cigarettes. Since he got the free daily Guinness he needed no money for drink, or indeed for much else.

In fact ours was a very temperate household. There was somewhere, under lock and key in a sideboard, a small bottle of spirits, whiskey or brandy, which was hardly ever produced except for Very Important Visitors or for medicinal purposes, or later to add to Gay's egg-flip, the story of which was blown on the 'Late Late Show' special programme on New Year's Eve of 1987/88. Young Gaybo was always thought of by his fond mother as being 'dawny' —delicate—and she presented him with an egg-flip every morning to build up his strength. The story is quite true. I *was* about 30 years old before I realised that all along she had been putting increasing amounts of whiskey into the egg-flip to try to disguise the taste of the egg, which I did not like, and I was 32 before I realised that egg-flips did not automatically taste the way my mother's had!

My mother had a curious attitude to drink. If you were important enough to be offered a drink and you asked for a whiskey or a brandy, you would get a tumblerful, filled to the brim. Just like reverend mothers in convent parlours all over the country who sent priests reeling into the night after their tea, she had no idea what constituted a measure. But if you asked for a bottle of stout you were immediately under suspicion as a drunkard. In later years, when Mary was pregnant and visiting home she would be offered a glass of Gilbey's invalid port, along with an admonishment that she was not to enjoy it: it was purely for the purposes of keeping her strength up. Yet, like a lot of Dublin women her age, Mam, if she was feeling a bit 'dawny', would indulge in a snipe—a miniature bottle—of Guinness mixed with milk and sugar.

In later years I once went on holiday with both of my parents, a driving holiday, which we grandly called 'touring'. Each day, once a day, we would stop outside a pub and Ma would allow Da to go inside for a pint while she

□

and I sat outside and waited in the car. The poor man must have had to open his throat and literally pour the pint into it, because Ma was not disposed to wait too long.

Her word was absolute law with him, and whereas he never lifted a finger to us on his own behalf, if she complained to him about our behaviour he belted us unquestioningly, even to the extent of waking us out of a deep sleep to hand out a clip on the ear. There was one occasion—and only one as far as I remember—when he went further than that. I had given 'lip' to my mother one morning, refusing to go to Mass in most uncivil terms. I was simply fed up with being expected to go to Mass and Communion every morning as she did. I made the fatal mistake of pretending that I had actually been in the church all along and she was meeting me coming back, as it were. As always, she recognised the lie, and began to harangue me. I cannot remember quite what I said, but it was something that in her terms was particularly nasty, like 'Sod off and get off my back with this bloody nonsense about Mass.'

She simply said quietly: 'Your father will hear about this.' I knew he would, and spent a most uncomfortable day in school in anticipation of what lay ahead of me. For that day, the Synge Street Brother and his andramartins was only in the ha'penny place.

When Da came home from work, I was in the front room. There was an uncharacteristic silence and tension in the house. He went down to Ma in the kitchen as usual, and then I heard the dreaded footsteps coming towards the front room. He came in and closed the door, and then beat me unmercifully—not for not going to Mass but for the way I had treated my mother. His hands were large and like leather, as tough as the barrels he handled, and I received a real battering. Afterwards I had to go down to the kitchen to apologise to my mother.

We all believed, and still do, that our Da did not like being a disciplinarian, but that he felt very strongly that he had to support my mother at all costs in her efforts to stay on top of us. He was quite gentle at the back of it all. I never had the opportunity to get close to him, since he died before I left school, and in the era in which we lived the only chance to get to know your father was later, in adult life, when you could approach him as an adult. One of my pals, Clive Culliton, has two sons, Simon and Peter. All their lives, but particularly from the time they were 15 or 16 years old, they were pals with their father. The three of them lend cigarettes to each other and buy pints for each other and go around with each other as equals. It is not that I envy the relationship, it is that I cannot fathom it. Just imagine, having a father that you could be close to and would call you 'pal' . . .

My father was someone I avoided as far as possible, because I regarded

☐

him as someone who would knock your block off. It was not that he was uncultured, or stupid: he was a big labouring man who thought he was fulfilling his proper role as a father. He was popular with his workmates and quite close to one of his brothers, but by and large, in my vision of him, he was a big, lone man. I suppose it boils down to the fact that he had no time for kids: that was women's work. But I am very sorry that he died before I had the opportunity to sit with him on a bar stool, to buy him a pint and to shoot the breeze. None of his sons ever had that opportunity: I was too young, Al was totally preoccupied with his studies, and Ernest and Raysie were away. My school pals who called around to our house remember him only as a big, quiet presence in our kitchen, clad in his dark Guinness jersey, but always silent. He was, simply, a man of his generation.

Although they were not particularly physically affectionate with one another—at least in front of us, in that I never saw them cuddling or with their arms around one another—there is no doubt in my mind that Ma and Da loved one another. We all kissed each other good-night and so on, and he showed his love for her by working around the house for her, washing dishes and cleaning, polishing all the shoes. I was brought up to do the same. It was only in later life that I discovered that all Irish men, all fathers, did not automatically make beds, chop logs, clean out fires.

All of us remember being woken up in the middle of the night by what we called 'Da's little turns'. In the dead silence, the air would suddenly be rent by the most appallingly violent screaming. The whole street was woken: the screaming was so loud and we all lived so closely together. I believe now it was *petit mal*, that mild form of epilepsy—but my mother was always convinced that Da's 'turns' had been caused by his experiences in the trenches of the First World War. She would say that at the height of the thrashing around and sweating he would be screaming about something coming in on top of him and smothering him, or trying to escape from something, or people being killed or dying all around him.

And always, after the shouting and thrashing around, he lapsed into a coma. No-one, not even the doctor when he was called, could wake him when he was going through one of these horrendous experiences. He would just have to be left in peace until he woke naturally some time during the following day. He never spoke about it and seemed to have no conscious memory of what might have caused it. Even if he had, he would never have spoken about it. He was obviously in huge distress and would be agitated for quite a while after he came out of one of these episodes, but this was in the days when men were supposed to be 'manly' and to keep feelings and fears to themselves. Many years later, while making a documentary about the war memorial at Islandbridge, I discovered that many men who had

□

fought in the First World War had similar recurring nightmares, visiting terror upon them at regular intervals throughout their lives.

The sad outcome of Da's 'turns' was that he had one at work one day, when he was loading his barge at Custom House Quay. And from then on, he was never allowed handle a barge again, but was given an indoor job. He was thought to be too big a risk.

Guinness's had a benevolent policy towards its employees. Those who became ill while still on the payroll were given whatever type of work they could still do comfortably. So Da became a sort of glorified dogsbody, rolling the odd cask around the vast warehouse, or taking messages from one part of the huge complex to another, or even going into town on his bicycle on an errand for one of the staff. He was only 51 at the time, and I believe that after the freedom and dignity, even status, of his labouring job, which he had loved, it must have upset him greatly.

He had been going hoarse from the time I was about 13. He never investigated it, because he was not in pain, nor did he feel sick. His voice simply got fainter and fainter. When it had at last faded completely and was merely a whisper, he went down to Dr Steevens' Hospital, where they discovered he had throat cancer.

He was treated with radium and everything that medicine could offer at the time, but it was already too late. He lingered on for about eighteen months and in terrible pain until he died. He had to have his larynx removed and a tracheotomy tube inserted in his throat, through which he breathed, each breath rattling horribly. Before he was removed to hospital he spent some time in bed in our back bedroom, lying quietly and un-complainingly in the depths of his appalling misery and suffering. All of us, I am afraid, are pretty finicky about blood and pain and sickness; but it was Al who overcame this and took it upon himself to perform the distasteful but loving task of changing and cleaning the tube. I think Al was superb at that time in dealing with a hateful job.

When Da was removed for the last time to Dr Steevens', a grim, forbidding building dating from the early eighteenth century, I found it extremely depressing each time I managed to pull myself together enough to go in to see him. One evening in July 1953 the four of us—Ma, Mary, Al, and I—went in to see him. He was visibly failing. The telephone rang in the house at two the following morning. It was the hospital, calling us to come back as Da's end was near.

I had never been out on cold streets before at that time of the deserted night. We drove along the canal and down Steevens' Lane in the family Morris Minor, and the journey was far too short. I was full of conflicting emotions: terror at what I might see in the hospital; terror if he was still alive

11

□

and that I would see him die; terror that he might already be dead; relief that he was at last going to be out of misery; relief that I would not have to witness this misery any more; guilt that I felt such relief.

Da had died by the time we reached the hospital. I remember very little of the funeral, out to Little Bray, and, as I remember, there was very little fuss made about my bereavement at school. I was absent for a day or two and then came back and life resumed.

Whatever about the manner of his death, which was slow and prolonged and hard, looking back on it now I often think that my father had a ferociously harder life than any of us. He worked very hard for Guinness's, long hours with comparatively little pay. And as far as I am aware from my observation of him, he got very little enjoyment out of life. Now I have no doubt that Mary and Al would say that he was a happy man, contented with his lot: but I am simply comparing the life that he had with the life we have, and especially my own. Our life-styles are so imcomparably different; my regret is that he wasn't a younger man and that he did not live a bit longer to join us when the better times came, so we could have spoiled him a bit.

Again I regret that I never got close to him. We never went together to a football match, because he wasn't interested. We never went fishing, because he didn't fish. I cannot recall ever going anywhere with him as father and son.

The only time we were ever in any way close was when I tried to teach him to drive. I learned to drive when I was about 14, because I was mad about cars and made it my business to ingratiate myself with a few older fellows locally who had bangers. I made sure to get myself into their driving seats. And when we eventually got a car, Dad wanted to drive—but he never made a very good fist of it. I keep on thinking: poor Da, he missed out on so much.

When one partner dies, there is obviously a huge gap. For my mother the gap was large, since they had gone everywhere together and socially had depended greatly on one another. Neither had any close friends that I knew of, and they always went together to the picture-houses or on visits to relatives.

Typically, Ma threw herself into being a widow. She made it her vocation to find a suitable monument for my father's grave. I had to draw plans and sketches, hundreds of them, while she deliberated and rejected and pondered and sought second opinions. We visited graveyards and monument works all over the city and county and assessed other people's headstones. Gravediggers and graveyard curators were consulted, people who imparted the unsettling news that no headstone should be erected until a year after the bereavement.

☐

I am absolutely convinced that half of the fervour was for the sake of the neighbours. The more splendiferous the monument erected by wife to husband's memory in those days, the more it would be a memorial to their unity in life and the greater the retrospective status of the marriage. Finally she plumped for something she considered worthy and splashed out £400, a huge sum, which she had managed to scrape together through her lifelong habit of thrift and scrimping. The headstone was erected, and Ma was at peace.

Then an amazing thing happened. My mother discovered freedom. All her children were more or less independent and working and earning good money, and she turned her attention to the greater world outside her own territory. She became friendly with another widow in the neighbourhood, a Mrs Parker, who had retired from teaching school. As often happens when widows are released from domesticity, the two of them began to have a whale of a time: going to the movies, taking bus excursions around the country, travelling to Spain, even to America on a Greyhound bus tour. Mrs Parker was a forceful woman and, being an ex-teacher, was considered educated and well-read above the average. One time they went to Rome (where else!) and were included in the standard tour. As part of a large party in the catacombs, Mrs Parker began correcting the guide, telling him he had the wrong dates, the wrong places and the wrong people. The guide, who'd obviously been doing the job for twenty years, got snotty at being corrected by a foreigner and arguments ensued. I think they were close to being thrown off the tour, but others intervened to calm things. Ma was utterly mortified and tried to pretend she wasn't with Mrs Parker, but they eventually ended up falling around the streets of Rome, laughing girlishly about the whole thing. And Ma dined out on the story for years.

She got herself onto a local committee that was set up to investigate the possibility of the tenants' buying the houses from the Dublin Artisans' Dwellings Society. There was an architect and a solicitor on that committee, and a senior inspector from Dublin Gas Company, a Mr Cooney.

As a matter of fact we had known Mr Cooney well; he was a good friend of the family and of many people in the area. During the 'Emergency' the use of gas was strictly rationed and there were very severe consequences if you were caught using gas during the times of the day when it was forbidden. And because pressure had to be maintained in the pipes, the supply could not actually be turned off, so there was a band of roving 'glimmer men': inspectors who entered people's houses to check that people were not using the 'glimmer', the tiny residue of gas that was left in the pipes during that period. People who took a chance on using the glimmer lived in dread of knocks on the door during forbidden times,

☐

because the inspector could enter your house and, by feeling the residual warmth of the gas ring, would know that you had been using the forbidden gas. You were cut off forthwith.

Mr Cooney, our friend, was in charge of the glimmer men, he was the *chief* glimmer man, and he was in our kitchen one Saturday afternoon, having a bottle of stout. Beyond the kitchen, in the scullery, to our heart-stopping horror, the glimmer was in use. We had been using it when Mr Cooney knocked and, knowing that he would be invited in, we had been afraid to turn it off because of the giveaway 'plopping' sound that followed.

It so happened that a horse-drawn Kennedy's bakery van was making deliveries to the shop next door, and there was another knock on our door. It was the breadman, who also knew us well. Something had got into his horse's hoof, and in taking it out he had dirtied his hands. Could he wash them at our sink? 'Certainly,' said my mother.

The breadman went into the scullery, washed his hands, came out, and said: 'Thank you very much, Mrs Byrne—and if I meet a glimmer man anywhere, I know where to send him!' We all laughed—not a lot. And he walked through the kitchen, down the hall and out the front door.

There was a deathly, deadly silence in our kitchen. Mr Cooney picked up his glass of stout and said: 'Well, as I was saying . . .' In those days, friends were friends.

When Ma joined people like Mr Cooney on her committee, she felt she had reached her proper element, communing with professionals, and grew in queenly stature. To be on equal speaking terms with people of such calibre gave her immense pleasure, not to speak of the community status she had always craved. And I must say it gave me a lot of pleasure to see her bustling around, puffed with her own importance.

She was a tremendous organiser, and very kind behind all the toughness. There was a particular family in our neighbourhood and somehow or other it came to Ma's attention that they were not getting enough to eat. None of us was exactly living high, but comparatively speaking we were well off, with the security of the Guinness's jobs behind us. Ma heard that this family was actually hungry. She used to contrive that members of the family would be dropping in just at the time when she would be taking bread out of the oven or carving the meat. Ma was a very good cook.

And there are cousins who are still grateful to her memory and will not let us forget her kindness. Her sister, Auntie Kathleen, another formidable lady but with an entirely different style, disapproved highly of the intended marriage of one of her daughters, Eva, to the extent that she would not and did not attend the wedding. The groom, Jack Flood, who also worked in Guinness's as a 'racker', was simply not good enough for her. Auntie

☐ Mum and Dad when he was home on leave from the First
World War (above) and many years later at Steevens'
Hospital (below). I took this picture with one of my first
cameras shortly before Dad died.

☐

Kathleen, who lived in Thirlestane Terrace, off Thomas Court, had managed to carve out an extraordinary life for herself. She was a dowager-duchess type, who sat all day in a chair giving instructions to her multitudinous family as they danced attendance on her. Kathleen managed to convey the idea that she could not be asked to do 'heavy' work because she was always, like, *sick*—and might drop dead. The wonder of it, for my mother, used to the grind of cleaning and washing dishes and the drudging part of housekeeping—Martha to Kathleen's Mary—was that her sister managed to get away with it.

Yet Ma herself contributed to the phenomenon. Kathleen was the only person who ever dominated her. It was an extraordinary thing to see. Kathleen was large, jowly, twice the size of my mother, a Hattie Jacques type who sat, not in a chair like ordinary folk but in a huge imposing structure that could only be seen as a throne and from which she issued her orders to all and sundry, including her husband, who submitted like everyone else. Uncle Dick was like his brother, my dad, a quiet, white-haired man.

Every time Kathleen had a bad turn, my mother would be out the door, coat on, not stopping no matter what was happening in our house. Kathleen was dying again, out, quick, go, and to hell with anyone else! As it turned out, Kathleen was the last of that family to die.

The only occasion on which Ma defied Kathleen was that of Eva's marriage. She organised everything, bought the girl's wedding outfit, arranged the reception, and ignored Kathleen's outrage. Later on, in a further gesture of solidarity, she asked the unapproved groom, Jack Flood, to be my godfather. They never forgot Ma. (And Jack had the last laugh. His son, Finbar, is now Personnel Director of Guinness's!)

So by any standards Ma was a tough woman, who ran her household with a rod of iron, who had plans for each of us, and was not going to let anything—even us—stand in her way until they were fulfilled. In contrast to my father, who just wanted peace, she pushed and pushed, wanting for us what she could never achieve for herself. She was certainly the dominant influence on my life, but then I was the youngest and, predictably perhaps, closest to her.

She was as tough on herself as she was on us, saving the penny bus-fare by walking, even in the cold and rain, even while seven or eight months pregnant. Malingering was never known in our house. Once, when I was still quite young and at school, I had to go to the dentist to get five abscessed teeth out. Dentistry was not as sophisticated then as it is today, and I returned home with my mouth in tatters, bleeding, in pain, and feeling very sorry for myself. She would have none of it. It was a school-day, and there were still some hours left before the closing bell. Education was to my

□

mother the golden key that would open all doors, and every inch of it was precious. I was sent packing out of the house and into school.

Her ambition drove us all and imbued us. Except for Mary, who is really the nicest member of our family—and like Ma in very many ways, except for that steely determination—we all drove and still drive ourselves very hard indeed. My father, who was not at all ambitious, tried to be because she was, and tried to drive us too because she wanted it.

But I am not sure how happy Ma was with her lot. She certainly dreamed of a better material life for us all, and this is probably why she pushed her children so hard. To say that she was actively unhappy or showed her unhappiness would be wrong and unfair, but I believe she was quite frustrated, seeing in herself the same standard of intelligence and qualities of application that had brought greater material and career rewards to people from a more privileged background.

As well as her dreams for us, Ma simply dreamed. It was something of which I was not too aware, although Al detected it. Perhaps by the time I had enough sense to see her as a person rather than simply as my mother, all the dreams had been worn out. She dreamed of wonderful things happening to us all. She was a great reader of romantic novels, Mills and Boon and Ethel M. Dell, and loved mushy, romantic films, escaping into them from the kitchen of her own life.

She was a hospitable woman, who regularly gave shelter to orphans of the storm. While he was at Trinity, Al had a tutor, Mickey Quinn, a fusty old bachelor who lived in a room on Clonliffe Road, Drumcondra. He was always clad in overcoat and scarf and gloves like a character out of a Dickens novel, and surrounded by books as fusty as himself, but was a great man for giving grinds in Latin and Greek. Mickey was thrown out of his room and, having no money, arrived around at our house perched in amongst the piles of his books on top of a horse-cart. My mother fed him up and put him in our parlour, where at night he slept upright in a chair for a number of weeks, until a place became available in Roebuck nursing home.

Ma's view of what was acceptable behaviour did not include the use of bad language, or any discussion about (ssh, not in front of the children!) s-e-x. In fact once, when I was a great big lad of 14 and my brother Ray brought his one-month-old daughter Shelagh on a visit to her grandmother, I was banished from the scullery, where the infant was being bathed. I must not have my pure young eyes polluted by the sight of a naked female, even if she was only four weeks old! It was the prevailing ethos, and I saw nothing peculiar in it. I rejoice in these better, more open days, when my own daughter Crona can hiss at her mother, who wants to hold her hand going down Grafton Street, that 'people would think we were a pair of lezzers!' The very existence of homosexuality would have been astonishing to my Ma. She had an absolute, blind faith in God and prayer. There was never any question in her mind but that she would get what she was asking for. In fact she did not ask, she demanded her rights.

I know that some of my school pals were afraid of her. She could be quite scathing if she detected weakness, with a lacerating tongue that struck precisely into the wound, like a scalpel. Tony Bennett from Inchicore, whose father worked with CIE, still has a mental picture of her as a small, determined little virago with horn-rimmed glasses, giving out yards to him when she thought he had stepped over the mark of her own high standards of behaviour. And quite often, even when I was a hulking teenager and Colm Campbell, who walked his two cocker spaniels past our house every evening, would call for me to join him, she would not let me out, not even for half an hour. Meekly, I succumbed to her dictates; I would not have dreamt of doing otherwise.

Ma was a very intelligent woman, sharp as a tack and highly organised. In other times and from another background she could quite easily have run a thriving business. Not having that opportunity, she substituted her family, and ran it with success and expansion in mind.

Given her pushing, I suppose it is not surprising that, except for Mary, we all aimed in one way or another for the communications business. Spurred on by her, we all wanted to get out and make some kind of mark on the world. We all expected to rise above our station, as she expected we would. The communications industry was a natural target: it tends to be classless, and success depends largely on hard work as well as luck. Given Ma's training, there was never any problem with the former.

And I suppose it is also because of her that none of us—again except Mary—has ever been quite satisfied with our own performances, always expecting more of ourselves. Whatever rung on whatever ladder was reached, there were always more to go. Complacency was a foreign country. (It might have been more peaceful.)

There were six of us born, but Joseph, the eldest, died when he was only a week old. It is a long-tailed family. I am the youngest, born on 5 August 1934 and two years younger than Mary, seven younger than Ernest, ten younger than Al, and thirteen younger than Edward, also known as Raysie-baby. (I have always found it fascinating how mathematically neat genetics can be. My grandfather produced nine sons and a single girl. The girl, Mary, married a gentleman called Laurence O'Toole, producing five sons and, again, a single girl. My father married a woman who produced five sons and a single girl.)

We lived in a little house in Rialto Street, number 17, off the South

☐

Circular Road, two up and two down, of the type now gentrified as 'town houses' and much sought after by yuppies. We, like vast numbers of working-class people, rented from the Dublin Artisans' Dwellings Society at seven-and-sixpence a week (35p—the price of a can of Coca-Cola). The whole family crowded into the two bedrooms upstairs, and yet we never knew we were crowded, being far smaller in number than a lot of our neighbours.

The downstairs was divided into a parlour and a kitchen, with a little scullery. Even with larger families than ours—sometimes as large as twelve or thirteen children—everyone in our street managed to keep the parlour as a sanctum apart from the hurly-burly of everyday life. It was reserved for visitors, for Christmas, for parties, for funerals—for all state occasions. Ours was typical, with the china cabinet, the thick velveteen table-cloth, and the musty smell of under-use, despite constant cleaning and polishing. We were all forbidden, on pain of death, to touch the china cabinet or its contents. In it my mother kept her treasures: two sets of china she had won in Bray for her prowess as a ballroom dancer, and some knick-knacks won for swimming.

Ray, or Raysie-baby, was, I believe, the handsomest of our bunch, in appearance very like the young film star Robert Taylor. Raysie-baby was a terror to his parents and always had his own ideas about which rules applied to him, invariably at odds with theirs. He sold his christening mug. He undertook to teach Mary and me to smoke if we went to bed quietly and did not 'rat' on him when he brought girl-friends home.

He went into Guinness's as a messenger-boy. The usual drill was that boys applied to work at Guinness's when they left school at 13. When they were interviewed they were asked to fill out a form that asked, among other things, their fathers' occupations. The form filled in by anyone who had a father in the company was rubber-stamped with the words 'Son of employee', and he or she had a head start over everyone else.

There were constant morning rows in our house about Ray being on time for his work. I was too young to be able to remember them clearly now, but Al still grinds his teeth, remembering the scenes where Ray seemed to delight in throwing down gauntlets in front of my hard-working, punc-tilious father. He had to be in Guinness's by eight, but instead of leaving on time he would drive my father right to the edge of dementia many a morning by waiting, deliberately it seemed, until seven, six, even five minutes to eight before sauntering out the door.

The rows were not only in the morning. My mother would not tolerate bad language under any circumstances. So Ray used it deliberately. When eventually we were moving house and we were all given things to carry and

□

jobs to do, Ray would not lift a finger but sat in the parlour, pounding and pounding on the piano. There was a constant stream of his disreputable friends knocking at our doors and windows at all hours. One had the nerve to ask for the loan of a bike at three o'clock in the morning when my father poked his head out of his bedroom window.

Ray moved from being a messenger into work in the laboratory at the brewery. He worked there until he was 18, the official age within the company when boys passed from being boys to being 'lads'. Ray hated with a vengeance just about everything to do with working in Guinness's laboratory, especially his overbearing, pompous bosses; but he also felt he was far too good for labouring (and he was right). He had already shown considerable musical talent, studying piano as far as his associateship of the London College of Music. He would have stayed on in the laboratory if Guinness's had let him, but of course they would not.

So in 1944 Raysie-baby ran away to war. But out of sheer cussedness, he joined the Irish army first. When he announced his intention of becoming a soldier my father implored him to join the British army, on the basis that if he was intent on taking up a soldier's life he might at least do something useful, like fight in the war, instead of hanging around in Collins Barracks.

Probably because it was what my father did not want him to do, Ray joined the Irish army. Then, promptly, he deserted and, like many of the boys from our street, joined the RAF. At the time there was a great deal of idealism in the air—freedom of small nations, fighting the Hun—but there was also the undeniable allure of seeing the world, and getting away from hefting barrels of Guinness all day long. However, before he joined the boys in blue there was the little matter of a discharge from the Irish army. He was the only person of whom I have ever heard who had the gall to come back in his RAF uniform to claim his discharge from the Irish army at Griffith Barracks. Sergeant Bolster, a neighbour, covered for him.

Of course there were ructions at home. It was all very upsetting. I was only 5, and to me Ray was this tall, handsome fellow who was very remote from the small doings of my life but who slipped me half-crowns on the rare occasions our paths crossed. But I do remember very clearly the atmosphere at that time of crisis and family conferences and slamming down of teapots. There were tears and appeals to his better nature and cries of 'We brought you into the world, why are you doing this to us? Where have we gone wrong?' But there was very little they could do about it. Ray was 18 years of age and of very strong mind.

My parents were aghast at the idea that anyone, no matter how wild, would contemplate leaving the safe, secure harbour of Guinness's. It was also a very dangerous war for the 'fly-boys', as they were called, who were defending their territory in the Battle of Britain. But Ma and Da need not have worried at least on that score. Raysie, being Raysie, ended up pushing a pen in a Nissen hut in Ruislip, outside London, nice and safe from any nastiness like bombs, or fellows shooting at him.

After the war, just when he was about to go for his commission, which he undoubtedly would have received, he went off with Jack Doyle and his companion, the film star Movita. The singing ex-boxer and his lady were touring England and Ireland with their musical show, and our Raysie became their official accompanist.

More ructions and andramartins at home. My mother did not know which was worse, the war or showbiz. Scandalous showbiz to boot! If he could have chosen, from anywhere in the world, a pair of companions who would have caused most scandal to my poor parents, they were Jack Doyle and Movita. To them, that pair, whose names and photographs were all over the tabloids and scandal-sheets, were the personification of Sodom and Gomorrah. Worse was to come.

Raysie announced that he was getting married. He had been engaged many times before, but this time it looked serious. Al was sent to London as an official delegation of one, to supervise the proceedings and to report back. He arrived and found himself being driven, not, as he thought he would be, to the swanky Catholic church in Spanish Place but quite a distance outside London to a beautiful cathedral at St Albans. He was impressed to find himself surrounded by all sorts of splendid chappies in bemedalled uniforms, and even an American major called Joe Longstreet. But something did not look quite right. Then he realised that there were no candles. No tabernacle. No Stations of the Cross. Horrors! It was a Protestant church!

From that moment on, Al's fevered brain was totally preoccupied with how to lie successfully to the Ma. It was one thing to go away with Jack Doyle and Movita; but to go into a Protestant church, to attend a Protestant service, and to marry a Protestant girl thereby was beyond even her wildest fears.

Al rehearsed his lies well. It had been a lovely wedding and the priest was very nice and sent his kindest regards and wasn't it a pity that more of Ray's family couldn't make it over for the big day?

But Ma was suspicious. She questioned him closely for weeks, coming back to him again and again. What's this the name of that priest was again? She would like to write to him to thank him for his kind wishes . . . Or she had had a terrible dream, and could he go over the ceremony again for her so that she could comfort herself that everything was okay?

Then the photographs of the wedding arrived. She perused them very

☐

closely—closely enough to see that the stones of the cathedral behind the wedding party were not Catholic stones. She renewed her attacks on Al. Eventually, at about one in the morning after the perusal of the photographs, she hauled the poor fellow out to the public telephone box outside St James's Hospital at Rialto bridge. She telephoned Ray in London, while Al stood helplessly by. She told her London son that she had had a terrible, an appalling dream about him and she was coming right over to London to visit himself and his new wife.

She went alone. Al was not allowed to go, because he was in utter disgrace, being an accessory before, during and after the fact. When she got there she packed the two newly-weds into a taxi and brought them to a Catholic church and had them married properly. They acceded for peace' sake. She told them she was not going home and was simply going to camp in their flat until they did.

Ray and Joyce, a lovely, very English woman, are still, years later, happily married and settled in Canada, where he has now retired from an executive job in Canadian television. His is the voice that announces to the nation every week, 'Ladies and gentlemen, to whom it concerns, it's the "Late Late Show"!'

Ray has always had a marvellous voice. He had been a school pal of Éamonn Andrews, and both were interested in broadcasting. Éamonn always said in later years that in fact Raysie-baby had more talent than the whole bloody lot of us put together. But whereas Éamonn was solid, reliable, hard-working, and dedicated, Raysie was the exact opposite: totally unreliable and volatile. But he could sing, he could play the piano, he worked as a male model for a while; he could write, adapt, and dramatise. He adapted books for the BBC's 'Book at Bedtime' series, and also very successfully dramatised Irwin Shaw's book about the McCarthy era in the United States, *The Troubled Air*, for broadcast as a play by the Beeb.

He is, I believe, currently engaged in writing his memoirs for publication. They will be a rattling good read.

Al was the next of the brothers, with a character that was the antithesis of Ray's. Throughout my life Al has been a solid rock and a great brother to me. Al was always hard-working and dependable, and a great favourite with both my parents. He went into Guinness's as expected, but my mother always thought that he should rise above labouring. In Guinness's, Al was what was known as a 'number-taker' on the wharfs and jetties, literally recording the registration numbers of the wooden casks as they were loaded for dispatch. There were 300 hogsheads on each barge, 52 gallons to a hogshead, and each cask debited against the account of whomever was

☐

getting it. At any given moment, the whereabouts of every cask that left Guinness's was on file.

The automatic progression from that, when he became old enough, would have been into heavy labouring. Al succeeded in actually getting onto a barge only once. One summer morning, at about 6.30 a.m., the number-takers on duty somehow missed an entire consignment, which was already loaded into the cavernous hold of the barge by the time they had realised what had happened. The only way to rectify the situation was to jump on the barge and go down the river with the consignment to where it was being offloaded onto the cross-channel steamers and there to take the numbers as the casks were being transferred to the ships. Al and his colleague were allowed to come on board and to sit tightly on hard pieces of wood.

The way he describes it, it was the most exciting experience of his youth. There was tension, because if the calculations about the tides had not been made correctly there would have been disaster. If the Liffey was too high, the barge could not have passed under the bridges even with the funnels lowered; if the river was too low, the barges could not travel at all. There was a great feeling of power—of being different. In those days, a barge going down the Liffey always made people stop and stare over the parapets. Inevitably, when the craft went under a bridge, people ran from one side to the other to see it emerging. To him the experience was like being involved in 'the real thing', like having been an amateur cricketer and suddenly finding oneself at Lord's, or from having been a knockabout tennis player and being seeded on the centre court at Wimbledon. The icing on the cake was when the crew took the two boys down below to share breakfast: bacon and egg and sausage and fried bread and tea, cooked on a solid-fuel stove stashed in among the barrels.

But exciting though that was, my mother had brought Al up with different expectations, and he did not fancy being a labourer. When he became old enough he announced that he wanted to join the RAF with a pal of his, Frank Nulty, and the droves of others who were going to war. He got on the train to Belfast to enlist, and actually did the medical. But my parents beseeched him not to. They said they would pay for him to go to Trinity College.

Given my mother's attitude to her own family's religious practice, and the fact that attendance at Trinity, a bastion of Protestantism, was proscribed by the Catholic Church, this was quite an offer. On the other hand, it must be said in her defence that Ma's attitude to Catholicism was strictly applied only to herself and to us. Never, in all the time I knew her,

☐

did I hear a single intolerant word out of her mouth. She totally accepted our Jewish and Protestant neighbours and the Jews and Protestants we sometimes brought home as friends. In fact, in common with a lot of people of her generation, she assumed that Protestants were somehow in a higher league of decency and integrity than us scoundrelly, raffish Catholics.

There was no problem when Mary brought home a Jewish boy-friend, David Bratman; and during the period that our long-time family friend, the Protestant Jack Prestige, lived with us, she insisted that on Sunday mornings he should get out of bed and go to his own church, on the basis that while he was under *her* roof he would practise his own religion. She had no problem with racism, either: a regular guest at our dinner table was Ariwodo Kalunte Onjejokwi, a Nigerian student who was a friend of Al's. Ma's attitude to him was that he needed feeding up, just like old Mickey Quinn, and she dished up heaping fries and mounds of chips in front of him.

So when she made her offer to send Al to Trinity, she made it, I think, on purely practical grounds: on the assumption that since Guinness's was a Protestant organisation, a degree from Trinity would have more clout.

Shortly after their trip to the recruiting office in Belfast, the letter accepting Nulty came, and he went away. There was no similar letter for Al, and so he assumed he had not been accepted. My mother had intercepted it and had burned it.

Al knew that despite my parents' offer to pay for him to go to university, they could not afford it: Da was earning only £5 a week. He decided to apply to Trinity and to keep his job at Guinness's, with whom he was now, officially, a 'lad'. (The next stage in the development of a labouring man was at the age of 21, when a 'lad' donned the overalls and rubber gloves of a 'man' and was listed for heavy-duty work.) The company agreed to extend the 'lad' period until he was 22, by which time he should have earned his degree. The company also agreed to allow him to work a split shift so he could attend lectures.

But before he could enter Trinity he had to get a letter of dispensation from John Charles McQuaid. He went to our parish priest, who went on his behalf up to the palace in Drumcondra. A few days later Father Meleady called at our house. To my mother and Al he read aloud the official letter from Archbishop's House, denying Al permission to attend Trinity College.

Al instantly said he was going anyway. My mother, to whom an edict such as this was Holy Writ, set up an olagón. (I suspect that when she offered to send Al she thought that the Catholic Church would have seen, like her, that the Byrnes were Different and would have let them get away with bending the rules.) The priest added his voice to Ma's pleading,

□

bullying and entreating, but to no avail. Al would not budge an inch. The priest then said, in his most formal tones, that he had to advise all present that since Albert Byrne was to set foot inside Trinity College, he was excommunicated from the Holy Roman and Apostolic Church. Al sat there, mutinous and intractable, while my mother's distress grew. The priest, sensibly, decided of his own volition to go again to Drumcondra.

He was back within five days, again reading formally aloud from a document—which he never let anyone in our family see—giving Mr Al Byrne permission to attend lectures. Only to attend lectures: not to join the Historical Society or the Philosophical Society or any of the immoral and depraved organisations or sporting clubs in the Trinity den of iniquity. Again, Al said immediately that he was going to join everything going. The priest retired, defeated. Mercifully, he left us to our own devices. The excommunicant felt that he had been reinstated.

For the next four years, Al got up at five every morning, was in Guinness's by six, knocked off at a quarter to nine, and cycled in to college for nine o'clock lectures or laboratory work. He also got private tuition from Mickey Quinn. He broke again at two or a quarter past, and went back to Guinness's to work out his eight-hour shift, usually until about six in the morning. Then he came home to study. He was usually in bed by nine o'clock, little Goldilocks, apple of my mother's eye—and we all had to stay as quiet as church mice. But for four solid years, that was one hell of a sustained performance.

Throughout those four years, Ma suffered agonies every Lent when the archbishop's pastoral letter was read from the pulpit of every church in Dublin. Everyone in our neighbourhood knew that Al Byrne was going to Trinity College, and as the renewal of the ban on the attendance of Catholics at this sinful repository of all that was harmful was renewed, she was convinced that all eyes in the church were turned in our direction. I was aware of it myself, young though I was, and sat there, part of a solidly packed Byrne phalanx, tight and rebellious, holding out against the neighbourhood and John Charles McQuaid.

The other side of the coin was that, like a lot of people of her generation and from her background, Ma was snobbish enough to like the idea of her son going to Trinity College, Dublin, and not to the institution for the sons of cattle-jobbers and big farmers and higher civil servants, UCD.

When Al got his degree, in science, he applied for what was known as the 'number one staff' at the brewery. The clerical and managerial grades were divided in descending order of importance: number one, number two, number three, and number four—plus an additional grade quaintly (and probably insultingly) named 'lady clerks'.

□

In those days the clerical staff in Guinness's went in at nine and knocked off at four. Lunch was provided in the 'lunch room' (*not* the 'canteen'), and a superb lunch it was. The clerks had three weeks' paid holidays, worked only nine to twelve on Saturdays, and had Sundays off. They also had weird extra holidays called 'privilege days': for 'Queen's Day' (to commemorate Queen Victoria's visit to Ireland) and to coincide with Punchestown Races. There was free medical treatment and other services. The number one staff in Guinness's at that time was the jackpot, the ultimate in jobs, dreamed of by most young men leaving school. Al was admitted to the grade of number one clerk.

It is difficult adequately to describe what that meant on the South Circular Road. No son of a labouring man from our street or our area had ever been invited to join the beautiful, exclusive club that was Guinness's number one staff. Al was the first Roman Catholic labourer's son to achieve the distinction. Guinness's was owned, managed and run by Protestants. Catholics loaded, laboured, coopered, drayed and crewed under their benevolent supervision.

The day he heard the news, Al was returning to the warehouse, floating down the metal stairs from the upstairs offices, when by chance, right at the bottom of the staircase, he met Da, who had just come in off one of the barges. The warehouse was vast, an endless echoing concrete cave where swarms of men heaved at the thundering, rolling barrels and the goods wagons shunted along their narrow-gauge iron tracks. Al brought Da into a little clearing between the stacked casks. He told him he had been accepted onto the number one staff.

Da was speechless. He gripped Al by the elbow, but could say nothing. The two of them stood there for about thirty seconds in an oasis of emotion, neither uttering a word, while all around them the clattering and noise swelled and abated. Then Da went back to what was known as the 'Tap', to get his free pint, and Al went home to tell Ma.

Her reaction was predictable. She fell immediately to her knees to thank God. Then she made Al kneel down too, and the two of them recited the Rosary. Al's thoughts were elsewhere, and so in truth were hers, because she kept stopping the well-worn prayers to ask him, Was he sure it was true? Could he have made a mistake?

For days, even weeks, afterwards, neighbours and friends called to our house to ask the same question. Could it be true that the Catholic son of a labourer was accepted onto the number one staff at Guinness's? By some curious quirk of memory I am convinced that bunting and flags were hung out up and down the street in celebration, as on the day of the

☐ My mother as a young girl and during her later years in our
living room on the South Circular Road.

□

Corpus Christi procession. Al swears that this is an exaggeration—but I am not so sure.

Al went from strength to strength in Guinness's, and on the side became a broadcaster in his own right. Selfishly, from my point of view, he has always been there when I needed him. And I suppose, after Da died, I cast him in the role of surrogate father, which he accepted willingly. Kathleen Watkins claims that after I married her it was a role from which she had to wean me. (With limited success. I still lean on him.)

Before he met Frances, Al had been engaged to a girl called Jeanne Edwards, the daughter of a Guinness's engineer—and proud possessor of a lovely Rover car, two-litre, circa 1935. Her arrival outside our door caused a sensation in our neighbourhood, where no-one at that time had any cars, good, bad, or indifferent. It was a beautiful machine, with a wide running-board and a step to assist entrance.

Al and Jeanne's engagement did not survive, a demise encouraged, I am sure, by Ma Byrne. She was assisted in her dispatch on one occasion by yours truly, when I was sent along as gooseberry while Al and Jeanne went for a drive in the Phoenix Park. (My presence had little effect, as it turned out, because once in the Phoenix Park they parked the car by the side of the road, put me in the front seat to amuse myself, and got into the capacious back seat themselves for a 'chat', out of which they galvanised themselves when I, who had by then become fascinated by motor cars, turned on the ignition of the precious vehicle.)

Frances, when *she* was brought home, turned out to be made of sterner stuff, and survived all Ma could do to dissuade her from kidnapping her little darling.

I have often wondered if Al has disappointed himself. He was always very ambitious. He has been successful—very; but with Ma's training there is always that elusive bit extra that is just out of reach. I wonder if Al believes that he has lived up to her expectations and to his own. If he does not, I understand it very well, because it is a syndrome from which I suffer myself.

The next brother was Ernest, who was always delicate and 'chesty' as a child. In fact he contracted rheumatic fever. I recently went to see our old family friend Jack Prestige, who, in recalling the old days on the street, remembered principally of our house the sound of Ernest's non-stop crying for a full year after he was born.

Ernest was always unfortunate. When he was 12 he was coming home from school one day, having taken a lift on the crossbar of a pal's bicycle. The wheels caught in the tram tracks on the South Circular Road and Ernest was thrown off the bicycle and into the path of an oncoming car. The car ran over him and smashed his pelvis. For the next two years he was

☐

in hospital, and he never really recovered educationally. But typically, my indomitable mother refused to accept the medical prognosis that Ernest would always have one leg two inches shorter than the other and would have a permanent limp. There was nothing that could be done, she was told. She hauled him around to one surgeon after another, and as each one shook his head she just moved on. She eventually found one who operated successfully. (In later years, when Ernest was caught in the war in Korea, she often lamented her persistence. If he had had a physical defect he would not have been taken into the American forces.)

When he left school, Ernest was apprenticed as a cinema operator in the Inchicore cinema, acting as dogsbody to the projectionist and anyone else who needed assistance or errands run. Each morning he lugged eight or ten huge reels of film from the Inchicore cinema into town, where he would exchange them for the next lot. Back at home base he would help to edit and paste them up for use that evening. His duties also included cleaning and tidying the projectionist's booth. His working day ran from about ten in the morning until after the last show in the evening, seven days a week. He would not get home until nearly midnight. Nevertheless he stuck at it, and after seven years qualified as a cinema operator.

But almost immediately after qualification, just as the war was ending, he ran away, like Raysie before him, to join the RAF. He was sent to Preston in Lancashire for training, and then to Valley in Wales, where he spent two and a half years.

He came home then and went back into his cinema work in various cinemas and theatres around Dublin, including the Queen's, but he never settled. He was a dreamer, like my mother, although in an entirely different way. My mother dreamed energetically; Ernest was content to sit and to dream in stillness. His dreaminess drove her mad: she would see him sitting, staring into space or out the window of the living-room, and demand to know what on earth he was doing. His answer, invariably, was that he was 'just thinking'. Yet it was quite clear that he wanted to live life and not simply to view it night after night on celluloid.

One day he simply packed up and got on a boat for Canada. He got a job as a hotel porter and began to work his way south, going from job to job and finally crossing the border into the United States. Still moving south, he eventually finished up in Dallas, Texas, where he applied for and got work in a television station. He started menially, doing odd jobs, but was on his way upwards through the organisation when the Korean War became a serious issue. He decided, sensibly, that rather than wait to be conscripted he would volunteer for army service, and he was sent to Korea. My abiding memory of that time is of my mother and myself listening anxiously to the half-past one news on Radio Éireann every lunchtime. Month after month the peace talks dragged on, and the phrase used monotonously by the newsreader every day was 'No progress at Panmunjom', whereupon Ma would straighten her shoulders.

There were letters, of course, particularly between Al and himself. Ernest's letters to Al were despairing. Even from the ranks of the lowly infantry he spoke of the impossibility of this war being won by America. He believed that the Chinese, who were fighting with the North Koreans, were drugged so that they had lost all sense of self-preservation and would come at the terrified Americans, wave after yellow wave, even though their own rifles were spent and all ammunition exhausted. The Americans would abandon their guns and retreat before this relentless, ceaseless flood.

His letters to my parents were more anodyne, and he tried to allay my mother's fears, writing that he was bored out of his mind doing a dull typing job far from enemy lines; but my father, who had himself been through the horrors of war, read between the lines and was very upset. (In fact it was Ernest who inadvertently sent my father at last to get medical help for his increasing hoarseness. Once, during an 'R and R' break in the Philippines, Ernest rang home, and it irritated Da that he could not speak to him because of his hoarseness. There was just no voice there.)

It was a great relief to us when Ernest was sent home with a shrapnel wound to the shoulder, the rank of sergeant, and a Purple Heart for bravery. But, as always in life, there is no pleasure without pain. Our Da died on the very day Ernest set sail to come home.

After a fortnight's leave he went back to America and resumed his job in television, again moving upwards and changing stations, moving from Dallas to Little Rock, Arkansas, and finally, very successfully, to St Louis, Missouri, where he worked with KMOX, a CBS network station. He married a beautiful woman, part-Indian, named Dorothy.

Then the whole story began to go wrong. He had a natural desire to come back to Ireland when RTE television opened and he realised what the opportunities were. It was the time when the one-eyed man was king. Éamonn Andrews, the first Chairman of the RTE Authority, was recruiting in the States for the brand-new station, and came back with the services of people like Ed Roth, who was to be the first Director-General. He went to see his old pal Raysie in Toronto, and also arranged for Ernest, who was Executive Producer of KMOX, to be interviewed. Ernest came home, just at the time my own career was beginning to flourish. He became Executive Producer with RTE. And since there was no Controller of Programmes, he fulfilled that function as well.

With all the other people who came home, or were recruited here, to work in the fledgling television service, Ernest worked long hours out of the temporary offices in Clarendon Street and the temporary studios in Abbey Street. It was a small, happy, select band of people, carried along by the excitement of being in on the ground floor of something new and glamorous. They could not wait to see the transmitter go up out in Donnybrook, and they knew every block that went into the building of the new studios. I was travelling back and forth to Granada in Manchester at the time and I was very aware of how much time and effort everyone was putting into the new venture.

Ernest's was a fireman's, hands-on attitude. The story is told that on the opening night of RTE, during the clamour and excitement in O'Connell Street and in the Gresham Hotel, and when Patrick O'Hagan was singing and there were snowballs flying and everyone who was anyone was present, including Éamonn Andrews as first Chairman of the new Authority, suddenly something went wrong with the main control desk back at headquarters. It is said that Ernest Byrne stood there for four and a half or five hours with his finger pressed, cemented, onto a certain button, the spring-loading of which had given way and without which the whole station would have gone off the air.

This is only one of many stories about him, and he is still held in high regard among the older members of the RTE staff. So he had fairly well-founded expectations that he would be appointed to the Controller's post when it came to be filled, since he had, he thought, been running the place well. When it was advertised, about a year after the station opened, he applied with confidence.

He was first devastated and then furious when Michael Barry from the BBC was appointed instead. Michael Barry was the quintessential old-school-tie, terribly British, BBC product. When he came to take up his job he realised immediately that the place had been set up on the American system, and set about changing it to what he knew best, which was to duplicate the home of good old Auntie.

Ernest, insulted, humiliated, made the grand gesture and resigned—entirely the wrong thing to do. (Never, ever resign: that's my motto. It is what 'They' want you to do!) If he had held his cool and waited he would have triumphed in the end, because within six or eight months Michael Barry had returned home. In his fury Ernest went to Welsh television, but that did not work out for him either and, disillusioned, he returned to the United States. Having left the rat-race, far more vicious than any on this side of the Atlantic, he found it very difficult to break into it again. The waters had closed over, leaving no trace of his former existence. The arena over there was always cut-throat and fit only for the fittest—and youngest.

☐

Things went from bad to worse. Remember, Ernest had been at the very top of his career in the United States, and the experience here was absolutely devastating to him. He began to drink very heavily, and so did Dorothy. They had four children, one of whom, the eldest girl, is seriously mentally retarded. Their youngest, a boy, is slightly so. Ernest died three years ago, a disillusioned, broken-hearted man. The year before he died, when Al last met him in Cleveland, Ohio, Al persuaded him to write something of his life. Instead he produced five 1,000-word articles about the 'American Nightmare', which he had thought at first was such a dream. Taken together they reflect a clear-eyed, horrifying view of what it is like to be sliding out of affluence and down the scale in the United States: a picture of a society where the 'haves' are blessed and distribute and re-distribute the resources amongst themselves and where life for the 'have-nots' —the elderly, the disabled, and the disadvantaged—is hopeless and undignified.

Although Ernest did not descend far down the scale and was, as he said in the first paragraph of the first article, approaching 'a sort of semi-retirement in fair comfort', clearly, like me and possibly the other Byrnes, he feared being poor and helpless, and his fear gave him an empathy with those who are.

He wrote that, all day and all night, as American people watched their television screens blaze with the American Dream of consumer affluence, the numbers of the jobless and the hopeless still grew. Thirty-one days after an American loses his job he will find himself with no health insurance. People who stand in line at the unemployment office still hear all around them from those who have jobs and who are holding onto their second cars, their Jacuzzis, and the private schools for the kids, the refrain that 'In America you can always get a job if you want one.' He knew that they were desperate for jobs, any jobs, but knew also that they were reduced to standing in line especially early when the government was handing out free cheese.

The soup kitchens were busy before Ernest died. He saw clearly that 'America has always had a "work or starve, survive or die" mentality. Even the old-age pension or Social Security payments are based on how much the worker paid into the system during the years of his working life. This is the great Free Enterprise system. What you put in you get back. No more; no less. We somehow never stopped to wonder, what about those who cannot put anything in?' Whereas America had always been and still is a great country for the young, healthy, and hard-driving, it was not for the old or the sick. The change Ernest observed between the time he arrived in the States and the time he wrote these articles was that it was suddenly the young and strong, as well as the old and the sick, who were in trouble.

☐

That was Ernest. By comparison, our only sister, Mary, has had a charmed life. She went into the Royal Insurance Company when she left school, and then, inevitably, made her way into Guinness's (which was fast becoming our Family Firm) as a 'lady clerk', where she met and married a fellow-employee named David Orr.

Of course it was not quite that quick. Mary had many, many boy-friends, and they were all brought home—and all had to pass scrutiny by the rest of the family. They all made themselves reasonably amenable to me, the kid brother: two especially so. Phil Newport was a very, very good model aircraft builder and turned me on to that for a while; but Eric Richardson had *a motorbike!* A 500 c.c. Matchless. And he went in for trials and scrambles! Hell, there was no contest in the popularity stakes! I wanted Mary to marry Eric. Who could turn down a 500 c.c. Matchless?

It is a wonder that Mary managed to escape our family. Ernest in particular took it upon himself to act as her protector and minder. She has a photograph, taken by one of those street photographers who are now a dying breed in Dublin, of herself coming out of an office near Trinity College, having been interviewed for a job. The interview had been scheduled for half-past five, and Ernest, suspicious fellow, had wondered about the motives of anyone who would interview a pure young girl at that time of the evening, after business hours. In the street snap there she is, bright as a button, and there, in the background, is the hulking, lurking figure of Ernest, who she had not known was present until she saw the photograph. After she met David, Ernest also took it upon himself to sit ostentatiously on one of the treads of the stairs in the hallway of our house while Mary and David were 'visiting' behind closed doors in the parlour. He never said anything, or made any noise. He just sat. Looming.

Young David Orr was a Protestant from Trim who worked in Guinness's. At that time, whatever about Ray managing it in apostate England, it was very, very difficult indeed for a couple of mixed religion in Ireland. Mary knew what she was up against, and told him. He loved her so much that he considered the possibility of conversion—and went ahead with it. In these more tolerant times it is difficult to understand just how big a decision that was for him, particularly coming from a small place like Trim, where his parents were highly respected people. His father was the local bank manager. They did not come much more Prod.

David initially told his parents only that he had fallen in love with a Catholic. But after he began to enquire into the Catholic faith he found that he came to a point, even if he was not to continue with the relationship, where he would have continued through with the conversion. It would not have made any difference to Mary whether he went through

☐

with it or not, because she had decided once and for all that she would defy Ma and anyone else who tried to stop her marrying him.

David wrote to his parents and told them that he was going to become a Catholic. Then he and Mary got on a scooter and went to Lough Derg. When they got back from their pilgrimage the letter of reply from David's parents was waiting. Although they were very, very upset at his decision and very strongly against it, they wrote that if that was what he wanted, they would go along with it. And to their eternal credit, having decided to go along with it they went the full way and came to the wedding, with his mother's sister and her husband from the North and a family friend who was the widow of a canon in the Church of Ireland. They sat in the church of Our Lady of Fatima, fifty yards from our front door, a small platoon of Christian charity surrounded by the legions from the One True Church.

Many years later, David's parents came to live with David and Mary in a flat in their house in Foxrock. About a fortnight before David's father died, Mary was sitting in the flat beside him. By then he had become totally blind and very feeble. It was the day of Mary and David's twenty-fifth wedding anniversary. Old Mr Orr took Mary's hand gently and tenderly in his own and said: 'All that foolishness . . . and it was such a good marriage . . .'

I have said before that Mary is the nicest of us all. She is certainly the most contented now. She did not react to our mother the same way we did. We all, it seemed, thrived on the pushing, whereas she resented it. She hated the way my mother was so gregarious with neighbours, announcing the family business to all and sundry.

It is always a source of amusement to me how it is the little, insignificant things we remember and not the great big important ones, which have perhaps shaped our lives. Mary is still indignant about the day when she was about 10 and was being brought in to see 'Daddy Christmas' in one of the stores in town. (We never had Santa Claus, it was always Daddy Christmas.) She blushed and squirmed with embarrassment as my mother announced their destination to everyone she met on the way.

When Mary was getting married, my mother did the tours of the shops with her, choosing material for the wedding dress. Finally, in Cassidy's of O'Connell Street, she found some they both liked, but there was not enough.

'Would you make the top out of another material?' asked the sales assistant helpfully.

'Oh, no, I wouldn't have that at all!' said my mother immediately. 'Show us something else.'

The assistant looked wryly at Mary: 'Who's getting married?' But Ma had her way as usual. Mary just found it easier to give in.

I do not think that she quite understood the relationship between my mother and father. Being closer to him than to her, she saw him only as the gentle husband of a domineering wife. But this was no problem at all for him. Only the willing can be dominated, and, loving her, he permitted it, not feeling himself at all to be subservient. There were ferocious rows between our parents, naturally, but that was par for the course in our area. All of us knew which husband had come in late and had battered which wife. We knew what the next-door neighbours fought about and they knew what we fought about, and that was the way our Dublin working-class life went. No-one passed any remarks. My parents' rows were verbal, a lot of sound and fury but nothing really serious.

Of all of us, Mary is the one who wishes I was not as prominent in public life as I am. I have learned only recently—to my regret, because there is little I can do about it—that she finds it very difficult to relax socially unless she is with people who do not know the connection. She says she sees people talking to her and making constant comparisons. She is very family-conscious: it is she who has kept all the photographs and clippings; and although she is absolutely loyal and admires what I do she would probably have preferred me to have a nice, sane, nine-to-five career. Then I could be more of a brother to her.

She says she now finds it difficult to differentiate between my on-air persona and my real self. She is very astute, because I find it difficult to make that distinction for myself. I believe I am me on-air. But is the on-air person the 'me' who walks around and has a life outside? When you have been performing for your supper for as long as I have, some confusion is inevitable . . . Mary rarely looks at the 'Late Late Show' but never misses the morning radio show unless she is busy with her catering business. Again, she has identified the difference with great astuteness. On television, she believes she has to share me with too many people. Radio is the one-on-one medium.

I think she was always aware of our mother's leanings towards the boys, and particularly towards Al and me. (In fact Al was so close to Ma that for twenty years after she died, he was miserable each Christmas Eve on the anniversary of her death.) It was not always easy to be the only girl of such a mother, and her memories of us as children are tinged with natural resentment of the favouritism shown to us. For instance, she has a very clear memory of the day we were playing outside and she hit me. I bawled, louder of course than was absolutely necessary, and purely for effect. It work-ed. She was yanked inside and sent to her room. She was ordered to pull the blinds down and not even to look out the window. She yanked down the blind with such a vengeance that she pulled it clean off the window.

☐

But strangely enough, this was quite an isolated incident. There were not all that many fights between us, and we all got on. Mary, who has a naturally sweet nature, never held anything against us. And there was never a question of 'girls' work' or 'boys' work'. All of us were required to follow our father's example in doing housework.

And Mary sees through all the flimflam I put up about treadmills and whirligigs and being trapped in this prison of my own making. Her attitude is, if I see this, why do I not do something about it? It is something I have asked myself . . .

CHAPTER 2
GROWING UP A DUB

ur first home, 17 Rialto Street, had a bright red front door that opened directly onto the street. In those days Rialto Street swarmed with kids skipping and playing relievio and swinging out of the lamp-posts, kicking forbidden footballs and playing forbidden handball against the end walls of the terraces. There were always parents on the war-path, spinsters confiscating the balls, and general Them-and-Us mayhem, but since the adults were so vastly outnumbered it was never long before we all surged cheerfully out again, sent out from under Their feet.

Most mornings I awoke before six o'clock in the back bedroom of Rialto Street to the sound of the Guinness horses, slow-moving trains of massive Clydesdales, twenty-five or thirty of them, clopping along the street on huge feathered hooves, going to start their day's work from their stables in Herberton Road. Up Rialto Street they went and down the canal to James's Harbour, horses and drays delivering stout all over Dublin. The horses were lovely beasts and beautifully cared for. In the evenings, when they were returning to their stables, they provided endless scuttin' opportunities for us children, who hung onto the backs of the drays, wheeling outwards like fairground chairoplanes as the horses swung around the corners. And part of our home chores involved collecting the copious piles of steaming dung they left in their wake, which our parents used to fertilise our flower-beds and our gooseberry bushes and, in the case of one neighbour, a Mr Dobson, to help provide the most delicious apples I have ever tasted.

Most of the families on our street were very large, five or six being on the small side, ten, eleven and twelve being not unusual; and, as always in poorer areas of any city, there was a rigid hierarchy of status in housing, tuppence-ha'penny looking down on tuppence.

At the bottom of the heap was Maryland, a flats complex down near the end of the canal. As far as we, the tuppence-ha'pennies, were concerned, the Maryland crowd were—well, *common*. But in our immediate ghetto, bottom of the league, although not as common as the Maryland element, were those from Rialto Buildings, about fifty yards from our door and at the

□

opposite side of the street. It was a big complex of flats with damp concrete entranceways and (quite pretty) wrought-iron balconies, always strewn with nappies and out of which we swung like reckless little Tarzans until we were caught. Then came the denizens of Rialto Cottages, little one-storey terraces ranged around allotments in the squares. These allotments were planted with potatoes, vegetables, and sometimes brave displays of wall-flowers, lupins, and even roses. (Recently a colleague in RTE astounded me by telling me he had bought one of the Cottages for £15,000.) Our houses were next, looking down both on the Cottages and the Buildings. We were two-storey, with back entries from the laneway running behind them into little individual yards, where we could grow geraniums in pots and lock up our bicycles instead of having them cluttering up the space inside the front door.

The height of it all was to be on the main road. That height, which we reached when we moved to 124 (later to be renumbered 512) South Circular Road in 1944, was where one was monarch of all one surveyed at a rent of £5 per month.

The story is told of an unfortunate man on 'the Street' who hanged himself in the attic of his house. For the purposes of the story we'll call him Mr Reid. And again for the purposes of the story we'll call the lady who lived in the Buildings across the street from the Reids, Mrs Pepper—a good woman, whose husband worked in Guinness's, but renowned all over the district for Putting Her Foot In It. Always and everywhere. Naturally, when poor Mr Reid hanged himself the whole district was agog. And when Mrs Pepper's husband came home from work, of course he was met at the door with the tragic news, whereupon he issued instructions to Mrs Pepper that she was forthwith to go across the road to the Reids' house and she was to sympathise. She was simply to say, 'Mrs Reid, Mr Pepper and myself want to sympathise with you in your terrible trouble.' *Then she was to come home without uttering another syllable.* Understood? Understood.

Off she goes across the road. It is a stormy day. *Knock knock.* 'Hello, Mrs Reid. Mr Pepper and myself want to say how sorry we are about your terrible trouble . . .'

'Thank you very much, Mrs Pepper . . .'

'Terrible weather, isn't it?'

'It is, right enough . . .'

'All this rain . . . !'

'Terrible, right enough, Mrs Pepper . . .'

'You wouldn't know what to be doing with the clothes to get them dry. Of course you're okay, *you* have an attic for hanging things up in . . . !'

The very earliest memory in my life is of one Christmas morning in Rialto

□

Street. Ernest came upstairs to me and announced that 'Daddy Christmas' had come. He took me on his back and piggied me down to the parlour. There, in front of the fireplace, was the most beautiful object I had ever seen. Even at that young age I could see what work and what craftsmanship had been lavished on it.

It was a covered wagon, about two feet tall and, from the nose of the little horse between its shafts to the rear entrance, three feet long. There was a little cowboy seated on the driving seat, holding reins of real leather. The horse had a padded leather collar and bridle. There was even a leather lead-rein attached to the bit, so that I could pull the whole thing along. The shafts were mounted on a tiny turntable so the wagon could turn, and there were wooden foldaway steps at the back for ease of entrance. Inside the canvas covering over the wooden ribs of the superstructure it was completely furnished, with table, chairs, pots and pans. All the wood was Canadian oak. I brought it out onto Rialto Street to play with it, and people going to Christmas Mass gathered around to admire it. I wish I knew who made it. In retrospect I think it had probably been crafted by one of Jack Flood's coopering friends. I wish I still had it—my mother gave it away eventually.

Another Christmas, Jack Flood sent me a rocking-horse. It arrived on our doorstep in a Switzer's delivery van, a lovely sight to behold. But there was no card with it, just my name and address on the packing label. The delivery-man argued with my mother, to no avail. There must have been some mistake, she insisted. No-one would go to that amount of trouble for little Gaybo. The rocking-horse, my beautiful rocking-horse, was sent back to the store with the defeated vanman. It was only much later in the year, when the Floods ventured to make enquiries about why there had been no mention of their gift, that the truth came out. My mother marched down to Switzer's forthwith, explained the situation, and took away with her, not a rocking-horse but goods-to-the-value-of, i.e. one hearthrug.

Beside us in Rialto Street lived the Killeens. One of them, Nan, worked in Denson's Shoes, but Florrie Killeen got TB and had to go out to Newcastle Sanatorium. We all knew she would not be back: TB was a death sentence, and it was greatly feared, the cancer of that era. (In fact, Ma saved regularly all her life to have money put by for the eventuality of any of us developing this dreaded disease. If it happened, the money was to be used to send us to Switzerland.) But until Florrie actually died, Ma regularly travelled out to see her, as did the other neighbours. It was a full day's trip to Newcastle, leaving at nine in the morning on the 19 bus into town, in time to catch the other, long-distance bus out into the Wicklow hills. She did not get home until tea-time.

☐

On the other side of us were the Hollingsworths—millions of them, it seemed. Nick was a manager in Clery's, and John went into Guinness's. Beside the Kennas on the corner were the Dunnes, who kept to themselves, and up the road were the Hoeys—millions of them, too—and the Heffernans, who included another special pal, Tommy, who lived with his family, including George and Teresa and Kevin. Tommy's father was a cooper in Guinness's, and Tommy himself ended up there too. There were the Griffins beyond the Cassidys, who sold milk for a living. One of the Griffins went away and came back to the neighbourhood in the canonicals of a Protestant clergyman. The neighbourhood was not amused.

I drove around the old haunts recently, up the busy South Circular Road with its venerable but dingy trees, past Griffith Barracks and up to the National Stadium. This was the road I traversed four times a day for approximately eight years. In some ways it has changed greatly, in some, not at all.

One of our pastimes was to loiter in front of the barracks, gazing in past the barrier at the front gate at the constant but fairly leisurely activity in the square in front of the big grey buildings, especially during the 'Emergency'. There was always a lot of marching and stamping, and clouds of belching black smoke from the exhaust pipes of the tinny armoured vehicles. Even at my young age I used to wonder how this little lot was going to save us all from nastiness like bombings and shootings and gassings, all the terrible things that were being written about in the newspapers and that I heard daily on our wireless. The height of our Defence Forces' activities, as far as we could see, was a tramping march from the barracks up to the Phoenix Park and back again.

Dublin, as has often been said, is a city of villages, and the whole South Circular Road area was a series of them—Dolphin's Barn, Rialto, Kelly's Corner, Leonard's Corner—each self-contained with its own pub, butcher, greengrocer, and general store. The citizens mixed around, but were loyal to their own tradesmen.

Mogerley's, the pork butcher, is still there, and all the little shops I used to know, some of them in the same hands. Al used to be sent up every Saturday morning to Honer's greengrocers and victuallers at Dolphin's Barn to buy two 'grazers'. A grazer was a fourpenny rabbit. Mr Honer would unhook the creatures from where they dangled from their hooks, part of a long row, pathetically and irrevocably dead. He would skin them with a huge knife in two shakes of their own tails. Then my mother would cook the most beautiful rabbit stew, and afterwards would remove the stewed meat from its broth, crisping it in butter in a large frying-pan. As I have said, Ma was a great cook.

On Christmas morning, when the smell of roasting turkey permeated the

☐ A very young Gaybo on a day trip to Belfast in 1949 with my mother and Jean and Pauline Edwards.

☐ A family picture in the back garden of Aunt Kathleen's house in Thurleston Terrace off Meath Street.

house and when the fire in the parlour was blazing brightly (reflecting so vividly off the trebly polished linoleum in front of it that Al always believed we had two fires on Christmas Day), Jack Prestige, now 96 years old and living in the Gascoigne Home, used to call in to our house at six in the morning on his way from night duty at Guinness's. He would unwind the strings from around his battered old leather purse and would give each of us children a half-crown. I never had mine long. Like all the other money I received, it was whipped away by Ma to be 'saved' for me. So, unlike a lot of my school pals, who could lavish pennies on Honey Bees and 'nancy balls' and fizz bags in the local shops, I had little or no pocket money.

This is perhaps why I stole the Apple. If you do not know the story of the Apple, you have not come within shouting or air-wave distance of me within the last ten years. *Crime and Punishment* has nothing on the Apple saga as far as I am concerned.

On the corner of our street was a little shop called Monaghan's. Mr Monaghan displayed his fruit on a stand outside the front door of his shop. Asking for it.

Little Gaybo in his short pants was 5 years old and could not resist temptation. Egged on by my pal Tommy Heffernan, I nicked an apple from the display. I was naïve enough to walk cheerfully into our house, munching on the forbidden fruit.

My mother pounced immediately. '*Where did you get that apple?*'

I lied that someone had given it to me. I might as well have saved my breath to cool my porridge. My mother could spot a lie at fifty paces. Clutching my precious piggy bank, in the shape of a red tin pillar-box, I was frog-marched back up the street to Monaghan's. The shop was full, bursting, it seemed, with people, all of whom stopped what they were doing to hear my mother ask in stentorian tones:

'Mr Monaghan, have you got apples on your stand outside?'

'Yes, Mrs Byrne.'

'I have to report to you that this *person*' (withering contempt) 'has stolen an *apple* from your stand. This is the very apple, Mr Monaghan!'

Christy Monaghan, who twigged immediately what she was at, as did everyone else in the shop, threw up his hands in shock. Everyone stopped breathing.

'Did you know this, Mr Monaghan?'

(Gravely) 'No, I didn't, Mrs Byrne.'

'Well, he did. And now he must make *restitution*! Here is his savings bank— ' (the miserable thing clanked treacherously) '*you must take it . . .!*' (High drama and handing over of the piggy bank, in the manner of Clara Bow renouncing Gary Cooper at the height of her melodramatic despair.)

I started to cry, the loud wails falling into the depths of the accusing silence in the shop as Christy Monaghan fetched a knife and laboriously inserted it into the small oblong slot at the top of the red pillar-box. Slowly, as slowly as the coming of Christmas, down the blade of the knife slid one, two, three of my precious pennies. I howled louder.

They were not going to let me off that lightly. Everyone in the shop felt it was their bounden duty to give me a lecture and to 'tsk-tsk' over the state of the world. What was it coming to when an honest man could not leave his apples outside his front door? What were boys coming to these days? And Mrs Byrne having reared such a nice, such a good, such an *honest* family? That was, up to this moment . . .

Then I had to place the apple butt on Mr Monaghan's counter before I could slink out of the shop like a whipped dog, all eyes still boring into me, forlorn little Gaybo, shame written along his back, having to walk every burning step back home.

I never stole another apple.

The first day at school is supposed to be extremely traumatic for everyone. Obviously I have no sense of drama whatsoever, because I remember not a blessed thing about it. All I remember is that I did not like my teacher, a Miss Leyden. Things began to look up the following year in high babies when Miss Leyden was replaced by Miss Sweeney. I fell in love with the lovely Miss Sweeney, who, I noticed, had terrific legs. I became her slave for ever when she correctly discerned that I was a true artist. She asked us all to draw a mountain. I drew an inverted V, with little squares hanging off each side of it. What mountain was that, enquired the lovely Miss Sweeney. It was the Big Sugarloaf, I explained gravely, and the little squares were all the lumps hanging off it. Miss Sweeney was really impressed . . .

I see now that the little Rialto national school is all boarded up and forlorn, with broken panes in its grubby windows. The principal was a man called Doolan, father of Dermot Doolan, who for many years ran Irish Actors' Equity. Mr Doolan was a tall, stately man with white hair who carried a comfortable corporation in front of him like an old friend. I was never taught by Mr Doolan, but after the Misses Leyden and Sweeney passed on to a teacher called Hearne, otherwise known as the Kipper, a long, thin, dark man who used the leather and the stick on us as he pleased. (Hearne—herring—kipper. Geddit?)

Everyone is also supposed to remember their First Communion day. I'm afraid all I remember is the money. The tradition, then as now, was that you were brought around, simpering, by the hand, collecting money from doting relatives who patted you on the head and said you looked gorgeous and what a great little man you were. This great little man collected nearly

□

eight pounds—a fortune—and could not *wait* for the next collecting day, which would be Confirmation. If you got eight pounds for your Communion, you could count on at least double for the Confo. As usual, the Ma immediately whipped the money away 'for safety' and put it into the post office. She had opened an account for me the week after I was born, with five shillings. Every time she had a spare shilling, she would put it in for me.

But if my memory of the Holy Communion day itself is mercenary, my memory of the preparations for it is frightening.

In first class we had a teacher called Duffy, but in preparation for our First Holy Communion there was a young curate from Dolphin's Barn who took us for catechism. One day, about a fortnight before the great day, he conducted a sort of examination of the catechism. One of the other kids in the class was asked a question and did not know the answer. Without any warning, this curate peeled off a box and laid out the child, sending him flying across the room, so that he actually bounced off the far wall. The blow was savage, with the full strength of a grown man, tall and young and healthy, behind it. Mr Duffy grew pale, and while the dazed and shocked child was still lying on the floor, he rushed over to the priest and bundled him out the door.

I cannot remember the child's name, but I would love to know now what his attitude is to religion. On the other hand, it is only fair to say that even at that young age I realised that the priest was extremely disturbed and unhappy, and indeed he was removed from our parish a short time later. Whatever happened to him after that I do not know.

From Rialto national school I went for a year to a sort of preparatory or bridging school to the nuns at Brown Street and Weaver's Square. Sister Rosarie, the head bottle-washer there, had taught Al, Ernest and Ray before me, so there was never any question that I too would be prepared for Donore Avenue at Brown Street.

One story concerning my stay at Weaver's Square was broadcast to the nation on the 'Late Late Show' in February 1988 by two of Sister Rosarie's pals-in-habit, Sister Columban and Sister Killian Horgan from Castleisland, a set of twins, known to generations of teachers trained in Carysfort as Mug and Gug. They were in the audience on the occasion of their golden jubilee. They reminded me that one of the finer practices in the school was that the poorer boys were given soup and sandwiches at lunchtime in order to supplement what was no doubt a meagre diet at home. Apparently I thought this was very humiliating, and I organised that we who were better off would bring in and distribute extra sandwiches from our relatively comfortable homes. I have no recollection of the event whatsoever, but am happy to bask smugly in its glory.

My friend in that school was a fellow called Christy Thompson from Maryland (he ended up in England as Sales Manager for Ilford Films). Christy and I had a wonderful source of entertainment right on our doorsteps. On our way home from school we would call in to Donnelly's meat factory in Cork Steet, next door to the school, to watch the cattle and sheep being slaughtered and gutted. Regularly in Cork Street in those days you would encounter huge herds of animals being driven to their doom, because as well as Donnelly's meat factory there was Keefe's the knackers, the odour from which is still in my nostrils. Keefe's performed the humbler end of the animal slaughter business. The burned-out and diseased animals that ended up there were slaughtered for what are euphemistically called their by-products. In other words, it was a tallow and glue factory.

I suppose there are Dublin city children these days who have never seen a farm animal in the flesh. But we were thoroughly familiar with them: working horses and cattle and sheep, (dead) donkeys in Keefe's—and pigs, which made an almighty squealing racket during the slaughtering process.

Christy and I became heavily involved in herding. Going to and from school, meeting a vast herd of lowing or bleating animals, we learned to raise our arms threateningly and to 'howup, hup' with the best of the drovers. In Donnelly's, we watched with semi-professional and totally heartless interest as our charges were driven one by one through the iron pens, coming inexorably closer to their deaths. It all seemed terribly easy. The animal's head was caught upwards and with one swift thrust, the knife went straight in and slit all the way down. Great fun. The steam and the noise, the water, blood and guts. Nice kids, we were.

After Brown Street it was on to the greater heights of St Teresa's in Donore Avenue. St Teresa's looked enormous. By the standards of Irish Catholic Dublin it was pretty ordinary—looming, greyly institutional, with many windows—but to my small, nervous eyes it seemed to be the biggest building I had ever seen. The rough concrete yard, with its bicycle sheds, was an endless prairie teeming with Big Boys and Bullies lying in wait for helpless victims like me. I don't know what I thought they would do to me—and in fact they were pretty harmless—but there was quite a delicious element of fear in the traversing of that playground. At least for the first few weeks. And they need have had no fear that I might challenge them. I was a hanger-back. First of all, I had no inclination towards the rough stuff, and secondly, I was under parental interdict not to get my clothes dirty.

The highlight of Donore for me was the day our teacher, Mr Moynihan, brought us all in to Radio Éireann to perform the play *Íosagán* as part of a series for children called 'Children at the Microphone'. We had rehearsed for weeks. I had already won at the Father Mathew Feis with a recitation

45

□

from *Séadna* (my prize for which was a copy of *Eachtraí Sherlock Holmes*, plus a bonus next day from Mr Moynihan of an English thruppenny bit). Therefore I was already regarded as quite a star in the Donore league of public performance. We lugged with us our 'set', which was a butter box with a semicircular piece of cardboard stuck around its outside. This was the little hillock on which one of the characters sat.

I was about 10 at the time, and when we got into the GPO I was struck dumb by the importance of the long, long carpeted corridor, the length of a city street, which ran from the front of Radio Éireann's premises all the way to the drama suite at the back. There seemed to be wires everywhere and microphones and strange, quiet people who walked around with an air of mysterious purpose, or who sat silently, twiddling dials and talking in quiet monosyllables. It was lovely, it was exciting, and I *wanted* it. Immediately, I knew I wanted it . . .

When I came home on the 19 bus after this wonderful performance, which was so earth-shatteringly important to me, I was expecting at the very least that there would be 'Welcome Home, Star!' banners hung from side to side of Rialto Street. At the very least there would be a brass band and a parish priest. To my surprise, no-one rushed up to me as I got off the bus. No-one lifted me shoulder-high. Alone among all the ingrates and ignoramuses in Rialto, only my faithful Ma had tuned in to 'Children at the Microphone'.

For my Confirmation, to be conducted by the late Archbishop John Charles McQuaid in the church on Donore Avenue, I was sent with one of my father's old blue suits to a local tailor on Mountshannon Road, a man called Carroll. Mr Carroll specialised in cutting down and turning—all the skills now, alas, lost. Mr Carroll measured me and in due course I collected my 'new' confirmation suit, a rather splendid suit in my opinion, one not to be sniggered at as a hand-me-down. I remember little of the big day itself, except that for some reason my mother was not allowed into the church. We went to the school first before the church, and the parents were to arrive independently. But when I came out of the church after the ceremony, I spotted her work-worn face pressed against the railings outside.

We re-enacted the visiting of the relatives and the collecting of the money. Sixteen pounds it was this time, I believe, and once again it vanished into the post office account. There are those who accuse me of still having my Confirmation money, one of the charming euphemisms for meanness in this mean country. In a sense they are correct, because I still have that post office book, long since emptied out, which was in my mother's charge up to the time she died. She kept adding to it in dribs and drabs, and when I began to work, so did I. (There was one occasion, quite early on in my

☐

career, when the Revenue Commissioners were dunning me for something and were pooching around in my accounts, going back twelve or fifteen years. They had noted that I had lodged £700 to a bank account after my mother died and wanted to know where it came from. Triumphantly I was able to produce the closed-off dog-eared little book, which showed her loving lodgments from the day I was born. I sent it to them with a note saying, in effect, 'Lose this, you rotten swine, and I'll have your guts for garters! It is an heirloom from my mother.' They returned it.)

Behind a high, very rough concrete wall at the end of our street, where Fatima Mansions now stand, was a big open space we called Bonzo's Field. Bonzo's Field was where superiority was asserted, the war zone for hostilities between our gang and the Maryland gang. The boys from Maryland were tough customers, but our gang frequently set out to show them a thing or two. This involved climbing over the concrete wall, grazing knees and tearing precious trousers, to stand face-to-face against them in Bonzo's. An arsenal of stones and rocks at the ready, we marched across Bonzo's from our end, they from theirs. The fighting was fierce and genuinely dangerous, frequently resulting in split heads and burst lips. When the Maryland gang were routed for another day, the wounded from our side were helped back over the wall by their gallant comrades, the more blood the greater the honour and the higher the heroism. Our mothers were never amused.

And to tell the really, really truth, although I did participate I was never all that pushed about the fighting. As well as being quite a quiet chap, there was my mother's edict about not getting my clothes dirty. I was reminded recently by one of the former desperados in our gang, now a respectable businessman, that I would always hang back: 'I can't do this (or that), I'd get my clothes dirty.' Knowing my mother as they all did, they were tolerant and put up with my little strangenesses.

Between us and Maryland was part of the Grand Canal, a busy boat thoroughfare from James's Harbour to the great beyond in provincial Ireland. It is now filled in, but to us was playground and swimming-pool. Your mother did not allow you to swim in the canal—there were rats and dead dogs and drowned cats in the canal and you would get terrible diseases out of it—but we got into it all the same. At least most of us did.

With little money and a lot of time during the holidays, Rialto bridge was the place where I spent hour after hour during my childhood summers, just listening, listening and watching, throwing sticks for the multitude of dogs that tagged along and swam with us. The drill was to congregate around the old stone bridge, which had a parapet and several lower ledges, and then, with great bravado, to jump in from the highest possible point. I saw at least one boy jump and miss. He was from Maryland, and we all watched

47

in fascinated horror as he splattered himself on the flagstones on the edge of the water. I was safe from such a fate. I did not jump, because I could not swim. Poor me.

Night after night, especially in summer weather, all the single—and some of the married—young men and boys congregated at the corner of Rialto Street: corner-boys, with nothing to do and nothing to go home to except rooms full of small children, no television, and nothing much else to amuse them. They eked out the minutes until they could respectably go to the pub, because they only had money for the one pint. We younger boys hung around too, a respectful distance apart from them.

One summer's evening we were all standing at the corner, watching the men playing toss-ha'penny and pitch-penny with fecks. A feck was a comb or half of a wooden clothes-peg, with which you 'fecked' off the coin. (If you were feckless, you did not possess even a feck with which to toss a coin, much less a coin . . .) Among the men's group was a fellow called Whitty, who was dropped into Arnheim as a commando parachutist, was captured, and had an awful time as a prisoner of war and who came home to a land fit for heroes but could find no work. One of our group was a boy called Seán Higgins, older than me and my immediate pals, who lived on First Avenue, around the corner. He was from a very tough household; we all knew that his father, a lorry driver in Guinness's, ran his family very strictly.

It was an exciting evening, because one of the older members of the group, who lived in a flat at the back of the Buildings, had just that day bought a brand-new 350 c.c. AJS motorbike, for all of us the epitome of all riches and the realisation of all material ambition. Cahill was allowing us to ride on his brand-new machine. My friends Colm Campbell and Tony Bennett and I were too young to be given the privilege, but we could all follow the progress of the chosen by the great roaring gear changes on the half-mile circuit from the corner of our street where we stood until it bombed back into view.

Seán Higgins was one of the lucky ones that evening. He got onto the bike and roared off up Rialto Street and down the canal to Rialto bridge. But at the bend beyond the bridge the motorbike went out of control and he veered right across the road and crashed into a lamp-post opposite Rialto House—McAuley's pub. He was killed instantly. He was the only boy in his family.

When Colm Campbell was with me, we always had his cocker spaniels with us too. My own first dog was a red setter, given to me from a litter owned by a colleague of Al's in Guinness's, A. A. Pakenham-Walsh. I travelled out on the bus to his house, Crinken Lodge in Shankill, and

☐

brought the puppy home with me. I brought him into the house and settled him down in front of a blazing fire, whereupon armies and legions of fleas began to torment him. The cure for fleas at the time was DDT, and I spent hours and hours driving the fleas towards his head by dusting the rest of him with DDT and then picking them off one by one from his snout as they marched in single file towards what they thought was safety. Greater love . . . Apart from anything else, I was allergic to the DDT and all the preparations lovingly lavished on all the Best Friends in our neighbourhood in an effort to control their fleas. I used to come out in a bad rash if one of these walking time-bombs came near me. But the poor setter did not live long. Red setters are scatty, and he was killed on the main road.

Our family, almost uniquely in our neighbourhood, had an Annual Holiday. Each year we went to Bray, bloody Bray . . .

I suppose I should not be too hard on Bray. I should be grateful that we had the privilege of actually going on holiday at all. In fact I am, and the appellation is just an affectionate groan. We always stayed with distant relatives of my mother, who had a big guest-house on Trafalgar Terrace that smelled overpoweringly of Mansion polish mixed in with rashers and eggs. Most memories of Bray are of this house, which I hated but which I know the others liked. Ma and Da spent hours sitting in the parlour, just talking. They went for walks along the sea front, imbibing the fresh air, and occasionally, very occasionally, they went to the Roxy cinema.

I spent most of my time hanging around at the railway gates in Bray, riding on them as they were opened and closed at the level crossing to let the steam trains through, enjoying the sun on my back. Sometimes I joined Ma and Da as they took decorous walks up and down Bray Head. I looked longingly at the amusement arcades, but I never had the money to go in. I prayed for rain on Sundays: a fine Sunday meant an invasion of city people off the trains. I was also resentful that I was not allowed into the sea. The strange thing was that although my mother had been a champion swimmer, she would not let any of us near the water. (I have only recently learned to swim, a distinction I share with, among others, the playwright Hugh Leonard, although he had fewer excuses than I, being brought up beside the sea in Dalkey. Hugh—known to his friends by his real name of Jack Keyes Byrne—and I actually learned together. Real swimming lessons. They were not entirely successful at first, because, although I learned to stay on top of the water, I kept swimming around in circles: I simply could not go in a straight line. It was Tony Bennett who later showed me in a swimming-pool in the south of France that the way to swim was not one long stroke with the right arm and a short one with the left . . .)

In the evenings I haunted the bandstand, where there was a variety show called the 'Coon Show', free except for those who paid thruppence for the use of a deck-chair. The acts were good: Jack Cruise was a regular, and it was at the Coons that Val Doonican got his first gig.

But there was one outstanding treat in Bray. Johnny Murphy, the man in whose house we always stayed, worked in CIE, and he managed to fix it so I would get a jaunt on the footplate of a steam locomotive, 'helping' to drive it. To this day I can remember her number, engine no. 436, as she bore me up and down the track to Shankill and then to Greystones. I do not remember why we were jaunting and doubling back—they were probably just turning the engine—but to me it was extraordinarily exciting to ride that big black machine, roaring and chuffing along the tracks, smuts flying past my head, the envy of every small boy in the counties of Dublin and Wicklow.

But I was always glad to get home to the South Circular Road and my pals. We all thought we were very fortunate to have such an important venue as the National Stadium right in our midst. This is where Éamonn Andrews got his start, both as a boxer and as a sports commentator. It was draughty and echoing and very exciting. It was here, on one celebrated night, that Éamonn won a hard-fought bout on points, and then scrambled up to the commentary box, still out of breath, to give his blow-by-blow account of the rest of the night's boxing.

All of us boys went along to the stadium on boxing nights. In my memory the crowd, like any Dublin crowd, was always good-humoured. There were standard gags, like when the two fighters were waltzing around one another, feinting and not connecting, and the roar would start: 'Look out! Don't touch him! The ref is watching!' Or someone at the back would start to sing the strains of 'The Blue Danube', 'La-la-la-la-*laah*!' and within seconds the whole place would be waltzing and singing and swaying along.

The crowd was charitable. If you were no good at boxing but you were trying, then they gave you full marks. But woe betide anyone who was lazy. Certain boxers, like Fred Teidt, had a huge following, and if he was fighting on a given night the place would be packed to the rafters. Other times there would be only a handful of people in the vast, echoing place, and the sound of the leather thudding onto bare skin was magnified a thousand times. At that time boxing was regarded as manly and was an official sport in many boys' schools. It was also a vehicle for dreams, as it is in Belfast today. A young boy with no education and no prospects dreamed of fighting his way out of his ghetto.

When I was a bit older and had become interested in jazz, Kenny Ball and his Jazzmen came to play at the Stadium once, and Colm Campbell and I decided to go and have a look. But as we approached we saw there were cars

☐

parked bumper-to-bumper all along the South Circular Road, and I knew we did not have a prayer of getting in.

'Come with me!' I said to Campbell. Adopting what I hoped was an official face, I marched up, past the queues ('Excuse me, excuse me!') and rapped importantly on the little wooden counter. 'Radio Éireann!' I said in my best 'microphone' voice, developed in the hours and hours of practice in our parlour at home. I was no more than a teenager, but the chap behind the counter was obviously impressed, and we were ushered in, straight through—no problem. Once in, there was the slight problem of seats: there were none vacant. So we spent the concert walking around, always looking as if we were coming or going to somewhere vital. But we did see the concert.

The fine red-brick houses that line most of the South Circular Road seem now to be so much more compact than they did to my child's eyes. Around the corner, approaching St Teresa's Gardens, the houses are either terraced red-brick or neat and grey with small railinged gardens. Éamonn Andrews lived in one of them with his family, so did the broadcaster Des Hickey and his brother Kieran, the film-maker. In the centre of them all is the huge grey . bulk of St Teresa's national school, which seems far less formidable than it did through my 7-year-old eyes when I first arrived there and when, in its dull concrete yard, I had to drill for physical exercise in long straight lines with all the others under the tutelage of a tough little sergeant from Cathal Brugha Barracks called O'Neill.

I had not been in the area for some time and somehow expected it to be run-down, but obviously the tradition of respectability still pertains. Most of the people in this area during my time would have been artisans, labourers or craftsmen in Guinness's, small businessmen, tradesmen, or workers in the nearby cigarette factory of Player and Wills. (That is one thing that has not changed at all: the area still smells of tobacco.) With few exceptions, all of their children would have left school at 11.

Yet out of here have come doctors and lawyers and physicists and scientists and all sorts of professional people. A lot made it. A lot did not. There was Jimmy Stapeleton, who is now a posh monsignor in Tucson, Arizona; and Professor Paddy Moore, whose Daddy sat on top of a huge bread-van behind a horse and who we *knew* was a brilliant guy since he walked around the neighbourhood talking to himself all the time.

Some escape from their environment, some do not.

The creeping and inexorable change in Dublin has covered the little hives of activity that were the White Heather Laundry and Maple Laundry with a sprawling, ugly complex called the White Heather Industrial Estate. Bowles's chemist shop is still there, but the Leinster cinema, where we cheered on the chap and booed the baddie, is now an ice-rink. And saddest of all in the nostalgia stakes is to see that the Rialto cinema, where we queued long hours to see Roy Rogers and Laurel and Hardy, is now the showroom of a main dealer for Nissan cars.

It was a fine cinema, which would have held between eight and nine hundred people. I did not have the money to go every single Saturday, but tried as often as possible. The queue for the 'fourpenny rush' started around the side of the building; the posh front entrance cost one-and-fourpence, way out of our league. Your stomach would be squirming if you were a bit down the queue for the fourpennies, because you never knew when Yer Man, the bruiser in charge, would lower the boom and say, 'That's enough—we're full!' and the rest of the queue would have to go home.

The Rialto was run by a Jewish gentleman called Maxie Baum, whom we all knew and who we thought was a millionaire. (It was a source of great disappointment to me in later life to find that Maxie ran greyhounds. On our peculiar scale of social cachet, running greyhounds was way down the list.) He was a low-sized, swarthy man of most forbidding mien, Crombie-coated and trilby-hatted, with jet-black hair and a small black moustache. We all crawled to Maxie. Being on the right side of Maxie meant sure admission to his cinema. But one word of censure from him and you were *out!* Barred. Banished. An outcast from civilised living—not to speak of ignorance as to how the chap managed to climb back up the cliff on which you had left him, dangling precariously by a single fingernail . . .

Barring occurred for bowseyism, like throwing ice-cream or not obeying the usher when he told you to shut up. These were the good old days when the usher in the Rialto cinema would take off his belt and whack us chisellers into line. There were frequent fierce ructions at the top of the fourpenny queue around the half-moon entrance window, pushing and shoving and general messing, and it was here that the usher's belt was mostly employed. None of saw anything peculiar in it. He was an adult, wasn't he?

Just beyond the Rialto were the wide open spaces of Madigan's Farm, which ran all the way from the main road to the canal. Madigan planted his acres with cabbages and rhubarb and potatoes. He ploughed his land with horses, and he kept pigs. Everyone kept their slops for his pigs. We separated the slops from the 'real' rubbish and kept it in a bucket in the yard, until it was collected by a character called O'Connor, who had one short leg with a built-up boot. In summer, O'Connor's arrival by horse and cart in your street was Reveilled by the smell and Last Posted by swarms of flies.

☐ *I remember my mother being very persistent about rounding us all up to go and have this family picture taken (above) and on New Year's Eve 1988 Mary, Al, Ray and myself met by total surprise on the set of the Late Late Show.*

RTE

□

In all my life on the South Circular Road I don't remember venturing to the north side. Perhaps we went as far as O'Connell Street now and then, maybe to Clery's, to one of the city-centre cinemas or over to Croke Park, or even, occasionally, to Dalymount; but the division between north and south of the city is a peculiar thing, I know, and one I have never understood, except instinctively. We from the south side simply considered that all northsiders were Injuns and blow-ins and runners and not real Dubs at all. My mother would have shopped in Meath Street, Camden Street or Francis Street if what she wanted was not available in our local shops. Occasionally she would have ventured as far as Henry Street—because Grafton Street was just too upmarket—but by and large we remained firmly anchored on the south side of the city. And I know that to this day in Dublin the distinction, despite intermarriage among the tribes, continues.

But in our time we were self-contained, a separate city, and in our particular part of it there was nowhere you could fail to notice the presence of Guinness's. There was the constant clopping of the dray-horses and the single-cylinder putt-putting of the big Dollinger engines on the barges, which, having come from the exotic ports of Portumna, Athy, and Tullamore, tied up in Grand Canal Harbour. There was all the busy activity in all the warehouses along Marrowbone Lane. If you were sick with flu and off school you were driven demented while on your bed of pain by the relentless, rhythmic 'crunk-thud!' of the local shopkeeper's apprentice bottling Guinness in the back yard of his shop; or if you were ambulatory, you walked to the Guinness dispensary, queuing up to see the Guinness doctor and receiving your medicine, which was dispensed, free, on the spot.

The fleet of barges continued to ply the Grand Canal until 1961, and I miss them. I miss the horses too. When Guinness's was founded, in 1759, there was stabling for only twelve horses and a loft to hold two hundred tons of hay. But in my father's heyday, the horse, the barge and the craftsman reigned in harmony, and the cooperage yard held as many as a quarter of a million wooden casks, each made by skilled hands. Somehow, today's sixty-five acres of gleaming technology in the brewery and the fleet of streamlined lorries on the roads of Europe have taken the soul out of my memories. But that is progress, friends, and today's brewery must compete. As well as stout, Guinness's now makes non-alcoholic lager and spiral staircases and runs a fleet of pleasure cruisers on the Shannon waterways.

When we moved to the respectability of 124 South Circular Road, I remember asking myself in wonderment how we were going to fill all this space. Before we moved in, naturally, I went up to explore, tramping up and down the wooden staircase, my footsteps echoing excitingly in the empty rooms. For instead of just the two-up, two-down of Rialto Street, we had

☐

an actual parlour and a separate dining-room and a kitchen and a scullery downstairs, with three bedrooms *and a bathroom* upstairs. Rialto Street had had nothing so luxurious as a bathroom. An outside lavatory in the yard and you washed yourself in the kitchen sink, and that was your lot. South Circular Road also had a little garden in the front with railings and a real gate, and a big garden at the back.

On moving day, we brought all our belongings with us in a handcart or by hand. It was such a short distance—about a hundred yards—and we had such a small store of furniture and possessions by the standards of today's middle classes that we did not need a pantechnicon or anything grand like that. Neighbours helped in relays, ferrying the lamps and the clocks and the ware, the pots, buckets, beds, and brooms, being careful with the piano and with Ma's precious treasures. We were really getting into the big time with this move. My mother would not actually have been satisfied until we ended up somewhere like Áras an Uachtaráin, but in the meantime 124 South Circular Road was a quantum leap.

There were two windows in our parlour, which overlooked the South Circular Road. An armchair in one corner faced these windows, and my mother used to sit in it for hours and hours, sometimes reading, sometimes just looking out at the street life. The parlour was a place for peace and quiet, a nice, bright, carpeted room with heavy curtains at the windows. I used it to practise on the piano, on the opposite wall to the windows, but it was not used much as a family room except for social occasions and at Christmas. There were a couple of mirrors on the wall, and in later years framed wedding photographs of Ray and Joyce, a photo of Mary going to her first dress dance, and one of Al on his conferring day. There was also one of Ray in his cap and gown when he got his music diploma, and his framed ALCM, of which Ma was very proud.

The only other major piece of furniture was the china cabinet, a good piece of furniture on spindly legs, totally dwarfed by the fireplace. My mother seemed to have a 'thing' about fireplaces. The one she put in the parlour was so ornate and so big that it seemed to be designed for a room four times its size.

There was a bus-stop right outside our house, a matter of only a few feet away from our parlour windows. Our front garden was so small that when it was raining, people were able to use our porch for shelter. It was Ma's practice while seated in her dreaming-chair to keep an eye on the bus-stop. If she recognised someone standing there, which was frequent, she could open the window and have a chat. I have vivid memories of all this neighbourhood chatting and commiserating and communal knowledge of everyone else's business. If a neighbour died, it was a personal loss. If a baby

□

was born, there was joy in every house on the street. We all knew who was having difficulty with money, whose child was clever and had prospects and whose was thick and the despair of his teachers, who was threatened with redundancy. We all watched the wider world together. And for seven years we all prayed for another neighbour's son, Father O'Reilly, who was trapped in a prisoner-of-war camp in the Philippines, and after seven years he came home and we all had a great time talking about how emaciated he was.

One incident that sticks in my mind and that illustrates some of the small joys of living closely happened at ten o'clock on a lovely summer evening at our front gate, when, on coming home, I discovered my mother chatting with a widow-woman from up the street, a Mrs Murnane. Mrs Murnane had just discovered Nelson Eddy and Jeanette MacDonald in *Rose Marie*. She was ecstatic about *Rose Marie*, standing at our gate telling Ma that she sat through all three showings in the Rialto cinema. While other neighbours passed by and greeted them, Mrs Murnane sang bits of 'When I'm calling you-hoohoo-hoo-oo-oo-oo!' to illustrate just how great was *Rose Marie*. 'Oh, you have to go to *Rose Marie*, Mrs Byrne . . .'

So next day, Ma went up to the Rialto. She started to sing 'When I'm calling you-hoohoo-hoo-oo-oo-oo!' to other neighbours, and *Rose Marie* spread through the women of our neighbourhood like the plague.

In later years, the dining-room on the South Circular Road became almost exclusively mine, for doing my homework but also, more importantly, for listening to the radio. For some reason our radio, a big Philips cabinet model with a little green eye shining with two moving crescents in the top right-hand corner to indicate when you had the tuning right, was placed in this hardly used room. From it a long flex ran to an extension speaker in the kitchen, where all the family listening to the news was done.

I also used the dining-room for practising and fantasising about my future life as a radio star. Da used to put his head wistfully in at the door as I played my jazz records and performed my linking scripts: 'Would you ever play a marching song . . . ?' But poor Da never bothered to come near the parlour on Sunday mornings, when there would be a 'jazz session' with me on the piano, Al on 'drums' —the bottom of an upturned chair, which gave a satisfactory hollow sound—and Colm on Jew's harp.

The South Circular Road was one of the areas in Dublin that housed a good proportion of our small Jewish population. They congregated in a small section, centred around the little synagogue on the South Circular Road, down Donore Avenue and on down into Clanbrassil Street. We were used to seeing them in their funny little round hats and dark clothes, and as far as I am aware they integrated very well with their Catholic and

□

Protestant neighbours, because right in the middle of the biggest concentration of them was the Protestant church that is now, strangely, the Dublin Islamic Centre. The other Protestant church, St Andrew's, was always, we thought, very posh and very successful. They ran exotic troops like the Boys' Brigade and the scouts we called the Bathing Powells. (Somehow I prefer to think of them that way rather than by their real appellation.)

In my memory there was never a marriage in our area between a Jew and a Catholic. However, Catholics marrying Protestants—which did happen, although only very occasionally in the days of John Charles McQuaid and Pope Pius XII—were the subject of gossip and even scandal. That was very, very serious. And if the couple managed to get a dispensation, they could not be married in front of the high altar in the church but in a side chapel. The whole thing was rushed, grudging, with no flowers. And then the whole neighbourhood waited with bated breath for news as to whether the Protestant partner would 'turn'. It was all a great pity. Such a lot of nonsense.

Having Jews in our midst was in fact a great bonus for the kids in our area, because, since Jews were not allowed to do any manual labour on the Sabbath, all the little Catholic gurriers made a mint by lighting their domestic fires for them or running errands or doing anything around the house that needed doing and that could not wait. There was an understood set of charges: so much for lighting a fire, so much for chopping wood, so much for this and that. All the Catholic kids knew and understood the Jewish traditions and the prayers, the yarmulka and the matzo balls, the seven-branched candlesticks and all. I do not remember any anti-Semitism: Jews were simply part of the scene. They were different, but they were just there. There were some catcalls of 'Jewboy' and gags made about Jews being mean—but I do not honestly believe they were serious, but rather were made in the spirit of dockers whistling at a pretty woman. It was sort of expected amongst ourselves. It was probably hurtful, but no harm was meant.

To my shame, however, I must reveal the story of Cokey's shed. Three doors from where Colm Campbell lived, opposite Dolphin's Barn church, lived the Copeman family, who were Jewish. Mr Copeman was a dentist, and his sister was the noted pianist Dina, a protégée of Esposito and teacher of Havelock Nelson and who had actually been part of the first transmission of 2RN in 1926. All the houses had long back gardens. At the end of Copeman's was a shed with a corrugated tin roof.

When we gurriers were teenagers, with little better to do, the suggestion was frequently floated, 'Let's raid Cokey's shed!' —a suggestion that always found instant and giggling acceptance from all of us. The ringleader was

□

Noel Campbell, younger brother of Colm, egged on by Tony Bennett and Yours Truly and a collection of maybe five or six others. We each equipped ourselves with an empty milk bottle, which we filled with water.

We would wait until about half-past eleven or near midnight, when the last bus had roared down the South Circular Road from Rialto and all was calm and bedded down. Then we lined up. We would take our milk bottles filled with water, one to a man, and we would have a count-down from fifteen. Fifteen, fourteen, thirteen, twelve, eleven . . . and, depending on how many were gathered, we let the bottles off one by one in hand-grenade fashion, so that they hit the corrugated iron shed one every second. Then we would hit the deck, smothering our hysterical giggles in the grass.

The noise of the 'bombing' was shattering: ten milk bottles breaking on a corrugated tin roof and showering broken glass all over the place. For three or four seconds afterwards there would be silence. Then all hell would break loose: lights on all over the place, in Copeman's and up and down the street, dogs barking, shouting and threats and imprecations, 'Get the Guards!' while we lay absolutely still in the grass before inching away, commando-style, on our bellies, totally convulsed. It went on for years, and we were never caught.

Sorry, Mr Copeman.

CHAPTER 3
SYNGER AND ALL THAT

■

The real world hit me in the shape of Synge Street Christian Brothers' school. It was housed in a series of tall old tenement houses that had been knocked together, and the boys were divided by year into A and B streams, the groups being divided merely by a notional partition. I was always in the B stream: but the Bs in Synger were of a pretty high standard. My examination results would have been typical. I got five honours in the Inter and seven in the Leaving. The As would have got, respectively, seven and nine.

The buildings were totally unsuitable for school use. There was even an ordinary family resident in the basement, from whose radio the strains of 'Housewives' Choice' wafted upwards throughout the upper floors. On a rainy day the stench from the wet coats heaped on the jumble of bicycles on the stairways and in the halls was overpowering, as forty or more of us scrunched up together on top of each other and the unfortunate teachers in rooms designed for single families. The A class would be in the living-room of one old house and the B in the adjoining dining-room. The din was frightful: there was no getting away from what the other class was doing. While the other class was doing maths, we could hear every word—and every beating—while we were trying to concentrate on Irish, and vice versa.

As an example of the chaos, there was the incident with a lay teacher, Tommy O'Rourke, who had us for English. One day in the month of March, during a Leaving Cert class, he asked a question about *Hamlet*. Tommy Giblin, a boy from Inchicore, put his hand up.

'Yes?' O'Rourke indicated him.

Tommy answered the question correctly.

'That's right,' said O'Rourke, and turned back to the blackboard. Suddenly he wheeled around again. 'Who are you?'

Giblin looked around and then back at him blankly: 'Me, sir?'

'Yes, you—who are you, son?'

'I'm Tommy Giblin, sir . . . '

'As God is me judge, son, I've never laid eyes on you before in me life!'

☐

This was March, and we had had Tommy O'Rourke for English since the previous September.

So let me say it first and get it over with: it is true that people like me would never have had a decent education were it not for the Christian Brothers. It is true that they laboured in Stygian conditions, which would not be tolerated now. It is true that boys were never turned away if they did not have the fees: it was a question of 'How much *can* you afford, ma'am?' It is also true that they beat the tar out of us. There was not a single day during the first four years I attended Synge Street Christian Brothers' school on which I did not creep in the door, my stomach sick with apprehension and terror.

We were beaten with straps, sticks, even the leg of a chair. We were beaten for failure at lessons and simply, it seemed to me, on principle. They were careful not to leave marks. They generally struck on the hands, the legs, the buttocks, and around the body. If they were thumping, they thumped on the body, where it would not show. They never hit us on the jaw but across the head; they twisted our ears and lifted us up bodily by the side-hair at our temples. I have often wondered why we put up with it—certainly in the later years many of us were bigger and beefier than the men who were doling out the punishment.

There was one incident, I remember, where one of the bigger guys, a boy called Colman, did take a swing at one of the Brothers. He arrived late for class, and this particular Brother, of whom we were all terrified, was waiting to pounce. But for once the boy did not take it: I think he was taken by surprise and simply reacted instinctively. 'What the fuck do you think you're doing?' he shouted as the Brother went to hit him, then he swung back. Naturally, all hell broke loose. The two of them, Brother and boy, went at one another, and went out in the hall. The door was slammed behind them and they fought their way up the stairs.

Three or four minutes later they came back to the classroom, breathless, but as though nothing had happened. The rest of us sat as if struck by lightning. There was no sense of jubilation but of sacrilege: we reacted as though this fellow Colman had stolen the Host out of the tabernacle or money out of the church poor-box. It was as if he had turned the world we knew upside down.

Naturally his parents were summoned, and there were grave discussions about expulsion, but he was allowed to stay on in the end, a chastened penitent. But that Brother never touched him again, and I think that after school Colman joined the RAF.

(I would love to have been still in Synge Street during the time the actor John Kavanagh was there. I was talking to him recently and he told me the most amazing story about a boy who actually pulled a gun on a Christian Brother who was beating him. The whole thing was hushed up and, as in the case of Colman, *that* Brother never went near *him* again either. I do not know who the boy was but he can be sure that there was a faint chorus of ghostly cheers ringing around the old tenements.)

Certainly I knew that life in Synge Street was unfair and unjust, but I think we just got on with it because there was little option. All of our parents were making sacrifices to send us there. The fees of £4 10s a year do not seem exorbitant by today's standards, but to the jobbing and labouring men around our area that kind of money, extra to the daily needs, was hard come by. People struggled to make ends meet, although some less than others.

Those Brothers saw it as their vocation to get us through our Inter and Leaving Certs with as many honours as possible. And if the information did not go in the easy way, it was going to go in the hard way. To this day I can recite the five Irish declensions and the poetry I learned by rote. I know that 'educationalists' throw up their hands in dismay at these methods nowadays, but I wonder if today's little gurriers are being educated any better than we were. Now I can see where the Brothers came from. They were taken from their mothers and any semblance of the gentler side of their own natures, at the age of 14 or even younger, locked up in gangs, and preached at that the world was a harsh place and a purgatory to be endured before the achievement of the real goal. Many of them were deeply unhappy and trapped people who had no way out, and were on such a short fuse of frustration that it was inevitable that they would take it out on us. Such is not the case nowadays.

So we all licked our wounds outside the school. We commiserated with the guy who had got the bad thumping that day, and we nursed him home. He was the walking wounded for that particular day—but each of us knew that his own turn was coming up. We had a special pity for the slow learners among us, because theirs was a particularly heavy load. They could count on being beaten every single day.

The one thing you did not do was go home and cry and whinge about it. It was in the era when, if you did, you would get another clip on the ear to be going on with, on the assumption that if you had been beaten in school, you must have done something to deserve it.

Sometimes, very occasionally, a parent might come in to enquire of the Brother what little Johnny had done to deserve such a particularly bad hiding. We never knew what went on on those occasions, but I knew that the parent was always sent off reasonably happy. We never wanted our parents to come in anyway; we were afraid of the consequences, the jeering and the sneering and the allegations that we could not fight our own battles.

In my memory it was that Brother who had had the dust-up with Colman who was particularly tough. In retrospect I wonder if his health was bad and if this was a contributory factor to his behaviour, because he arrived into the classroom each morning, flung open the windows and stood in front of the freezing air, drawing it in through his clenched teeth, seemingly with some difficulty. Then he would turn around to face us, slapping one fist into his palm, his face an impacted mask that always seemed on the verge of rage.

He taught for a great portion of every day in third year, and we could not wait until that year was over. He knew very well what we thought of him. But he waited until that delirious day, the day of deliverance, the last day of the summer term, when we knew we were about to be released from his tyranny. We were going into the Intermediate Certificate class and would have a different, perhaps more humane, teacher come September. That last June afternoon before freedom dragged on and on, and just before the final bell he raised his hand. In his hateful, nasal voice he announced: 'Well, boys, ye'll be delighted to hear that ye have me again next year . . . ' I will never forget the glimmer in his eyes.

After Inter Cert, I had had enough. I applied to the Royal College of Surgeons for a post as a lab assistant, and was even called for interview—but was rejected, although very kindly. I can still picture my mother standing in our kitchen, brows furrowed in puzzlement as she read my rejection slip. The RCSI wrote that, although I was not being offered a job, I had 'made an impression'. I suppose my mother's attitude could have been, 'Well, if he made such an impression why the hell was he not offered a job?'

I then applied to Findlater's for a job as a messenger-boy, was accepted, and saw my future. I had not given up the dreams of radio, but Findlater's was freedom, a few shillings of my own—and escape from Synge Street.

Findlater's was not a bad choice for someone from my background. (And although I could not have known it then, Ms Kathleen Watkins, from a much superior background, thought so too. She was later to become secretary to Findlater's Managing Director, J. A. McGrail.) This old Protestant family firm, which opened the first of its twenty-one branches in O'Connell Street in 1823, operated in the same benevolent, paternalistic manner as did our Family Firm, Guinness's. They even owned a church— still called Findlater's—at one corner of Parnell Square. The company had a policy of taking people straight from school; sometimes country merchants sent their sons as apprentices; and it was quite common that once in, a boy would stay until he retired.

The O'Connell Street branch was the largest food hall in the country, with great echoing tiled surfaces and bustling, dexterous assistants who had served there since they had left school. When you entered Findlater's your nostrils were teased with the overpowering scent of freshly cut cheese, spiced with the cool scent of bacon from Matterson's, Denny's, or Buttle's, loose Jacob's biscuits in rows of glass-topped tins, and the faint whiff of alcohol. The firm operated its own wine cellars and stout bottling plant, bottling a stout called Mountjoy and XX porter for Guinness's in caverns under O'Connell Street.

At one time Findlater's stables for its dray-horses were the largest in the country, even bigger than Guinness's, but the horses were being phased out and being replaced with vans, and I applied for one of the new jobs occupied by the messenger-boys who sped around Dublin on big black bicycles with square iron receptacles in front of the handlebars to take the boxes of provisions. All in all, the prospect of whizzing around Dublin on a black bicycle, with my own money at the end of every week and no more Christian Brothers, was very attractive. Especially no more Christian Brothers.

My parents begged me to continue school, but I was adamant. So they bribed me, with the only bribe that would have worked. They offered me a brand-new bicycle. I was tempted, and then fell for it. They went out and, with money they scraped together, bought me a Hercules Kestrel in the most wonderful shade, polychromatic gold, for £15 7s 6d. I recall the day I walked to the Hercules shop in Capel Street to collect it. Oh, ecstasy!

I went back to Synge Street. To my utter joy, we had a completely new situation in fifth year. We had a Brother called Brother Lucey, nicknamed 'the Guck', who was sweetly cracked. (The origins of the Brothers' nick-names were, even then, lost in antiquity. For instance there was one called Jiggers, who had hair as black as jet, the blackest I have ever seen, slick with Brylcreem. In reality he was not a bad old fellow, called Ryle, whose constant and kindly advice to us was, 'Now, boys, ye must work hard to get a fine job in the Civil Service.')

Brother Lucey, the Guck, tried to teach us Greek, with no success. He tried to teach us everything with no success. He inhabited a pleasant world of his own, and if we did not care to join him, that was our business. We did absolutely no work. It was even possible, in those happy, lazy days under the rule of the Guck, for Colm Campbell to leave the classroom, go to the local shop, buy a cream bun and return to his desk without his absence being detected. Colm Campbell's father was Works Manager in the *Irish Times* and came home from work every morning about three or four, bringing with him a few copies of the newspaper. Colm always brought a copy with him to school to give to the Guck, which saved the

☐

Guck the price of it. This gave Colm the licence to come to school whenever he liked: half an hour, an hour, even an hour and a half late, on the pretext that he had to wait for his father to come home from work with the *Irish Times*. At the morning break, at around eleven, while we were all let out to 'the yard', the Guck would disappear down to a little back room in the house to read the *Irish Times* and to smoke a fag. It must have been his little moment in heaven. It was important for us all, therefore, that Campbell turn up every day with the paper, to keep the Guck sweet.

If you misbehaved you were brought up to sit in the front row of the class, where you could be watched. The trick then was to sprawl, with your feet, which on all of us by that time were big and ungainly, out in the aisles so that poor old Lucey would trip. You would look utterly stricken and surprised: '*Sorry, Brother!*'—and it was only a matter of time before you were moved to the back of the class again. All the hardchaws wanted to be at the back. In the fifth-year winter, when the windows were locked tight, those at the front could barely see those at the back. All you could see, through a dense blue cigarette fug, were the little red lamps of cigarette butts flaring and waning as their owners dragged on them.

From out of the fug, from the desks behind me, came the sounds of the card school, including Jim Culliton (the present Chairman of the RTE Authority) and a fellow from Greystones called Whiston. They played pontoon for the entire year. All I ever heard from behind me, rising above the convivial chatter all over the rest of the room, was:

'Twist!'

'Fuck you—I owe you a ha'penny . . . '

'Twist!'

'Ah, shaggit!'

It was St Trinian's with trousers.

While reading his *Irish Times*, Guck would let us out for a breath of fresh air. We were in a separate tenement in Heytesbury Street, where the new school now is, and we were instructed to walk nicely, two by two, out of Heytesbury Street, around the corner of the yard, and back in through Synge Street. The Guck watched benevolently as we walked docilely, Our Boys, out of his sight. What he did not see was the wild scramble the moment we were out of his sight. The pushing and the shoving and the racing into the corner shop, where cream buns, gur cake and sweets were purchased, the cramming of said cream buns into our gobs, and then the magical re-formation of our docile crocodile as we got back around the corner into Synge Street.

He was a lovely man, the Guck. One time he decided that my behaviour in the classroom was getting out of hand and he sent for my mother, who,

☐ One of the most treasured pictures in the collection of my mother and father. On a visit to London in 1951, Éamonn Andrews brought them to Sugar Ray Robinson's training camp where he was preparing for a title fight with Randolph Turpin. They always remembered it as a beautiful and outstanding day in their lives and they were on the radio, BBC radio, with Éamonn as well, so there!

☐ Al, Ray, myself and Ernest on one of the few occasions when we were all at home together.

□

taking this very seriously, sped in at the first opportunity. The Guck engaged her in earnest discussion: 'What's the matter with kids today?' and 'Where are we going wrong?' —the perennial cry of those on the other side of the generation gap. The Guck had a theory about the cause of all the mayhem. Speedway. That was what was driving all the young fellas mad: it was definitely speedway. This motor sport, which had just become very popular in Shelbourne Park, was the cause of the complete breakdown of all moral values among young people, a spur to all decadence.

Even for my mother, for whom the word of a Christian Brother carried very considerable weight, this was a little peculiar. Like, speedway? *Speedway?* She looked at him with the first dawnings of understanding of the Guck's true, harmless condition.

Sixth year was a different kettle of fish. Sixth year was when we got down to business, with a Brother called Bill Ó Laoghaire, a born teacher, who made up for the hell of the first four years. He never laid a finger on us— somehow he did not have to. If any of us stepped out of line, he had only to look at the miscreant, more in sorrow than in anger, over the tops of his glasses and the recipient of the Look would shrink back to size. None of us had any problem with Bill Ó Laoghaire. By then, of course, we were in the big league. Seven honours in the Leaving meant a sure executive officer job, eight meant you could aspire even higher. Brother Ó Laoghaire died only three years ago, and he kept tabs on all his former pupils until the day he died, sending Christmas cards, writing notes of encouragement on any achievements or sympathising on a bereavement. (At his funeral his brother gave me his little finger-ring Rosary, which had belonged to him all his life, and I have carried it with me ever since as a mark of liking and respect for a fine man and a superb Christian Brother.)

I found that I had a great aptitude for Latin and English; I loved history and geography, and was competent in Irish. Maths passed me by. Maths is something you either click into or you don't. If at any stage you lose the thread, you are lost. I lost the thread and never picked it up (and of course this will come as no surprise to anyone in the light of subsequent events in my life . . .)

On the credit side for the Brothers, a love of the English language was passed on to me by Synge Street, where Frank MacManus, a notable novelist in his own right (in fact one of his works, *The Greatest of These*, is on the present curriculum for Inter Cert), was the first of a long line of English-teachers of excellence. Frank eventually left teaching and went into broadcasting, becoming in 1948 Head of Features in Radio Éireann, where he was a great mentor of the broadcaster John Bowman and, to a lesser extent, of mine. His heritage in Synge Street was the inculcation,

☐

through his successors, of a similar love in people such as the novelist Cornelius Ryan, Éamonn Andrews, James Punkett Kelly, Milo O'Shea, and Ronnie Walshe, all of whom share my love and respect for the English language and literature.

But there was one episode, from one of the earlier school years, that is still baffling to me. I really enjoyed writing English essays, and on one occasion I really pulled out all the stops for a teacher I'll call John-Joe, a man who had brought sarcasm to a fine art. He had set us an essay on 'The War', and I decided to write about the First World War.

I went home and asked Da to tell me a little bit about his experiences. Now he never talked about what he had gone through; but to my utter surprise, for the first and only time, he opened up. He talked about experiences I now know were standard but were a revelation to me. He described the cloying, sucking mud, the filth, the wet, the perishing cold, the rats, and the slippery wooden planking they had to walk on in their sodden boots. He told of his comrades who ventured to raise their heads above the level of the trenches and had their heads shot off. Exhilarated, I took copious notes and wrote what I still believe to be a very good essay. Since I was only a teenager, I suppose I wrote in highly dramatic form, highlighting the little details Da gave me, the passing from hand to Irish hand of Rosary beads and miraculous medals and so on. (Many years later I was to read Robert Graves's *Goodbye to All That*, about the poet's experiences in the trenches. Da had been spot-on.)

I brought it in to school and, well pleased, handed it up to John-Joe. Normally, if John-Joe did not like an essay he would just intone 'Five out of ten' as he flung the copy-book back at the perpetrator. For some reason, he went to town on me. He made me stand up while he read extracts from my essay to the class in the most sneering tone he could adopt. He made an absolute mockery of me. He went on and on and on. I was at first utterly shocked, and then devastated. My face burned, and I just wished the ground could open up. I had tried very hard to write a winner: it must have been obvious to him; but the worst part is that he was making fun of my Da's true experiences.

I went home in bits and confessed to Ma what had happened. She simply said: 'Show it to me!' and she sat down and read it. For the next ten days, to give her her due, anyone who came to the house was given my essay to read and asked was that, or was that not, a terrific essay. Everyone agreed and was most supportive and comforting. But the damage was done. I retreated even more into the safety of my quiet shell and resolved never to make any more waves. I still do not fully understand what happened. The only thing I can surmise, based on some of the appalling letters I get to the radio programme from Irish patriots every time there is any reference to the First World War or to Poppy Day, is that John-Joe was a closet nationalist and abhorred the idea of the father of a pupil of his having been in the British army.

But during this time there was life outside those dingy walls. To write about it does not make it appear very exciting, but there really was a balance. Synge Street was to be endured, but friendships were maturing, and there was radio: AFN and Luxembourg, Geoffrey Everett and Pete Murray.

I listened to AFN a lot, because they had American radio shows like the 'Bob Hope Show', the 'Jack Benny Show', and the 'Bing Crosby Show'. Later on, when I was doing my MC work, I was listening to Bob Hope, and one of his gags went like this: 'Is Bing Crosby mean?' And Hope said: 'Is he *mean*? I'll tell you how mean he is. He got married in his own back-yard so the chickens could get the rice.'

And I thought this was a wonderfully funny gag and immediately began to use it in my MC act—usually about someone local whom the audience would all know. I had no scruples: I'd nick a gag from anyone then, and everyone else nicked them from me. It's called free circulation.

Anyway, time moved on, and many years later Bob Hope was a guest on the 'Late Late Show'. He was a most pleasing, courteous, easy man to deal with. We ran the show in the form of a press conference, and in the middle of it one of the press people asked Hope, 'What's this about Bing Crosby being mean?' And, so help me God, Hope sat there and said: 'I'll tell you how mean he is. He got married in his own back-yard so the chickens could get the rice.' And he dared the audience not to laugh. They dutifully rolled around in hysterics of enjoyment at this quip, but I sat there to one side, thinking: I don't believe this. It's twenty-five years later and he's still using the same gag. He can't do that! He wouldn't dare! Even Bob Hope. That one has whiskers on it! But he would, and he did, and he got away with it.

I have a sneaky admiration for all stand-up comics, and of the breed, Hope is the acknowledged king. He is also the living embodiment of the maxim that if the public at large had memories, no politician would stay in business longer than six months and no comedian would be in business longer than a week. People in general don't remember funny stories and gags; only those in showbiz do.

Apart from the American programmes, there was 'Round the Horn' with Kenneth Horne, and 'Hancock's Half Hour', 'Variety Bandbox', 'Variety Night', 'Opportunity Knocks' with Hughie Greene, and later the 'Goon Show'. (It is extraordinary now to realise that almost all of the people I listened to were interview guests of mine in later life. The late Kenneth

◻

Williams was delightful, and Kenneth Horne, to whom an entire generation of Irish families listened along with their Sunday dinners, once filled in personfully for forty-five minutes on the 'Late Late Show' when the guest scheduled to follow him failed to show up.) There was a great world outside, borne into my house through the Philips radio in my dining-room. I dreamed up scripts like theirs, wrote them, talked them across the dining-room table.

There was also the fresh air and the canal in summer. We all had bicycles, and thirty or forty-five minutes' cycling would bring us out of the city and right into the heart of the countryside or the mountains. Dublin itself was a city full of character and of characters, and, almost without knowing it, I was absorbing what it was like to be living in a terrific city. Mícheál Mac Liammóir, splendid in purple suit and yellow tie, flaunting full stage make-up and very obvious wig, could be seen perambulating daily in the streets, which were teeming with authors and poets. At the other end of the artistic scale, Bang-Bang from Inchicore rode the open platforms of the buses and aimed his great iron key at the stripey-suited businessmen in Dame Street: 'Bang! Bang!' whereupon they would fall to their elegant knees on the pavements, dropping their briefcases and clutching their chests in simulated agony.

Colm Campbell's family always had dogs, and Colm walked them every evening past our house. I would often join him as he passed, and, walking the red-brick road, we would share our dreams. The communal view of me seen from those days is that I appeared to my mates to be more serious, more gentle, more vulnerable than they were, more conscientious about my work. And more anxious to stay out of trouble.

Tony Bennett and Colm Campbell are the two friends from school who are still my friends. My idea of a great day out then was for the three of us to voyage on the number 19 bus from Rialto all the way to the terminus at the other side of the city. And then to get the next one back. That is how imaginative I was. On the other hand it was I who persuaded Colm, Tony and a fellow called Tommy Langan to set out with me one Thursday afternoon on a 'grand cycling tour' of Ireland. We set off bravely enough, but when we got to Clondalkin, one of them, I forget which one, said: 'Hump this! I'm going home!' And that was the end of the cycling tour.

But then when I was 14, I discovered jazz. There were two guys in my class, called Gerry Tierney and Harry Fitzpatrick. Gerry Tierney was the only child of his widowed mother: she worked in the American embassy, and they lived in Terenure. He was a chronic asthmatic, small and thin, with generally lousy health. He was also one of the funniest guys in the class, and lived his life through his imagination and the movies he saw in the local

☐

cinemas. It was always a joy to visit the Tierney house, to see the terrifically close, warm and witty relationship between himself and his mother. Gerry wanted nothing more out of life than to *be* Gene Krupa, the jazz drummer.

Harry Fitzpatrick lived on Harold's Cross Road, and if Gerry wanted to be Gene Krupa, Harry wanted nothing except to be the trumpet player Harry James. Tierney actually had a drum kit and practised his rhythms while listening to records. I had always been bored by linear music; it simply did nothing for me. But when I first heard this exciting, spontaneous, improvisational way of zooming up, down and around the old boring tunes, I was riveted. I loved the brilliance of those jazz players who could follow the chord sequences of a melody on their own instruments and then bring that melody up into the stars and beyond.

Tierney and I clubbed together to buy the Philips double album of the 1938 Benny Goodman concert at Carnegie Hall, which was written about as a watershed in the history of jazz. Neither of us would have been able to afford the set, but we scraped up the seventeen-and-six that each of the records cost, and swapped as necessary. Many years later that double album became the basis of one of my first jazz programmes on Radio Éireann: I made a complete programme out of it on the occasion of the twenty-first anniversary of the concert. And I repeated the exercise on 16 January 1988, making a complete 'Gay Byrne Show' out of it. So I reckon that double album does not owe me a penny change out of my seventeen-and-six.

What still excites me about jazz is that every jazz player plays every tune differently each time he plays it. He can be on or off form. He can react to his environment or to the band on stage and can start swinging straight away—or can miss. But I have let life and busyness overtake me to such an extent that I have lost touch with jazz. When I was really into it, for instance during the period when I was presenting jazz programmes for Radio Éireann, I had a remarkably good ear and could distinguish many of the top players by listening to a few bars of what they played. On most occasions I could tell a black player from a white player.

It is a great regret that I am out of touch to such an extent that I do not know who the new young international players are or what the local scene is in Dublin or what developments have taken place in recent years. And in some ways those early times with Tierney and Fitzpatrick were the most exciting, when we were all discovering jazz for ourselves as we banged our drums and pianos and dreamed of musical careers.

I know that people nowadays react in horror to the stories of the cruelty and beatings of those school-days, and I believe strongly that they are right. Under no circumstances would I tolerate a teacher beating Suzy or Crona. On the other hand I am not against a sharp, fast thump—not a beating—

☐

for some of the young male thugs encountered today. We were all fairly tough customers; bloody noses were badges of honour. And it is only in retrospect that I can see what we went through. I remember the rare and wonderful days when our Christian Brother was in jolly form and, instead of biffing us, would tell heavy-handed and sarcastic jokes, at which we fell about sycophantically and in wondrous delight that the day was a holiday from beatings.

And, of course, nowadays an education with the Brothers is so much different. They simply would not get away with that kind of carry-on now. It is astonishing to think that in my day there may have been, say, twenty Christian Brothers in Synge Street and half-a-dozen lay teachers. Now the proportions are completely the other way around.

I have wondered desultorily about whether I have been psychologically damaged as a result of my days in Synge Street. I know I am reserved and do not take emotional risks. My world is bounded, and I stick with what I know. I am not a man who wants to see the Amazon or to stretch myself with adventure. Safety is paramount. But was this caused by Synge Street? Would I not have been that kind of person anyway? My mother was tough on me and on all of us. Her influence has left me with a terrible puritanism, which I find very difficult to shake. Even today I feel guilty if I go to bed early without being sick; sometimes I feel that if I am enjoying myself or having a good time I must be committing sin. But why should I blame her for that any more than Synge Street? That is to whine and not to take responsibility. Synge Street was tough. But the world was tough.

Tony Bennett, who is now Bursar of UCD, strongly believes that our background, and particularly our mothers, had far more of an effect on us than any walloping we got at Synge Street. He, like me, is 'dead scared of being broke', and it is this that drives him. I once heard a very astute comment about our communal background. It marvelled at the 'extraordinary enclave of mothers' that pervaded it.

I know that there are other boys who were hugely damaged by Synge Street. I cannot honestly say I was. It certainly bred caution in me and a desire always to keep my nose clean and not to invite trouble. Maybe I lack imagination . . . I know of a man who was caught behind enemy lines for nine days in the Korean War and survived by eating earthworms. He managed to re-join his comrades, and from that moment knew with certainty that he would never again know fear. All of us who came through Synge Street together—Colm Campbell, Tony Bennett, all my friends—have agreed that having got it, we could survive anything. It has also created a bond between us that exists to this day. After Synge Street, the rest of life is a doddle. And we never forget that without the Brothers, none of us would have had any chance of any education at all. We owe much to them.

71

CHAPTER 4
A FOOT ON THE LADDER

■

I have always made it clear how deep was my admiration for Éamonn Andrews. I think he was one of the finest all-round broadcasters in the world, and without doubt the best sports commentator that I ever heard.

Éamonn, the Third Playwright of Synge Street (the others being Synge and George Bernard Shaw!), wrote a play, at the early age of 17 or 18, called *The Moon is Black*, in which Raysie-baby had a part. There was great excitement when it was to be performed by one of the local amateur groups. We all went along of course to support our brother the actor, and our friend the author. The main chap in the play was an anti-hero, a poor, unfortunate, seedy, run-down, decrepit fellow who suffered from TB. Unfortunately, at the last minute the boy who had been cast in this part could not play it. His mother made him go home to do his homework.

So Éamonn had to play it himself. Even from the height of our hero-worship it was a little hard to swallow: to see this young, well-built, bustling junior amateur champion boxer whinging and whining under the burden of TB. But we were charitable, and the Byrne family led the thunderous applause at the end of the play.

When Éamonn Andrews began to broadcast, my mother thought it her bounden duty to control the size of his head. It was a type of game she played. She told him that he should not be getting ideas above his station, just because he was now famous. She made him suffer when he called into our house on a Sunday morning for the ritual drink and visit. He was not a drinker, or so she thought, and he would be served with a concoction known as Bird's Crystal Lemon Drink, which looked and tasted like a watery fizz bag, or with real red lemonade. Even when he was well into adulthood and taking 'real' drink, which she knew very well, she would continue to serve him with this stuff, and he had not got the guts to tell her. She figured she would let him suffer until he was man enough to do so. Of course when he eventually cracked, she poured him whiskeys of such large proportions, by the tumblerful, that it was a great source of wonderment to all of us that he managed to get home to his mother for his Sunday dinner.

□

The parallels between our two careers must be quite obvious, although I, in my quest to be him, forced some of them. Although it was never in my grand career plans to go into insurance, yet, like him, this is where I started my working life. I discovered later that he found it just as difficult to get a 'proper' broadcasting job in Radio Éireann in the early days as I did. In those spartan, puritan days, ambitious people were frowned upon as being too pushy. Somehow it was not 'nice' to be ambitious, and there were numerous people available to slap down any upstarts who might want to do more than they were asked.

His initial entry into radio was relatively simple. He was earning about £5 a month in insurance, the salary thus pegged on the understanding that gentlemen in the insurance industry were training to be professionals. He read, during a break from studying *The Principles and Practice of Fire Insurance*, that the only way to get into broadcasting was to be an expert on something. So he wrote to RE telling them that he had been a schoolboy boxing champion and had studied elocution. He was therefore, he felt, their ideal candidate for boxing commentator. They wrote back, gave him an audition, and then his first commentary job. But from then on he found progress more difficult. He wanted to get officially into RE, to broadcast generally and not just in sports, but found it impossible; so he took himself to London, to the BBC, 'as a stick', he once said, 'to come back to beat them with and to say, "Now will you let me do the things I want to do here?"'

Éamonn's breakthrough came with the show 'Ignorance is Bliss'. He had gone to London with very little to sustain him, just the promise of the occasional sports programme. At the time, the king of BBC radio—which for us here in Ireland was king of the world of radio—was Stuart McPherson, who was a sports commentator and also host of 'Twenty Questions', 'This is Your Life' (on radio), 'Ignorance is Bliss', and almost anything else that was going. He was a Canadian, with a very crisp, sharp style. He was very good and had the BBC tied up. And then, suddenly, his father died. Stuart announced that he was quitting the BBC and going home to Toronto to look after his father's newspaper empire. He gave the BBC seven days' notice, and flew off.

Our Éamo was man-on-the-spot. Just as I was later and, in his own time, Terry Wogan, Éamonn was the right guy in the right place at the right time. Success is all a matter of luck (if you don't believe me, ask any failure!). Éamonn got his astoundingly lucky break—but he had the talent, energy and moxie to grab the ball that was handed to him and to run with it.

He was first of all pushed into the Saturday afternoon 'Sports Report' programme, followed closely by the other two programmes that had been done by McPherson. It was almost miraculous. Now he was coming into

□

our homes—and into the Byrne home via our radio in the dining-room and the extension speakers in the kitchen—at all hours. Whenever he came home now and paid us his Sunday visits, I hung around with even more stars in my eyes.

It was not only my ambitions and fantasies that were being appealed to: it was my vanity too. Éamonn had a Thunderbird car, a long, low beauty that purred under her shining bonnet and that seemed to be longer than the entire frontage of our house when she was parked outside. The sight of her outside our house on the South Circular Road did our image no harm . . . Even before he had risen to the heights of the Thunderbird, he had one of the first Ford Prefects (known in our area as a 'Perfect') ever to be seen regularly parked outside any of our houses.

Éamonn met his wife, Gráinne, in the Theatre Royal while doing a 'Double Your Money' quiz show. Gráinne, or Gracie as she was known then, was a member of the famous theatrical family of Bourkes. There was Lorcan and Jimmy and Rick, later Chief Barker of the Variety Club of Ireland. (Lorcan later became the Deputy Lord Mayor of Dublin.) The stories about Lorcan Bourke are legion, and the best stories are in the memory of Bill O'Donovan, of RTE FM2. Bill is Fred O'Donovan's brother, and dines out on the Lorcan stories, complete with wickedly accurate mimicry. For instance, Lorcan was producing a show in the Olympia, which, of course, had a pit band. Lorcan, as was his wont, was busy-busy-busy, and was dashing past the orchestra pit when he noticed that the brass section was not playing. He leaned over the rail: 'Hey—why aren't yous playing?' And the leader answered that it was okay, that the music said they were supposed to be *tacet* for these sixteen bars or so . . . 'I don't give a' (deleted) 'what yous are, yous are paid to play—*play!*'

My mother was invited to Éamonn and Gráinne's wedding. Lorcan had pulled out all the stops, and it was a very lavish affair. Everybody who was anybody was there.

The story is told that there was Lorcan in his tails and top hat, very upmarket on this great occasion, talking to two titled ladies: call them Lady Mary and Lady Geraldine.

'Yes, Lady Mary and Lady Geraldine, we are very pleased to have you here this evening on this auspicious occasion, and of course Éamonn and Gracie are going to set off, as it were, on these totally uncharted seas of matrimony in this delicate barque of . . . Excuse me, Lady Mary, Lady Geraldine—' (turning his head to address a third party) 'Wha? No . . . no—Yes, as I was saying, Lady Mary, Lady Geraldine, Éamonn is a very fortunate man; although she is my own daughter I have to tell you—' (again responding to a tug at his sleeve) 'Wha?—Excuse me, Lady Mary, Lady Geraldine—*Wha?*

☐ *The Guinness barges on which my father worked for most of his life.*

GUINNESS

☐

No . . . I said, *No!*—Sorry about that. Well, as I was saying, Éamonn is very fortunate, Lady Mary, Lady Geraldine, to get a girl like Gracie, because she will be a great adjunct, as it were, to his illustrious and professional career, because she will be entertaining all these—Wha?—Ex*cuse* me, Lady Mary, Lady Geraldine— ' (then loudly) 'No, I've *told* you: there's *no* fuckin' stout!'

But my own fondest memory of Lorcan is of the day we were all together visiting in Éamonn and Gráinne's house in Portmarnock. Kay and I had our youngsters with us, and so had many of the other guests. At some time during the party all the kids came waltzing in to the adults, full of excitement, each waving a pound note—which was a lot of money at that time. Adults react in shock-horror: 'Where'd you get that money?' followed by a cacophonous chorus of 'From Uncle Lorcan.' We all remonstrated with Uncle Lorcan. But he turned around: 'Don't ever forget, the day will come when they will remember me. My name will be mentioned, and they will always remember the day their Uncle Lorcan gave them a pound in Éamonn's house.' He was perfectly right. They still do.

During my final year at Synge Street I had had some hopes of going to Trinity like Al, but because Da died while I was in the Leaving Cert year that put paid to that. I had to earn my living. I did the clerical exam for Guinness's after the Leaving Cert, because of Mary and Al and the short hours and long holidays and the restaurant and the privilege days and all the rest of it, but fell at the interview.

The Guinness version of the failure is that I failed. My version is that I did not fail. Sir Charles Harvey looked across the board-room table at me during my interview. What were my hobbies, what did I read—all the usual stuff; and then he said: 'I am of the opinion that there is an elegant sufficiency of Byrnes on the Guinness staff.' I swear that is what he said.

I probably failed.

I applied to the Royal Insurance Company, where Mary had once worked and where I probably got the job in fond memory of her. Ma was, predictably, delighted.

Recently I came across some chronological notes I had made at some stage about my ascent, or descent, to my present state. I cannot decide whether or not it makes me depressed or happy.

From about 14, the influence of Éamonn Andrews; wanted to be what he was—sports commentator, 'Imco Show', etc. Started doing amateur drama and shows, National Arts Theatre, Dublin Shakespeare Society, MC at concerts in Arch. Byrne Hall, St Francis Xavier Hall, St Anthony's Hall, etc. General interest in showbiz and listening to radio all the time. Special interest in comedy. Stock-car racing commentator, Shelbourne Park.

Asked to stand in for Pat Layde reading commercials on Urney Chocs show.

□

Then asked to do dance-band show on RE, Christmas Night, 11.30 p.m., 1958. Got into GPO, having been turned down many times. Newsreader, conty anncr., recitals, orchestra, jazz programmes. Left insurance and went to work for Wilson Young Advertising as radio producer, Bird's Prog. (3 per week), 4 other sponsored programmes as well.

Heard of job in Granada TV, Manchester. Pestered Tim Hewitt until he asked me over for audition as newsreader. Read the news on air that night. Started flying over each week. Then vacancy came to co-host 'People and Places' 5 days a week, and got it. Settled into Monday–Thursday Manchester, reading news, hosting 'People and Places' 6.30 p.m. and regular stints on BBC Radio Manchester. Home to Dublin Fridays for 'Top of the Pops', 'Late Late Show', '17 Club', and some sponsored programmes.

The brief résumé seems to show a life filled with frantic activity, but in reality it was blissfully filled one day at a time.

Shortly after I began work I joined the Dublin Shakespeare Society, where I greatly undistinguished myself as an actor, although I was a passable assistant stage manager in a production of *Julius Caesar* with District Justice J. A. McCarthy as Caesar, Al as Brutus, and another man from the business world who was longing to get out of it, T. P. McKenna, as Cassius. I also hawked my talents into the National Arts Theatre, where I continued to be undistinguished, carrying spears in plays like *Deirdre of the Sorrows*. The director of the National Arts Theatre was Frank G. O'Neill, who took me aside and confirmed for me what I had always dreamed. He said my future lay in my voice. Well, I knew it certainly did not lie in my acting.

I had always taken the quality and production of my voice seriously. In school-days I had already had formal elocution lessons ('Ode on a Grecian Urn' and the like, detested by others, loved by me for its sounds) from 'Miss Buhke' in Synge Street. (No-one ever thought to enquire whether Miss Burke had a Christian name. All over the Christian Brothers' schools of Dublin, the most uncouth and unkempt chisellers and gurriers shot to their feet when she entered their classrooms, trained to chorus, as if strolling around the playing fields of Eton, 'Good mohning, Miss Buhke!')

During this period of peripatetic activity on the fringes of the Dublin stage, I went for voice training to Coralie Carmichael, the actress at the Gate Theatre, who 'took' people if she liked them (and if she needed the extra cash), and finally I landed on the doorstep of the doyenne of Dublin voice teachers, Elizabeth Graves, a frail, unhealthy little woman who lived in the back room of a splendid old house in Appian Way, fusty with velveteen and tassels, crammed with souvenirs of her long and illustrious career as a voice coach.

She is credited with taking the basic and undistinguished voice of the

☐

actor Patrick Bedford and developing it into the rounded and sonorous instrument it is today. She also 'took' Mícheál Mac Liammóir and Hilton Edwards, and any actor who felt his voice was ailing and who needed a refresher. Miss Graves did not like elocution. She was into voice production, with the aid of little plaster casts of heads, complete with hinged jaws and full sets of teeth, showing the voice soaring from the chest and up, up through the larynx, careening around the ears and sinuses and cranial cavities. She had a theory that most voice teachers had it all wrong: that they were teaching that the voice had to be produced in the front of the mouth, whereas she believed that it should be 'thought' up into the cranial cavities. I can never hear Perry Como, Frank Sinatra or Laurence Olivier without thinking of Miss Graves.

I discovered very early in life that the best way to achieve anything was to keep trying. And that hard work and practice helped as well. While I was still at school, Raysie-baby was sending me copies of disc shows copied from Canadian radio, and Ernest was sending me spent news-scripts from his television station in the United States—scripts all about negroes being clubbed to death and busing and the school debate, and Governor Wallace: real life, far away. I practised and practised in the dining-room. I sent tapes of myself reading this stuff back to Ernest, and he would send back encouraging letters, saying 'Yes, you're good—but do this a little faster (or slower), more emphasis on such-and-such . . .' I sent tapes to Éamonn Andrews as soon as his commercial studio was opened in Henry Street, and got the same reaction. I practised harder, in front of mirrors, without mirrors, with or without the use of my records.

Just when I needed a boost, a man called Coyle staged a radio exhibition in the Mansion House. It was purely a display of the latest radio technology, but he had also rigged up a closed-circuit television system. This was at a time in Dublin when only a very, very few people had television sets, and even those who had could get only a snowy BBC if they happened to live, by geographical fluke, in the very small pockets along the east coast where BBC could be received. I had never seen television in my life, but I knew, like everyone else, that it was the coming thing.

I went along to the Mansion House to see the radio exhibition, and saw that Coyle was holding auditions for someone to 'read the news' every hour on the hour on his closed-circuit television, which for the rest of the hour was to be occupied with people standing in front of the stationary cameras, waving like idiots and watching themselves wave on the accompanying monitors (something like the 'Late Late Show'!)

I joined the queue for the 'newsreader' auditions, and won the right to read extracts from the *Evening Herald* every hour on the hour for the

□

great closed-circuit audience. All those hours in the dining-room paid off. People, even Mr Coyle, said I had a great future. He did not have to tell me: I knew I had a great future. I just had to let the world know about it.

In the meantime there was the little matter of earning a living. So I worked as assiduously as I could at the Royal Insurance Company, even sitting for, and passing, the first part of the Chartered Insurance Institute examinations (ACII), but always casting around for some way out.

A way out seemed to present itself when I heard that there was a job going as a trainee cinema manager with Irish Cinemas. (Well, at least it was on the periphery of show business!) But if the insurance business was tedious, it had nothing on being a trainee cinema manager in the Strand cinema on the North Strand. I discovered it had nothing at all to do with movies and everything to do with sales of popcorn and not falling foul of chief ushers, chief operators and the sales-girls.

Only when the weather was absolutely awful did I think of travelling to work by bus, so six mornings a week I cycled to work from the South Circular Road to the North Strand, arriving at ten.

Then I cycled back across the Liffey to deposit the takings from the previous night in the Bank of Ireland, College Green.

I cycled back to the North Strand.

I cycled home for dinner.

I cycled back to the North Strand for the afternoon.

I cycled home for tea.

I cycled back to the North Strand for the evening shows.

Then I cycled home, arriving at about midnight.

I became a very good cyclist.

I had one half-day a fortnight and every second Sunday free. I got cheesed off. I knew I wasn't going to stick cinema life, so I continued my insurance studies during the day in the dingy little manager's office at the back of the balcony. It was not sound-proofed, so you got the sound-track of whatever movie was playing.

Many, many years later (in September 1988) one of my guests on the 'Late Late Show' was Audrey Hepburn. I had the pleasure of thanking her for a long-distance good deed to me when I was in the Strand cinema. It was big for a suburban cinema: 1,500 seats. And we got *Roman Holiday*, with Audrey Hepburn, Gregory Peck, and Eddie Albert, right after its city-centre run. It was *the* movie of the year. We ran it for three weeks, and for that three weeks, seven days a week, we emptied and filled *three times a day*. We broke all records for admissions, and for ice-cream and confectionery sales, and I got a bonus (I think it was £10). All those years later, I thanked Audrey for the tenner. She kissed me.

□

And because I heard it so often, I still cannot think of the conditions, terms and exceptions of the standard motor policy without hearing the voices of Audrey, Gregory, and Eddie—and the theme music of *Roman Holiday*.

After a year, when I was about 22, I could not stand being a trainee cinema manager any longer. I had heard there was a job going in the reservations department of Ryan's Car Hire that paid £20 a week. The firm, which was owned by Dermot Ryan and run by Joe Malone and Alan Glynn, had a garage and office in Hawkins Street. I still hankered for showbiz and was still practising and pestering every bit as hard as I had been, but this job would do as a stop-gap until I became a star. At least Ryan's offices were rubbing shoulders with showbiz: they were beside the Theatre Royal. And there were great advantages to the job. When they were not in use, staff were allowed to hire the cars from the firm's fleet for one penny per hiring. No more cycling—and status with the opposite sex . . .

I enjoyed the job, but the old Byrne caution struck again. I felt, somehow, that Ryan's was not secure enough to last (which feeling, of course, turned out to be total rubbish), and I started to look around again. On the one hand I craved the excitement of the most insecure business of all; on the other, I wanted the steadiness of pensionable, lasting jobs. Weird.

I applied to the Guardian Insurance Company in Kildare Street, and the then manager, Ken Metcalfe—impressed, no doubt, with my 'dedication' to insurance in passing the exams while listening to *Roman Holiday*—gave me the job. I really did try to settle down, studied some more, and did my finals in the insurance exams. But I was also spending a lot of time spraying Radio Éireann and commercial studios with applications and tape-recordings of myself, so far with little success. I knew, however, that when Éamonn had applied to RE someone perspicacious had pencilled all over his application, '*Completely unsuitable for radio work of any kind and should never be allowed near a microphone,*' and I pressed on.

I have found that, remarkably, it often works if you decide what it is you want to do and then offer your services to whoever owns it, no matter how long it takes you to force them to say yes. At the time, Joe Lynch was compèring the Urney sponsored programme in front of an invited audience in the CIE Hall in Marlborough Street. The sessions were held every fortnight, with two or three recordings being made at a time. Norman Metcalfe was on the organ, and the commercials were read by the Abbey actor Pat Layde.

I had been hounding Desmond O'Kennedy of O'Kennedy-Brindley and had auditioned for him. OKB was one of the biggest agencies in town and had a lot of sponsored programmes. I hung around the CIE Hall during

□

the recordings and frequently ran into Eileen Bowers, the daughter of Urney's Sales Manager, who, I soon realised, appreciated me if no-one else did. So when Pat Layde had to be unavoidably absent because of an Abbey tour, I was Johnny-on-the-Spot, helped into it, I am sure, by the lovely Ms Bowers. So my first actual paid broadcast on radio (as opposed to my star performance in 'Children at the Microphone') was made standing in front of a live audience in the middle of the CIE Hall, one commercial in Irish, one in English. And when Mr Layde's tour was extended, I did it again. I became the official stand-by, and finally, as these things usually work out, the official official.

In those pre-television days the sponsored programmes were very popular. Nowadays, when I am walking along a street, the smart-aleck thing to do is to hum the tune, 'It started on the "Late Late Show" . . .' while pretending not to look at me; but in those days people used to shout the Urney slogan across the street: 'Any time is Urney time . . .'

I became 'Have Microphone Will Travel'. I insinuated myself into the variety scene and began compèring shows, linking the acts and telling gags in places like the Archbishop Byrne Hall—a big deal in those days, with people like Cecil Nash, Seán Mooney, Val Fitzpatrick, and some of the Happy Gang from the old Queen's Theatre. The other venues on the 'circuit' were the St Francis Xavier on the north side of the city, and St Anthony's Hall on the quays.

Having started small and for charity, I then moved on to the Sunday night variety scene, and was getting paid to host really big shows starring people like Jack Cruise, Maureen Potter, and Hal Roach. My policy was still to do anything that smacked of show business in general and anything in front of a microphone—any microphone—in particular.

In Dublin, once you are involved in theatre at all it is such a small scene that you are quickly assimilated and get to know everyone and everything that is happening. Dermot Doolan, whose father's school I had attended in Rialto, told me that Stanley Illsley and Leo McCabe were casting *The Remarkable Mr Pennypacker* in the Olympia. Big-time stuff: professional theatre. Pennypacker himself was played by Stanley, and there were dozens of children, it seemed, including one Larry Gogan, child actor.

'Of course you're not paid during rehearsals,' said Leo loftily to me, 'and you will get five pounds a week during playing.'

It did not seem like an awful lot of money to me, and I said so.

'How much are you getting on wireless for reading commercials on the Urney programme, Mr Byrne?'

'Three guineas.'

'Isn't that interesting, Stanley? Mr Byrne gets three guineas for reading the commercial on the Urney programme.'

Stanley's lip curled theatrically.

Even if I had been very good, which I was not, I do not think I would have lasted in theatre for very long at those rates.

Around 1956, following a temporary craze for speedway racing—the very dangerous sport of racing around a dirt track on motorcycles—stock-car racing came to Ireland. The king of public announcements at that time was Les Thorn, a man who presided over most of the 'serious' motor and motorbike racing all around Ireland. I went a lot to speedway with Tony and Colm, and of course I was the kind of young pup who always thought 'I can do better than that!' So when I heard that the stock-car racing was coming I rang one of the men in the motor trade: 'My name is Gay Byrne and I'd love to be your commentator at Shelbourne Park for the stock-car racing.' The poor man had not had time to consider whether or not he wanted a commentator. But he said okay. Thus I became the commentator for the races, broadcasting internally around the track at Shelbourne Park from the little wooden eyrie on top of the stands, learning how to use the (very good) public address system. There was a three-second delay between what you said and the time your voice came back to you, so it was a very good discipline, and meant you had to think on your feet. I was getting something like twenty pounds for the Sunday afternoon's work—to tell the truth, I would have done it for nothing for the training. I felt I was one teensy step closer to the style of my idol, Éamonn Andrews. And from the commentary position, for about an hour before the races began, I also had the opportunity to broadcast a record request programme, using my own discs, mainly 78s, although I did have a few long-playing records. The equipment was minimal: I had a microphone and a turntable. To fill in between the records I would tell gags and mention Auntie Julia from Roscommon. I became quite popular, and people started arriving early on Sundays to hear the 'radio show'.

The races were organised by the Stock-Car Association of Ireland, the members of which were mainly drawn from the motor trade. At the end of the first season they held a celebratory dinner in what was then the Four Provinces ballroom at the top of Harcourt Street. I was invited along. There were the usual speeches and tributes, and then, at the very end, there was a tribute to me. I was blushing and demurring, probably not very convincingly, when, out of the blue, having done a whip-round, they handed me £250. In *cash*. This was in recognition of what they reckoned was my contribution to a great season of racing.

□

I had never, ever seen so much money before. For once in my life I was almost speechless. I know that they were all motor dealers and they had made a tidy profit on the season, but the idea that they thought so much of me as to give me that kind of a tribute was the most wonderful boost I could have had.

That evening, after the dinner, I walked all the way home to the South Circular Road. I could have got a bus, or a taxi, or three taxis, or ten taxis. I could even have bought a car. But I simply wanted to savour every step of the way home. I knew exactly how Gene Kelly felt in that wonderful dancing sequence in *Singing in the Rain*. Every touch of my foot on the golden pavement reminded me that I had £250 bulging in my pocket. Sweet money. Those tough men thought I was great. To tell the truth, so did I.

Still on the Andrews quest, I decided I wanted to be a soccer commentator. The fact that I had managed to get through my entire school career and leisure life afterwards without kicking or hitting a ball of any shape or size was immaterial. It was not that I was interested in soccer. It was not how you won or lost, it was how you talked about the game . . .

I took a grind from Colm Campbell, who played rugby and had more than a passing interest in ball games of all sorts, and I read the rules of the game of soccer, studying them as if for an examination. Replete with theory, off I went to see Philip Green, who was Head of Sport in Radio Éireann. I told him I wanted to be a soccer commentator. Phil has eaten, slept, dreamed and nightmared soccer for his entire life. He is a very kind, diplomatic man, and after a few general questions about sport, during which it became perfectly evident that (*a*) I knew nothing about sport and (*b*) I cared less, he suggested gently that perhaps I might like to go away and spend a couple of years actually watching soccer matches and other sports, and maybe then I could make another appointment with him.

Many years later, on the 'Gay Byrne Show', I interviewed Phil on the occasion of his birthday; he recalled my 'audition' very clearly. I had the manners to apologise to him for wasting his time that day so long ago in the GPO.

By then the work for the sponsored programmes had begun to mushroom, and one of the most exciting events of my life so far had happened. Kevin Roche, the Assistant Head of Light Entertainment in Radio Éireann, who had been at the receiving end of a lot of my attention, rang me in late November 1958 to tell me that he had arranged for me to present a programme of live dance music on Radio Éireann at half-past eleven on Christmas night, with Peter Cusack and his orchestra. It was an adventurous offer from a station the idea of whose bosses at the time was that to string together 'The Rose of Mooncoin', 'Va Pensiero' from Verdi's

□

Nabucco and a few records from the Gallowglass Céilí Band with just pre and back-announcements constituted the height of a jolly night's entertainment. I hope that Kevin knows how grateful I was and still am to him for taking a cocky, red-raw rookie like myself and allowing him to develop. Because shortly after that Christmas broadcast, he offered me a series of similar programmes.

At the same time, Desmond O'Kennedy of O'Kennedy-Brindley, to whom I am also very grateful, was beginning to offer me more work in sponsored programmes. I was up and running.

John Young, of R. Wilson Young Advertising, the agency that was buying proportionately the greatest amount of advertising time on Irish radio, contacted me. His agency was handling three programmes a week for Bird's, three for Beecham's, one for Brittain's Motors, two for Maxwell House, one for Prescott's, and one for Bradmola Mills. He wanted someone, a producer-type, who would handle the day-to-day running of these programmes. I was his man. He offered me the job of radio producer in R. Wilson Young Advertising. Just about the same time, Arthur Tutty, the then manager of the Guardian Insurance Company, had decided that he had had enough of me ducking out the back door in Kildare Street to do a quick recording session several times a week and thus not being available to our customers. I was under the impression I had not been spotted. Arthur realised he had a showbiz man on his hands, and he wanted an insurance man. He encouraged me to decide. 'We think you ought to leave,' said Arthur. 'Don't you?' I left to take on the advertising world.

Then I met Adrian Cronin, with whom I was later to work for so many years on the 'Late Late Show', which was still only a glimmer in the eye of Tom McGrath, since we had not yet got a television service in this country. Adrian was doing for a firm called Radio Publicity what I was doing for Wilson Young, writing and broadcasting sponsored scripts. Our paths crossed often at Peter Hunt Studios, which at the time was taping most of the sponsored programmes going out on Radio Éireann.

Adrian had a wheeze. He went to a German, a man called Max Ammon, who he knew was a bit of a boffin. Would it be possible, asked Adrian, to produce a flexible, unbreakable record that could be sent through the post. (This was, of course, in the pre-cassette days.) 'It would indeed,' replied Ammon, and he produced a machine that cut small discs onto very thin plastic, which could even be folded.

So Adrian and I formed ourselves into an ad hoc company called Personal Recording Services—that is Personal *Recording* Services, if you please, and long before Cynthia Payne's activities hit the headlines—and

☐ Ernest during his time with the US Army in Korea, a period of great tension for my mother.

☐ Ma, Mary and Frances decked out in their finery on the occasion of Al's conferring with the MA in Trinity.

advertised our presence. We advertised in the small ads of the newspapers and distributed leaflets in hotel lobbies. The idea was that for a small consideration, Adrian and I would come into your home, your very own living-room, and would record your messages, of up to five minutes' duration, to your loved ones far away. Then we would transfer the taped messages onto these little flexible discs and either deliver them back to you or post them directly to whoever you wished. All part of the service. Distance no object. Satisfaction guaranteed.

So for six to eight months we lugged our big, heavy reel-to-reel tape-recorders up and down the city, from Glasnevin to Rathfarnham, plugged the recorders into the mains, and looked on encouragingly as people stumbled through their messages written painstakingly on grubby bits of paper.

The first problem was that most people, confronted with gadgetry, were very nervous and stuttered and stumbled, necessitating re-takes. The second was that the messages were so unutterably banal: verbal seaside postcards. 'H-hello, Auntie B-b-bridie. I h-hope you are w-w-w-well . . . We are all well here. H-how is the w-weather over there? It is fine here—now' (with relief) 'here's Donie . . .' 'H-hello, Auntie Bridie? How're things? Don't do anything I wouldn't do—haha! Well, that's all, here's Dinny . . .' And so on. We could have died of boredom. The third problem was that we were using as the address of our 'business' the premises of my advertising agency and Adrian's father's shop. Neither my Managing Director nor Adrian's father was amused.

The company folded after about eight months, mainly, I suppose, because we were putting in a lot of time and effort for very little reward. The whole process was long and tedious, and, in any event, by that time Adrian had become involved in the management of a jazz club in Grafton Street, the Blue Note, which was taking up more and more of his time, while I was getting busier with my own extracurricular activities.

I was at long last in full-time broadcasting. I was working with all the contemporary broadcasters: Joe Linnane, Cecil Barror, Ronnie Walshe, Eddie Byrne. I wrote their scripts, held microphones for them while they interviewed people, and stood in for them if they could not be there. Even Radio Éireann capitulated and allowed me onto their precious 'official' air waves, as opposed to the slightly tainted sponsored ones, as a part-time newsreader and continuity announcer.

I do not mean to denigrate the early Radio Éireann. I was young and brash, into pop music, and céilí was not my thing; I was not interested in Irish 'culture' per se; my father had not been in the GPO in 1916, and I would have been anathema to the powers-that-be in RE like Mícheál Ó

☐

hAodha and Roibeard Ó Faracháin. I was the very antithesis of what they and most of the establishment had up to then been looking for in a broadcaster. Yet once I actually got my feet under the table, the station was impeccably generous to me. I was allowed to read commercials *and* to play the 'station voice' roles, and no-one made an issue out of it. When you consider that I was a continuity announcer, I was reading the news, I was introducing orchestral programmes, I was introducing recitals by visiting musicians, I was doing programmes in Irish and English, I was playing jazz records, reading commercials and doing everything possible, it is obvious that the leeway allowed me was considerable, and the training and experience were invaluable.

I made sure I was always punctual, sober, and neat, and if I said I would do something, I always did it, even if it meant staying up all night to write a script or to finish a project. I still operate on those principles today. It is surprising how much they mean to other people, who are just as busy as I am. But when I was starting, I got the reputation of dependability and was offered more and more work. I was usually first to be called on to fill in if anyone was sick or absent, and I was always available. It took me only fifteen minutes to get from home to the GPO in my latest vehicle, a little Austin A30.

Dónal Stanley, who was Commercials Officer in Radio Éireann, slipped me the wink that Granada Television was looking for a newsreader. I am sure that the last thing on Granada's corporate mind was to hire a Paddy from Dublin, but I wrote immediately to one of the station bosses, Tim Hewitt. (Kathleen accompanied me to the post-box.) I got the usual non-committal reply.

Then I started in earnest. I constantly wrote reminders. I rang Mr Hewitt once a week. I found out who might be meeting him and I beseeched them to mention my name. For about four months he could turn nowhere without hearing or seeing my blasted name. One day, in weary desperation, he finally caved in and agreed to bring me over to Manchester for an audition. The audition was on a Tuesday afternoon. I read a mock-up of the news headlines at four o'clock.

At six o'clock I was live on air reading the actual headlines. That night, at eleven, I read the longer, Northern news. They asked me to come back the following week to read the news for two days. Then they asked me to come back the following week again, for three.

They had a nightly current affairs magazine programme called 'People and Places', which was co-hosted by Chris Howland—who also did a stint on German television—and Bill Grundy. Howland was a singer as well as a journalist, and out of the blue he had a big hit with a record called

□

'Fräulein'. He decided to capitalise on it and to settle in Germany. There was a vacancy.

I auditioned to take his place. The producer, David Plowright, offered me a three-month trial contract for 'People and Places', four days a week, a combination of early and late newscasts and a good deal of film reporting. They paid me a vast amount of money, more than I had ever dreamed about, plus my air fare and hotel expenses; and since it was only from Monday to Thursday I was still free to do my work in Dublin: all the newsreading and continuity, sponsored programmes, commercial-reading and the Wilson Young work. It was a huge work load, but I thrived on it.

For instance it was around that time, in 1958, that I produced Joe Linnane in a radio documentary that, in a way, broke new ground. At the time, most radio broadcasting was scripted and rehearsed by presenters but, with a foretaste of what was going to become the norm, for 'Last Tram to Howth' I had Joe talking and talking off the cuff, with 'actuality' in the background—real live sound—as the tram, clanking and ringing, laboured up the Hill of Howth. The programme was a sponsored one, for Prescott's Cleaners and Dyers. It was a little gem, recorded on the Tuesday of the week the last tram ran on the Hill of Howth. I recall the day vividly, though I little thought that day that I would one day be living on the Hill and would love it so much. Occasionally, I've played part of that little programme on the 'Gay Byrne Show', for the sounds of the tram are extraordinarily authentic.

I continued in the commuting-and-working whirl right up to the time it became clear that the Minister for Posts and Telegraphs, Michael Hilliard, was going to authorise the setting up of an Irish television channel. I knew that Ernest was coming home, that Éamonn was to be the Chairman of the Authority, and that people like myself and Adrian were among the few in Ireland who could walk in and start to work in it straight away. Adrian and I had already made a 35 mm film together, *A Day from the Sea*, which I produced and Adrian directed. We acted in it (sort of); Mr Cronin was in his Fellini period, and everything was—well, representational. It was one of our more lunatic endeavours. Our leading lady was a girl called Linda Foley, Mike Monaghan was on cameras, and Janet Wynne was production assistant. (It is a measure of how small this country is and how young and tight the circle of media people that the same names still run throughout the history of Irish television.)

Adrian did walk into a job, but there were a few hitches for me. With all the experience I had under my belt I expected to be offered something in the new station; but it was getting perilously close to opening, and there was no word. So I wrote to the new Controller of Programmes, Michael Barry, and applied for the job of part-time newsreader at weekends. I was

□

really disappointed to receive a rejection—without interview, audition, or meeting. (I was later told that the then Head of News, Des Greally, had said that I was 'too professional' for the new service—whatever that means; but in the light of what was happening between Michael Barry and Ernest, I suspect I was caught in the cross-fire.) I was upset, but decided to take the long view. I wrote back politely to Mr Barry, saying that I was very disappointed but that I completely understood his decision, and added that should he ever change his mind I would be instantly available. Afterwards, all misunderstandings were forgotten and I ended up reading television news for RTE.

So, reviewing the year coming up to Christmas 1962, I could see that, despite RTE's feelings about me, my career was really progressing. The Christmas plans were that I should fly out to Granada on Christmas Eve, record two shows, and fly back as early as possible. Ma and I were going to drive to visit Mary and David in Ballinasloe for Christmas. We were full of plans and presents as I set off for the airport that morning. When I got to Granada there was a message for me to ring Al. Ma was dead.

Al had gone to the house to bring her to the bank so she could get Christmas money for the trip to Ballinasloe. He parked his car outside the house, and en route to Ma's hall door Christmas-greeted one or two of the neighbouring women as they passed. He opened the door and closed it after him without at first noticing the crumpled heap on the floor at the other end of the hallway. It was Ma.

Since there was no-one else to do the programme in Granada, I had to go ahead with the recording before I could return home. I do not remember much of what I felt: 'numbness', I suppose, would be the best word to describe it. I got home at about five o'clock. The house was crammed with people. Al and Mary and all the relations were sitting in the parlour. I went upstairs to her bedroom to where she lay in bed, smaller in death, all that activity stilled. Then she was removed to the local funeral home.

We cleared the house and Al brought me to his in-laws' house in Drogheda. The Larkins owned a chemist shop in the town and lived over it. Someone gave me a glass of green chartreuse, and I kept drinking it until the bottle was empty.

Christmas Day was, understandably, a rather low-key affair.

The funeral to Little Bray, on the day after St Stephen's Day, passed in something of a blur: I cannot remember clearly anyone who was there. I know that Kathleen came, and that my accountant, Russell Murphy, sent a representative, as was his custom.

CHAPTER 5
KATHLEEN

■

I do not remember the first time I kissed a girl. I know that this is the kind of thing on which women dine out, but for the life of me the memory of the occasion refuses to come to the surface of my brain. Perhaps it was not all that memorable. I know I was, like all my pals, feverishly wondering what it would be like and all of that, but the actual event passed me by somehow.

While we were still in Synge Street we all had a communal crush on Breda Shaw, a girl gorgeous in her green Loreto College uniform who got out of school slightly later than we did and who, as usual, fancied Colm Campbell far more than me. Ten or fifteen of us would cycle as far as the lay-by outside Dolphin's Barn church, ostensibly for deep discussions but in reality to wait for Breda and her gang of hockey players to come by on their way home.

They would stop and we would 'talk' to them, while the heavy lorries and the traffic pounded by. We discussed all the deep utter rubbish in the world, while the blood pounded in our veins and what we were really saying to them was that we wanted to swing them up behind us on the saddles of our charger-bicycles and to carry them off deep into a bosky wood. (The picture got a bit vague after that. But none of us had the slightest doubt but that we would be able to extemporise if ever we actually got into the situation. For 'bosky wood' substitute the back row of the Rialto cinema . . .)

Later I fancied another Loreto girl, the blonde Patricia McCusker. She was semi-approved at home, because her mother, a most imposing, wonderfully statuesque woman, went to Mass every day, and her father was the local Garda superintendent. But the most painful crushes I had around that time were, naturally, unattainable. (What are crushes for! Or is it only me?) There were two doctors living beside one another at the corner of the South Circular Road, a Dr McKay and a Dr Foster. Dr McKay had a lovely daughter. I was 15, she was 24. Day after day I loitered around the bus-stop where I knew she would wait for her bus to go to her work, which, I just *knew*, was something deeply fulfilling and important and even spiritual. (In fact, I think she worked for an insurance company.)

☐

I fantasised about her, in and out of bed; I dreamed about our lives together on some desert island, where I would look after her and she would be demurely grateful and would murmur about my maturity despite my tender youth and how age never mattered in the course of true love. Then she would cover me with soft kisses. The crush went on for quite a while, but if the poor woman ever noticed this sheep-eyed child staring at her, she never gave any indication. If she had ever looked directly at me I think I would have swooned.

That crush was replaced by a similar one on a girl behind the counter in Hafner's in George's Street. Hafner's was another of those institutions that to me symbolise what was good about my childhood Dublin. It was established in 1882 at 37 George's Street, near the corner of Fade Street, but by the early twentieth century it had expanded so much that Mr Hafner, a German gentleman, moved the business across the road to a bigger premises at number 50. The family lived over the shop in George's Street, and because of their excellent reputation and long history of service to Dublin they were not interned by the British during the First World War, unlike other residents of German nationality. Hafner's had a reputation for scrupulous cleanliness and attention to its customers' needs, and a visit to the tiled premises with its aroma of spices was on the itinerary of country people when they visited the city. City children like me loved to scuff our shoes and runners in the white sawdust that covered the floor, heaping it into little piles while we waited to be served with sausages, thick or thin, black and white pudding, thick or thin, pork chops, or sides of bacon, all of impeccable presentation and superb quality.

My Hafner's love was blonde, and I never objected to being sent to George's Street on Saturdays, sometimes as early as half-past eight, to have a head start on the morning queue, first from the door and then, after the shop opened, from the counter all the way out the door and down the street, beyond Cassidy's and towards Dame Street. Sometimes the queue was so long that it could take up to two hours to be served. At the counter itself the queue was usually two or three deep and there was fierce jostling for attention. The Battle of Agincourt had nothing on the strategy I adopted while in that queue, trying to place myself so that when My Love shouted 'Next!' I was properly placed to respond and to be served by her.

The fantasy was that I would at some future date quietly acquire ownership of Hafner's. No-one would ever know how I did it—it would be written about for years to come in the business columns of our national newspapers—but after stealthy use of a combination of guile and brilliant business acumen I would one day walk into Hafner's dressed to the nines. In front of the rest of the startled employees, who would pause in mid-chop or mid-wrap, I would take her hand, and then, gazing deeply into her lovely eyes, I would offer her my hand and my empire.

Then there was Maureen Callaghan, who lived in Haroldville Avenue. At least she was my own age, but, as usual where girls at talking distance were concerned, Colm Campbell got there first. Doggedly, I stuck around until she began to notice me . . .

When I think of it now, we were very backward. When we went to the 'fourpenny rush' in the local cinemas on Saturdays and Sundays, it would be in gangs of lads together. There was the later, occasional 'date' with a girl when you did not see a single frame of the movie but would sit beside her, heart battering at your rib-cage, wiping your sweaty palm on your trouser leg before you would risk taking her hand. Having got that far, the next stage was to drop something on the floor and thereby have to let her hand go to pick it up. On straightening up, casual-like, instead of taking her hand again you would drape your arm along the back of her seat. The next half-hour would be spent trying to get up the courage to drop your hand on her shoulder. If she let you, it was a signal that she would allow you—oh, bliss!—to *kiss* her.

My first real, reciprocal arrangement with a girl was after I left school and began to work. Lorna Blackmore, from Churchtown Road, worked in the Royal Insurance Company with me, and we went around together for a while. There were other girls I would meet at dances with whom I went out a few times. Then, as today, it was easier to 'click' if you had the use of a car. Sometimes generous Al would give me the use of his; sometimes Colm Campbell's father, who worked a night shift in the *Irish Times*, would give us the use of his Vauxhall. We were 'set up' on those nights for the hops at Bective and Palmerston, and could select the best of what was on offer. Dances usually went on until long after the last buses left the Pillar, and taxis were very expensive for young working girls, so any fellow with a car who could offer a lift home was likely to be very attractive.

The dances we attended were mainly in the clubs all around our area: Pembroke, Wanderers, Bective, and 'the Mhuire', which was run by the Oblates in Inchicore. We ranged far and wide around those club dances. If it was one of the nights when we did not have a car, we had to be content with our local dance in the Dolphin's Barn Hall with its dreadful squeaky trio.

My friends Tony Bennett and Colm Campbell were far ahead of me in the women stakes. I was extremely bashful and shy and in mortal dread of rejection, although, in fact, Colm credited me with having the best taste of the three of us, a compliment he gave with one hand and took away with the other, christening me 'First Gear', because this is as far as I ever got!

□

My function seemed to be to introduce women to the others. Colm remembers one holiday we took in Salthill where we were driving along in the little Austin A30 I had then, and I spotted two females walking along the promenade. I screeched to a halt with great squealing of brakes and burning of rubber, jumped out, and, leaving the engine running, rushed over to the females and shouted: 'Quick, quick! Have yous got a glass of water, my friend is very sick!' As an approach it might have been more subtle, but it worked. Bennett and Campbell had a wonderful time with the girls.

I had a girl-friend when I was working in Granada—several, in fact—but I was never all that serious about any of them, jogging fast, ambitious with my growing career, enjoying relationships with women only casually, for relaxation and fun. Except for one Kathleen Watkins.

I first set eyes on Kathleen Watkins in the Safari coffee-house at the top of Dawson Street, where Harry Moore's electronics shop now trades. It was the yuppy haunt of the fifties, a very 'in' place, patronised by students from UCD and young workers like ourselves. Later we were all to move to places like the New Amsterdam in Duke Street, but at that time the Safari was still the most fashionable place to be seen at night and at weekends. I was still working at the Guardian Insurance Company but getting nearer my goal by compèring the variety shows and working on the sponsored programmes.

At one stage I had formed a sort of unofficial variety company with Dónal MacNally, a man who had gone away to be a priest but who left gratefully to become a wages clerk in the Shelbourne Hotel. Dónal's brother, Tom, had been a good friend of mine in Synge Street. (As I write, Tom is now a colonel in the army, serving in Lebanon as chief dentist to the troops there. Dónal's business is MacNally's the opticians. Another of the five MacNally brothers is the singer, John.) Dónal and I, under the aegis of our little 'touring' company, brought variety shows around the halls. I was the compère, he was one of the star acts. Using the stage name 'Les King', he whistled like Ronnie Ronald. Ronnie Ronald was well known at the time on the English show circuit and would have been known in this country from his records. He used his whistling ability like a musical instrument, to very lush orchestral accompaniment. Dónal also played the piano and violin—the MacNallys were a very musical family.

There was only one disaster, as far as I remember. We arrived at the Father Mathew Hall in Church Street (Injun territory) to find that the patrons had stayed away in droves and that there were only twelve people in the auditorium. The twelve made up for their rarity value by being obstreperous. Even my dress suit had no effect. When 'Les' could not make his

☐

whistling heard, I took an executive decision. We let down the tabs and ran for it . . .

I was also by then doing the Urney programmes and others on a regular basis. I had heard, and read, about this gorgeous girl with red hair who played the harp and sang. There were three of them who came out of Sion Hill convent school at around the same time, pupils and protégées of a famous music teacher there, Sister Angela. There was Mary O'Hara, who I knew was in a monastery in England after the death of her young husband; there was Deirdre Flynn, and Kathleen Watkins. In retrospect it is extraordinary that Kathleen and I had not bumped into one another on the show circuit, although my orbit was far humbler than hers. The papers were always full of Kathleen Watkins flying off to Holland, or America, or representing Ireland somewhere in some folk festival or competition.

Dónal MacNally was an occasional visitor at the Watkins household. His (accurate) assessment of me was that I was always a little bit scared of women, so he took me in hand. He informed me that Kathleen Watkins was asking for me. That was the great phrase of the time. If someone was 'asking for you', you were well in, you'd be 'all right there'.

I found out later that he had told Kathleen that *I* was asking for *her*. Mr Dónal MacNally had taken it upon himself to act as matchmaker: Miss Watkins was not 'asking' for me at all. In fact, although I myself fancied that the whole nation knew me from the Urney programme, Miss Watkins told me afterwards that she was always running for a bus at the time it was on so she never heard it. She had heard of me through the grapevine though, however vaguely, and she succumbed to MacNally's conniving and agreed to meet me. Apparently what clinched it was that MacNally told her I was 'very musical'.

I arrived at the Safari with Dónal on the appointed day and at the appointed time, 5.30 p.m. after work. Kathleen was already there. Somehow I knew before I met her that this girl would be different. I cannot pretend that I had some psychic premonition that this was going to be It, that this was going to be the woman for me for the rest of my life, but I just knew in my heart that this meeting was going to be significant.

Her version of it is that I arrived wearing a brand-new raincoat with big epaulettes, which, she felt with some satisfaction, I had probably bought for the occasion. I remember the coat: it did have epaulettes and it was the colour of a Marietta biscuit; a big, important, Humphrey Bogart coat with a touch of the Robert Mitchums. I really loved myself walking up the South Circular Road in that coat. But although it was new, unfortunately for her story I did not buy it to impress her. Nevertheless, she has told people since that she was immediately impressed with how 'spic-and-span' I was.

☐

Furthermore, she says that she saw immediately that I was quite obviously a young man in a hurry. It probably says something about our relationship that she remembers more detail than I do, or maybe that is one of the great advantages women have over men. What I remember is precious little, except for sitting there, drinking coffee and admiring her. She was really gorgeous.

Dónal MacNally's version of that meeting, as compère, so to speak, is probably the most accurate. The Safari was dim and dark, with the lights kept deliberately low to create the proper atmosphere of intimacy. When we entered, Kathleen was seated at one of the small round tables, with her long red hair flowing across her shoulders and down her back, every inch a queen.

We ordered cream buns with the coffee. He noted with satisfaction that I messed them. I spilled the sugar all over the table. I talked gobbledegook. The more flustered I became, the more regal did she. Since I was so clearly flummoxed, he kept the conversation going in the higher realms of music. His brother John was by then achieving some reputation as a *lieder* singer, and he and Kathleen continued with a lofty conversation about this while I sat there, mummified, all thumbs, covered in cream bun and slop and crumbs.

I wish I could say that I floated down Dawson Street after that first meeting, convinced that at last I had encountered the Real Thing. No such recklessness for me. In my less-than-daredevil way, however, I did recognise that my hunch had been correct. This girl was different.

We started to date. I left what I thought was a respectable period between the meeting and my first telephone call to her. Didn't want to appear too eager. (She, however, remembers that I called almost immediately. Within two days, she says.) In the meantime we had each been in eager contact with Dónal MacNally, each asking him what the other thought. 'Did she like me?' 'Did he like me?'

I remember our first date. We took a walk down Dún Laoghaire pier. She remembers our first date. We went to the pictures. But what I definitely remember with awful clarity is the long, long road out to Saggart, where she lived with her family in a big house called 'The Laurels' —and the big, big harp I had to lug around as she travelled all over the country. With the extra few shillings brought in by the gigs in the Archbishop Byrne Hall and other venues, I had risen to the price of a scooter. I first bought a BSA Bantam, and it was followed by a 197 c.c. Francis-Barnett. By the time I met Kathleen I had a Lambretta, those little whiny machines that were so popular in the more penurious times of the Dublin fifties. Night after cold night I would scooter out to Saggart to collect her. Sometimes her father would lend us his car—but that meant, after I left her home, a hair-raising ride back into town. The great urban expansion had not yet happened in Dublin. The journey from Templeogue out to Saggart was traversed on narrow, winding country roads, rising into the Dublin mountains. On that return trip I was, to put it mildly, reckless. I know it is hard to believe now, from the *éminence* of my *grise*-ness, but I treated the run from Saggart as sort of a downhill slalom. Crash helmets? Never. Helmets were for sissies. (Five years ago, for old times' sake, we hired a Lambretta while on holidays in Crete and scootered all around the island. We paid for our sentimentality with appalling sunburn.)

From the very beginning, I had to be conscious of my mother's attitude to Kathleen. Ma scented danger. She had met other women I had brought home from time to time, but with the Irish mother's unerring instinct, she knew that Kathleen was in a bigger league. There was one occasion when we had been to a party in Mary and David's flat, just after they were married. Ma rang Mary in the early hours of the morning, wanting to know where the hell I was and what was Kathleen doing with Ma's baby. Of course I was somewhere out in the Dublin mountains, Galahad on my Lambretta with my lady on the pillion. In fact, if the truth were known, there was no-one in the world who would have been good enough for any of Ma's children. The only exception was David Orr, whom Mary wanted to marry. It is entirely probable that since Mary was not a son, approval for her choices was not so hard-won.

From the very beginning, I would never have dreamt of being anything but chivalrous with Kathleen; there was something about her that demanded it. I always made sure she had a safe way to get home. I would never have been drunk, or rude, or dirty or unkempt in her presence. To this day, she hates foul language. If it is used in a joke or a funny story and is in context—well, that's acceptable. But I have rarely if ever heard her say anything worse than 'Damn!' or 'Godalmighty!' or 'Curses!' And from the very beginning, I was totally aware of her high principles. (If I hadn't been, she would have let me know, pretty sharpish . . .) I think it is innate in her, this ladylike expectation of high standards. She was probably born with it: and a combination of her upbringing and education just served to confirm it in her.

So despite Ma's best attempts, there was nothing at all she could find to criticise in Kathleen; but often I felt she would have liked to. She was certainly far more charming to other girls I had brought to meet her, knowing perfectly well that they posed no threat to her little darling.

Kathleen herself comes from a close, happy family, with two sisters and a brother. She and her sisters still talk on the telephone all the time, every

□

day it seems to me. For the life of me I cannot think what they must have left to say to each other after all these years. Her father, Tom Watkins, ran a quarry business beyond Brittas, later bought by Roadstone. He had a bit of land around the house in Saggart, on some of which he raised cattle. His daughters, Kathleen, Phil, and Clare, all went as boarders to the Dominican Convent at Sion Hill, an expensive business, even in those days; his son, Jim, now a vet, went to Blackrock College. Many were the days Kay stood beside her father as he leaned over a ditch, looking at one of his animals: 'There's a lovely whitehead: that's next term's fees!'

He was a big, bluff man, a great storyteller, who surrounded himself with characters who complemented his large personality: people like John McCann, the playwright and ex-Lord Mayor of Dublin, father of actor Dónal; Louis Byrne, who owned the Downshire Arms Hotel in Blessington; and Michael McNamara, who was Principal of the Municipal School of Music. The Watkins household was a very musical one.

Tom was, in appearance, extremely like Pope John XXIII, a great drinker, smoker; a most convivial man. In my memory I see him always surrounded by his Fianna Fáil cronies and other men of jollity. (Like many of the seed men of Fianna Fáil, Tom came from a staunch republican tradition—and was actually married to Kay's mother, Dinah, while on the run during the Black and Tan period. The ceremony, I believe, took place somewhere in the Dublin mountains.)

Eventually, courtship serious, the day came when I was to meet this man. 'How do you do?'

'Fine, thank you, Mr Watkins. How do you do?'

'Fine. Will you have a drink?'

'No, Mr Watkins, I don't drink . . .'

'Will you have a smoke, then?'

'No, thank you, Mr Watkins, I don't smoke . . .'

(Pause) 'Ah, musha, why doesn't God call you!'

He was probably right. Proper little prig . . .

Kathleen was very happy in school. She has a theory that children who have a happy home life will be happy as boarders. When the time came for our daughters to go to secondary school, Crona was very anxious to go as a boarder to Loreto Abbey, because one of her pals was going. We tried to get her in, but there was simply no room. One of the nuns told us that, short of one of the community giving up her bed, accommodation just could not be found. Kay was just as pleased. She wanted to keep Crona at home with her. Her own parents came to visit every Sunday in Sion Hill and she made friendships there, with other pupils and with nuns, that have remained

☐

with her ever since. And it was there, of course, that she learned to play the harp, as well as the cello and the piano. So she is in favour of boarding. Still she wanted Crona at home.

Kathleen only has one unhappy memory of those days, and that is directly related to her developing TB. She was only 16 and was in great pain; but the pain kept shifting, and doctors found the disease very difficult to diagnose. Eventually they did, and she was removed to St Vincent's nursing home for six weeks, before being sent home for a long recuperation. Naturally, she fell behind in her schoolwork; and in an Irish test after she got back to school, she achieved the mighty mark of 3 per cent. She will never forget the humiliation of being told off for this in front of the class. And in her dealings with Crona's and Suzy's teachers these days, she can tolerate their being disciplined for bad behaviour—but never, ever unfairly for something that was not their fault.

After school and after the spell as secretary to Findlater's Managing Director, she took a clerical job with the tyre manufacturers Dunlop, and began this other night life of touring with her harp. She had a standing invitation, I remember, to play in the Great Southern Hotel in Galway any time she pleased. And she was a regular with Din Joe on his travels around the country with 'Take the Floor'. In those pre-television days, Din Joe, a big Corkman called Denis Mahoney, was a huge star. He packed in full houses everywhere he went. His show was a mix of céilí music and variety, with Irish ballads thrown in. (It was Din Joe who performed the feat, marvelled at by other radio organisations, of pioneering 'dancing radio', with the Rory O'Connor dancers. Their hornpiping feet became a regular accompaniment to the Irish Sunday dinner.)

Kathleen was also beginning to become interested in broadcasting, not only with Din Joe but in her own right, with her harp and songs, and also in the operational end. She had sung and played some fifteen-minute slots for Radio Éireann in Henry Street, in the course of which she had noticed that one of the disc operators was a girl. In the days when feminism was not yet popular or profitable, a girl in any operational job like that would have been instantly noticeable. Kathleen became interested, and in due course was trained for the job herself, playing discs into the old (and very popular) 'Hospital Requests' programme. She was a regular on the Gael-Linn cabaret scene as well.

So by the time I walked into that Safari coffee-shop, she was quite a star and already a seasoned broadcaster, something that I only aspired to. And she already knew what I did not, that broadcasting is not at all the glamorous, glitzy life that sometimes the public think it is. It is exciting, certainly; and addictive—for some. But not long after we met, I was already sensing in Kathleen that she was getting a little tired of it. She was certainly getting tired of the slogging around the country.

(Nevertheless, she will always have the distinction of being the first face ever to appear on Ireland's brand-new television station. When the fledgling RTE television service advertised years later, in 1960, for continuity announcers, Kathleen applied. She got one of the first three jobs, along with Nuala Donnelly and Marie O'Sullivan. It was tough enough for her. The TB had recurred and she was undergoing a painful course of injections, one every single day for nine months, which was the new treatment. She certainly gave RTE full value for its few shillings. It has probably been forgotten now, but in those early days of continuity there were a lot of breakdowns between programmes, and the announcers had to 'fill' a lot, usually talking, through their smiles, about promotional material. Kathleen did more than that. She kept her harp beside her, and when there was a breakdown, instead of talking about the great treat in store, 'Tarzan and the Elephants' or whatever, she plinked away on the strings and sang a little song. If the studio light blinked, she knew things were back on course. If it did not, she merely began another song.)

By no standards could the courtship of Gabriel Mary Byrne and Kathleen Watkins be considered as 'whirlwind'. I first met her in 1957, and we did not get married until 1964. It was an 'on-again, off-again' kind of courtship. I was reluctant to commit myself.

It was during one of our 'off' periods that my mother died. I rang Kathleen to tell her, and she came to the funeral. I was lonely and I had missed her, and we got together again. In fact, very soon after the funeral we went together to stay with Mary in her home in Ballinasloe. Over the years, Mary had met all the girl-friends in this way. The house on South Circular Road had become a very cold and empty place after Ma's death, a very unattractive home when I arrived into it each week from Manchester in the early hours of Friday morning. Very quickly, within a few weeks and on the urging of Al and Frances, I decided to sell it. It was Al who found for me a small, recently modernised flat opposite the sales kiosk at Lansdowne Road. Michael Viney of the *Irish Times* lived upstairs in the penthouse, and the comic actor Jimmy O'Dea lived next door with his wife, Ursula Doyle. It became quite a little showbiz enclave when Olive White, the beauteous Miss Ireland who was playing hostess on the television game show 'Jackpot', moved in too.

Kathleen and I began to go out with other people. Every so often, on the Viscount in which I regularly travelled from Manchester I would see this very attractive Aer Lingus hostess named Ann Tolan. She would be seated

☐

in the jump-seat, the little pull-down seat against the forward bulkhead, while I was usually in the front row of the passenger seats. Ann and I got to know one another and began to date. On one occasion we went out for a meal to the restaurant on the Dún Laoghaire sea front we all called Mickey the Greek's, the really 'in' place at that time. At a certain point in the evening, the owner, who was genuinely Greek, would entertain his customers with songs, accompanying himself on the mandolin. Going there with someone was like putting up a poster on O'Connell Street: it guaranteed that all interested parties would know who you were with and how long you stayed, and that you were serious about one another.

I heard some time in 1964 that Kathleen had become or was about to become engaged. There is never any shortage of 'friends' around Dublin to be the first with news like that. I cannot remember who told me, but in any event I was speaking on the telephone to Kathleen herself on one occasion around that time. In the course of the general conversation she stitched it in that she had heard all about Ann Tolan and what a lovely girl she was and that everything about her was lovely—and by the way, she herself was getting engaged. As it turned out, the relationship between Ann and me had already run its course, and although we were still friends I knew that we would progress no further. I did not, of course, tell Miss Watkins that . . .

I had begun to take flying lessons at the time, operating from Weston aerodrome, and was logging up the hours towards my private pilot's licence under the instruction of a man called Mick Flavin. One Friday morning, after one of these lessons, I stepped out of the plane and thought to myself that it was now or never with regard to Kathleen. I was going to drive, there and then, to Saggart to sort everything out. The other man's ring was on the finger, I knew that—but I was going to give it a try.

I know now that I was just plain jealous. So I was going to barge in and reclaim what was mine. Nothing is that simple, of course. In almost losing her, what had happened was that I came to my senses. But I also found out that my timing was perfect. She herself was beginning to have doubts about her engagement, and I arrived at the right psychological moment. Although I do not remember precisely what happened next, Ms Watkins claims she does. According to her, I went into her house, into the dining-room, where she was sitting in a low chair; then I went down on one knee and asked for her hand.

I did all the old-fashioned things. Just like in *The Quiet Man*, I told her how much money I had in the bank and what my prospects were. And after she said 'yes' and it was all newly exciting, we went for a walk behind Baldonnel aerodrome, where she had the big ego-boost of seeing an old friend of the family coming towards her, with every intention of

☐ Weren't we a handsome couple, then, on the day of our engagement and her showing off her sparkler on the steps of my apartment in Pembroke Road and later on our wedding day at Saggart?

□

congratulating her on her engagement to the other chap, only to screech to a halt at the sight of her walking, obviously otherwise occupied, with me.

Soon after we went down to Grafton Street and bought the ring in Louis Wine's. But it was the protocol of the time that the girl did not wear the ring until the 'official' engagement: in other words, when it was publicly announced. So Kathleen put the little ring-box in her handbag and came out to Dublin airport to wish me a fond farewell on my way to Manchester. I was going only for the day, and was due back late that evening.

This was during the period when I had permission from Aer Lingus to travel with the crew in the cockpit on their late-night freight planes. That night it was a Carvair, the four-engined DC6 with the huge bulbous nose that swung open to take vehicles, horses, and other freight. On this particular night there was nothing down in the cavernous back except a few coffins and lettuces and mushrooms. I was up front as usual, with, unusually, two senior captains, David Hood and George Castellaine. When we came in to land at Dublin airport the nose-wheel collapsed. There was a full-scale mayday, with screeching sirens and fire engines racing towards us. None of the three of us in the cockpit panicked. I am a pretty fatalistic person, and there was nothing I could have done anyway; but the two captains coped calmly and brought the aircraft under some sort of control.

My brand-new fiancée was waiting to meet me in the terminal building. It was a quiet night, with not much activity. All of a sudden this siren began to wail with the most scarifying racket, and people began to run everywhere. Desperately, she kept asking people what was going on, and eventually someone said, as he ran by, 'There's been a plane crash—the Carvair's down.' She knew I was on it.

Kathleen could not see the tarmac, and no-one was about to bring her out to it. So she clawed her way into the customs hall, forcing her way in through the outward-opening doors. And when she got inside she sat, in a dreadful state, on one of the benches then used for the examination of luggage. There she was, with her brand-new engagement ring burning a hole in her pocket, and it looked as if her beloved fiancé had just snuffed it out on the main runway. Then . . .

In I strolled, with the two captains and a few more officials, cool as a breeze. She did not know whether to hug me or hit me.

By then I was what is usually known as a 'celebrity' on this little island, as indeed was Kay; and all the newspapers began to get in on the act. To try to defuse the interest, and in the (vain) hope that if we did they might leave us in peace, we held a photo-call on the steps leading to the front door of my flat. That we were engaged was not the end to it, of course. There was the little matter of the wedding. As the date for the wedding drew

☐

inexorably closer, Gaybo began to get cold feet. Extremely nervous and panicky. To be perfectly frank, I was a reluctant groom.

Part of my panic was also to do with my move from Granada to the BBC. I had signed on with Éamonn's agent, with a company called Teddy Summerfield; and Éamonn's personal agent in that company, an Irish lady called Sheila O'Donovan, agreed to add me to her personal list. Granada had been very good to me, paying me a salary that was very high for a beginner. They paid my hotel expenses while I was in Manchester and my return air fare every week from Dublin, and two fees, one for doing the programme and one for reading the late-night news. But old Sidney Bernstein had an inflexible rule. He would not allow anybody to be on Granada television and BBC television at the same time, although he did not mind my combining television on Granada with radio on the BBC. However, Teddy Summerfield persuaded me to sign the contract with the BBC. When Sidney heard about it he called me in personally to his office, a rather large and lavish office, very darkly and heavily furnished in the Jewish manner.

He was a tall and very striking man, stereotypically Jewish-looking, with a broad, slightly flattened nose. He was very kind and flattering. The exact expression he used was: 'Well, if you want to get your feet under the table here, please say so; if money is troubling you, that will be no problem.' But I told him I had signed with Teddy Summerfield, who had already concluded this deal with the BBC. Mr Bernstein, who obviously thought (correctly) that I was wet behind the ears, said: 'Teddy Summerfield is a man of the world who knows exactly what he is doing; and he would know about my rule.' He was sympathetic but inflexible.

But I had this inflexible rule myself: that one must be honest in business dealings. I had already signed the BBC contract. Sidney said he could not waive his rules for me, sorry and all as he was to lose me—and that was that. I left Granada and moved to the BBC.

I only knew how happy I had been in Granada after I got to the BBC. Granada was not very big: there was a small-family feel to it, with Sidney as the father-figure. David Plowright had been my producer there, a brother of the actress Joan Plowright and a particularly kind and mannerly person. He was one of the few producers I have ever had in my life who had a post-mortem and advisory session after each programme, always conducted in gentlemanly and constructive fashion, and his advice proved invariably to be correct. Johnny Hamp was another guy extremely good to me, as was Bill Grundy, the co-host, who had the name of being irascible and who con-ducted an on-air act of irritability with my supposed greenhorn incom-petence, so much so that people would stop me in the street to say the equivalent of 'Don't mind him, luv . . .' He was actually very sweet with me and I knew it was an act, and we got on very well.

The BBC, on the other hand, was a vast conglomerate. The new television centre at Shepherd's Bush had just been opened, and although it was very impressive—and they were paying me very well—it was over-powering. I arrived at a time when BBC2 was very new and was not working with the public. The Saturday afternoon programme I was hosting, 'Open House', was not working. It was on against 'Grandstand' on BBC1. It started during a beautiful, hot, sunny April, and in addition, ninety-five per cent of the British public did not have sets that were tuned to the new station. So really we were broadcasting to ourselves. And I did not like the people with or for whom I was working, with the exception of Jacko—T. Lesley Jackson—himself a man from Dublin, who had brought me to the BBC as he had brought Éamonn Andrews before me. He was known in the business as the man who had 'created' Éamonn. I think he wanted to see if he could create another.

But while there is no way I could allege that anyone at the BBC was other than cordial and mannerly towards me at all times, I simply could not click to the new situation. I was introduced to my producer Stewart Morris by Jacko as a *fait accompli*, he having had no say in the selection of who was to present this highly expensive and prestigious show. Any producer worth his salt would resent such an imposition; in his situation, I would myself. There was no easing in either. I simply arrived at the new BBC premises in Shepherd's Bush one day, went up to Jacko's office, and was brought down onto the floor and introduced by him to everyone. Then we all went immediately to work.

The programme itself was a fine programme, over two-and-a-half hours long, with major interviews with big stars, a big orchestra under Tony Osborne, and a very large budget. The interviewees were top-class: we attracted people like James Mason and Deborah Kerr—with whom I fell instantly in love. (If we had only had such a budget and line-up for the 'Late Late'! On Saturday nights, after finishing 'Open House', I would fly in to a 'Late Late Show' where we might have two of the three Bachelors. If we could have managed the third, they might have sung!)

After Kathleen and I had the wedding date fixed and the two-week honeymoon booked and organised, the BBC powers cancelled the break that I had been given. I simply had to be there for the two Saturdays and the rehearsals. This meant that our lovely honeymoon, which we had planned and talked about, was going to be ruined. However, we were going ahead. I even had a stag party—not much of an event: I was not much into drinking at that stage, and it was pretty sedate. I do not remember all that

□

much about it, merely that it should have been a more memorable occasion than it was.

The wedding day itself was grand, although I know that Kathleen enjoyed it far more than I did. I hated being dressed in tails for a start; and to this day I will not attend a wedding where I am required to wear them. There was a huge turn-out. In fact there were so many people, the curious along with the well-wishers, that the police were on duty on crowd control. The crowds and the press photographers were there to see us, of course, but also to see who was at the wedding. Éamonn Andrews was a big star, and so were many of the others we had invited. Ernest and Ray were not there, unfortunately: they were both away. Fr Brendan Heffernan, the priest who officiated at the marriage ceremony that day in the little parish church at Saggart, was later moved to be parish priest in Portmarnock. The last two times I met him, he was officiating at Éamonn's funeral and then at Gráinne's.

We held the reception in Louis Byrne's hotel in Blessington, the Downshire Hotel. That was happy too; but I was still uptight and nervous, and I was glad to escape to the airport and our flight to London, where we spent the first few days of married life in the Westbury Hotel. Then we went on, as planned, to Sitges.

Poor Kathleen. There is no such thing, I suppose, as an ideal honeymoon. But ours was less ideal than most. After a few days in Sitges I had to leave her to her own devices and fly back to London for four days to record the BBC2 programme. Then I flew back. It was a dreadful mess. We had chosen Sitges because it was one of the few holiday resorts that I knew, having been there previously with 'the lads'. It was also relatively unspoilt, a small old town with a real heart, not custom-built like one of the strip developments on the Costa del Costa. As it turned out it proved to be a wise choice, because it was very popular with Irish people, and during the times she was on her own, Kathleen was taken under some very kind Irish wings.

We set up home in London, in a lovely flat in Onslow Square (we have called our house in Howth 'Onslow') that was owned by a grand-aunt-in-law of the broadcaster Brendan O'Reilly. Julia Ward (whose original name was Holzapfel, until the family, which had lived for a long time in Britain, prudently changed its name at the outbreak of the Second World War) was a wonderful old lady, very wealthy and with great taste. She had a succession of beautiful houses in Geneva, La Roquette, outside Cannes, and on the outskirts of Montreux. She married a German, George Deutsch, who was also wealthy; and when she died, early in 1988 at the age of 83, she left four-and-a-half million pounds to the World Wildlife Fund. The flat she rented to us was absolutely wonderful, with a garden back and front, one of those lovely communal and secluded London

□

gardens for which tenants have keys. It was an oasis of peace in that thundering city.

Kathleen loved London, and still does. She loves the anonymity of it and being able to shop unrecognised; she loves the theatre, the ballet, the shows. Her idea of perfect joy is an unfettered weekend in London during which she can organise herself to include as many shows and exhibitions as possible. But while she revelled in the city, I did not. I hated and still hate London, in hot weather particularly. And I was still very unhappy in the BBC.

After a year, Mrs Deutsch sold the flat. We were devastated. The price was only two thousand pounds, and had she asked us, we would gladly have bought it. In fact when I heard she had sold it I wrote out a cheque and brought it around to her by hand, but it was too late. She said she never dreamt we might have been interested, and was quite upset too. The new owner wanted possession, so we had to get out quite fast. We moved to another flat, in a place called Rosary Gardens, which was not at all as nice, and all my misery was simply compounded.

My commuting was in the reverse direction to what it had been before I got married. For two of the three years that we lived in London I was travelling to Ireland every Saturday evening to present the 'Late Late Show', and sometimes it was touch and go whether I made it. Ronnie Walshe, the actor and presenter of the radio show 'Sunday Miscellany', would be on stand-by in case of fog or other delay, and there was one occasion when he had to go on. He was about thirty minutes into the show when I sprinted in to the studio.

It was a messy set-up and clearly could not continue. I was not surprised, therefore, when it was announced that from the autumn of 1966 the 'Late Late Show' would be presented by Frank Hall. I was very sad, though, to see it go. Frank told me afterwards that my sadness was as nothing compared with his! The 'Late Late' milieu was just not his forte, and he struggled in it. During the summer of 1967 the Controller of Programmes, Gunnar Rugheimer, came to London to see me. He had heard on the grapevine that the BBC was about to drop its ailing Saturday afternoon show. He also knew of Frank's unhappiness on the 'Late Late' and of his eagerness to present a magazine programme of his own in the early evenings. He asked me to go back to Ireland as presenter of the 'Late Late Show'. I accepted with alacrity, but only on condition that I could be my own producer as well.

I had very definite ideas about what I wanted to do with the show. I wanted continuity in it, and I did not want each week to be in the hands of a different, perhaps inexperienced, producer, who would have his own

Announcing three new

summer shows . . .

the LATE late SHOW

FROM 11.15 p.m. TO 12.15 a.m.
ON FRIDAY NIGHTS STARTING JULY 6

**GAY
BYRNE**

**DANNY
CUMMINS**

**VERONA
MULLEN**

**LIAM
O'BRIAIN**

THE 'Late Late Show' is a new idea on Telefís Fireann — a relaxed late-night show of an informal kind. Gay Byrne, already well-known to viewers, will be the man in charge. Anything may happen, anybody may drop in.

Spontaneous talk . . . idle chatter . . . controversy . . . all unexpected, all unrehearsed. Helping Gay to keep the ball rolling will be Professor Liam O Briain, comedian Danny Cummins, and fashion model and ballad singer Verona Mullen. And, of course, the studio audience.

RTE GUIDE

☐ *If we had only known then what we know now and how long it would last...*

THE TIME OF MY LIFE

ideas that were perhaps at variance with my own. Gunnar was also anxious that Adrian Cronin should direct the show, believing that it needed someone with local knowledge. Some of the other directors who had joined the station from abroad when it opened were occasionally slightly at sea with the subtleties of the Irish mind, particularly with regard to politics. (The director is the person who sits in the gallery calling the shots and being generally in charge during the running of a show. The producer is the person who organises the content of the show and runs its budgets and administration. In RTE the functions, except in the case of the Presentation Department, are usually combined.) Adrian at first refused to direct me, believing that he knew me too well, but Gunnar persuaded him to accede with the aid of a letter, which Adrian still has, guaranteeing him that the assignment would be only temporary. It lasted for almost twenty years.

I was anxious to get back to Ireland in any case. Apart from my general unhappiness in London, and the absolute conviction that I had made a very bad mistake in moving from Granada to the BBC, the impression in London among us expatriate Irish was that things were happening across the Irish sea. Seán Lemass was Taoiseach and there was an economic boom. The Programme for Economic Expansion was in full swing. Ireland was *happening*! It was apparent to me and to others like me that 1967 was a very good year to be young, ambitious, and in a position of some power and influence in Ireland.

Kathleen was not as happy about the move as I was. But she has always regulated her life according to its different stages. Marriage was now her prime concern; and we moved back to Ireland.

CHAPTER 6
PRIVATE LIVES

■

When we first came back from London, we lived for about a year in a small but comfortable flat at 40 Elgin Road. It was one of those flats with a shared entrance underneath the imposing front stone stairway. We shared our entrance with the late James Dillon of Fine Gael. It was a nice flat, underneath a very nice road, even if it was a bit of a come-down after our lovely place in Onslow Square in London.

James Dillon and his wife used this flat when he was in Dublin for the sittings of the Dáil. At that time I had a Triumph Vitesse, which I parked zippily beside his huge Ford Zephyr in the communal driveway outside our door. One morning he bumped into my Vitesse and broke one of the stop-lights. During the course of that day Kathleen answered the door. Mr Dillon stood there, with all of his old-fashioned country stature. In his sonorous, rounded tones he said:

'Mrs Byrne, I regret to inform you that in moving my Ford car this morning, I accidentally knocked against Mr Byrne's stop-light. I am ashamed to tell you that I broke same. You must have it repaired and you must send me the bill.'

'Don't worry about it,' said Kathleen, 'it'll be all right . . .'

Three or four days later he again knocked on the door. "Mrs Byrne, I perceive in passing the Triumph Vitesse that Mr Byrne has not had his brake-light fixed. I insist that this be done and the bill be sent to me . . .'

A few days later I happened to be passing the Triumph depot in Baggot Street and I picked up a stop-light cover for seven-and-ninepence (about 36p). I replaced it myself.

Two days later: 'Mrs Byrne, I perceive that Mr Byrne has indeed repaired his stop-light. How pleased I am it worked out so elegantly, and you must allow me to pay the bill. Pray, where is the receipt?'

'Mr Dillon, please do me a favour. It was an accident, we are neighbours. Please forget it. It doesn't matter. It was a small amount of money. There is no bill.'

Next day he knocked again, with a huge bouquet of roses and a card

☐

expressing the sentiment that we were, indeed, wonderful neighbours. Days long gone.

We always knew that we wanted a house, and we set about house-hunting. One of the disadvantages of living in Ballsbridge, although it was very central and close to the Montrose studios, where I was working, was that a lot of other people I knew lived nearby. It was just too close to work for comfort. Even if I arrived home in the middle of the day for a sandwich or a snack or just to rest, there was always someone dropping in, or some punter to accost me with some request. We saw a newspaper advertisement for a small house in Howth, which was being sold after the death of the owner.

Howth, to me, was the sticks, even if it was the nobby sticks: miles away, out beyond the north side of the city. Being beside the sea attracted me, although up to that time my only acquaintance with the sea was in Bray, bloody Bray, and my only experience with Howth so far had been the day I went out there with Joe Linnane to record the 'Last Tram to Howth' radio documentary.

Kathleen and I set off on a Sunday afternoon. We travelled through the countryside—endless miles, it seemed to me—and climbed the hill. It was a glittering day, and the sun danced on the waves far below the cliffs. It glanced off the Baily lighthouse and lit up this little unpretentious yellow house and its acre of gardens that we were going to see. We knew immediately that this was where we wanted to live.

I believe now that the move to Howth has quite literally saved—or certainly prolonged—my life. In the world I inhabit, exercise is essential if I am not to keel over; and the walks and pathways around the Hill of Howth are impossible to ignore. The sea air is bracing and stimulating, and while I walk or cycle I can actually feel its rejuvenating sting. I walk, alone, sometimes for as many as three hours, every weekend. I could not do without those sessions now, but I could never see myself tramping around Dublin suburbia, however leafy or lawned, for that number of hours; nor could I see myself driving for miles to reach the countryside or the seaside just in order to take exercise.

All I have to do in Howth is to walk up my own driveway and out onto the road. After that I can choose to walk along the cliffs or through the little woods or across the bracken of the summit walkways. Sometimes I walk across the golf course. I know every fence-post on every house; I note where a wall is collapsing or a tree has been felled. My heart sinks if I hear heavy machinery: in Howth we are selfishly jealous of our beauty and the peace of our wild places. (I think that if we do not look after Howth and our other areas of high amenity, generations to come will put a curse on those of us

☐

who allowed them to be destroyed.) And everywhere I am, I only have to turn my eyes and the whole of Dublin Bay is mine, with the city pretty in the distance, its problems shrunk.

Each morning when I drive to work it is a gentle descent towards Dublin, always with the sea in view, along the Black Banks Road, towards the twin stacks of the Pigeon House chimneys and the low outlines of the oil storage tanks in Dublin port. At dawn even they are pretty, silhouetted hazily against a pink sky. And in the evenings I escape from RTE and Dublin as fast as I can, leaving the grime and the jostling and all that busyness behind.

I had one brief moment of doubt about the house. I had asked the solicitor who was then acting for me, the good and courtly Jack Maloney, to bid on my behalf at the auction; and I gave him my financial limit. He was a most conscientious and cautious man, and I trusted him completely. When the auction was over he rang me. He was quite distressed. He had, he said, gone over my pre-set limit by three hundred pounds. 'But', he said, 'you have your house in Howth.'

I put down the telephone. I should have been thrilled to bits that I had acquired such a gem. But typically, all the Mammy's early training in frugality and thrift came bubbling into my mind. Three hundred pounds more than I thought I could afford! How appallingly extravagant! This was during the very first bank strike in Ireland, and if I had had half the sense that was displayed by half the population, I would not have given it a titter of thought. Needless to remark, Jack Maloney had done me one of the greatest services I ever received in my life.

I should thank him every day I pull in to the driveway, which slopes steeply towards the house and from which can be seen the whole wide sweep of Dublin Bay. I should thank him each time I go inside, past all the familiar and homely objects that families accumulate, and sit in 'my' chair in the little extension off the kitchen. It is big and brown and comfortable, and is placed to one side of a picture window facing towards the bay, with Dalkey and Killiney set against the Sugarloaf mountain in the distance. I can watch as freighters make slow progress through the white-caps towards the Liffey, or follow the planes as they make their final approaches to Dublin airport.

Arising out of my work on sponsored radio programmes, and during my courtship of Kathleen, a very good friend, the late Larry Cassidy, whose family were the Cassidy fabric people in George's Street, began to invite us to visit him at his holiday house in Donegal, in the townland of Tubberkeen. The house had been left to him by an old aunt, a very religious lady, who allowed it to be used as a base for her Legion of Mary friends when they went on pilgrimage to the local shrine at Kerrytown, where the

☐

Virgin Mary is supposed to have appeared. If Larry did not want it, it was to pass to a community of nuns. Nuns? That would have been too much for our Larry. He took the house.

One day while we were up there he showed us a little cottage, called Dan Jock's, which was up for sale just a little way from his own house. It was set a little back from the shoreline with its wild land sloping into the sea, and was basic to say the least, but it had the sweetest well in the area: fifty feet above the house, so that the water supply was gravity-fed and did not need any pump. It had electricity, it was slated, and had two small bedrooms, one on each side of the front door. It was only a mile from the town of Dungloe, a very comfortable walking distance, but it sat in its own peaceful capsule of isolation, on a mini-peninsula in Dungloe Bay, with a view across the little harbour and the outside water towards the island of Arranmore.

We had already fallen in love with Donegal, and by that time I had also met the man who was to become one of my dearest friends, a solicitor in Dungloe, Patsy Sweeney. Patsy is one of twelve, seven sons and five daughters, born to a court clerk. He is the wisest and kindest of men, a wonderful granddad to his grandchildren, his pockets always filled with sweets and other treats. Each year he brings gangs of them to Portstewart on holiday for a week. Their fussy mothers pack suitcases full of pristine clothes, which are never opened, and the children come back from Portstewart, happy little ragamuffins, in the same clothes in which they left. 'There's no point in trying to keep childer clean' is Patsy's motto. He was handling the sale of the little cottage, which had been empty for about three years. No-one else wanted it; he was strongly urging us to buy it, and so was Larry. I dithered around for a while, but then, in 1967, we bought Dan Jock's.

Slowly we improved it, adding a big glassed-in veranda at the front, which is now the main living area, enlarging the bathroom, and covering the inside walls with plasterboard. It would not win any awards from *House and Garden*, but from the very beginning I found it magical. Each time I get there I feel that I can drop 'Gay Byrne'. There is no telephone, so I can read uninterrupted, and I can walk and cycle for miles across the mountain roads and past the quiet black lakes when, for hours at a time, the only living creatures I meet are black-faced sheep and an occasional rabbit.

Kay and I walk along the lake shores or beside the sea, watching as the light shifts constantly across the brown-and-purple landscape. There is history here, beside the Bread Wall, a huge structure about twelve feet high, built from smooth boulders of brown and black on two sides of a sandy pathway, starting nowhere and guarding nothing, bounding only a little bit of bogland before petering away. This, like Connolly's Folly in Co.

Meath and other fantastic structures of no useful purpose, was built by the poor and starving in times of famine for wages of loaves.

Times are better now, and the houses are snug (and there are more and more of them), nearly all with glassed-in porches as lines of first defence against the fierce north-westerlies from the Atlantic. People marry locally, and stay here if they can.

We were taken in as honorary members of the community. As we move around Dungloe, people shake our hands and welcome us, and then leave us in peace. I can settle in a corner of Beedy's bar with Patsy for a drink while we talk the world through. I can eat in peace in Sweeney's Hotel across the road from Beedy's. The happiest times are beside the stoked-up fire in Patsy's cottage beside the sea at Termon, or, on a calm evening, pottering in his boat around the islets in the bay. He brings us freshly caught fish, and Kathleen, his wife, brings us fresh brown bread or blackberry jam. When I get back to Dublin I send them books.

As part of the community, we know who is expecting a baby, who is coming from America to get married, who has died. We mourn the tragedies acted out on the pier-side at Burtonport, from which first the *Evelyn Marie* (named for the skipper's two daughters) and then the *Carraig Una* set out to fish but foundered on the rocks of Rathlin O'Birne. The scenes at the pier were reminiscent of Synge's *Riders to the Sea*, as everyone from this close-knit community waited for the bodies to be brought ashore. Not long before the first accident happened we had been out with the *Evelyn Marie* as she hunted salmon one night, and in the darkness we had even had a ship-to-ship concert, swapping songs in Irish with another trawler.

We have had the best of times and the worst of times in Dungloe. We have sat in our cottage through a week of non-stop rain and seriously considered slitting our wrists for laughs; we have enjoyed seasons of Mediterranean sunshine and warmth, fishing and swimming in the sea, walking and cycling and tramping the mountains. I have been more depressed in Donegal than anywhere else in the world, and I have laughed loudest and longest there in the company of my friends. I suppose precisely the same comments could be made by anyone who makes a point of holidaying regularly in Ireland and for whom good weather is important. It is for me. I vacillate between disliking the place thoroughly when I am there and being madly in love with it when I am away from it. But I am happy that Crona and Suzy love it so much, and several of my own male pals are crazy about the place, whatever the weather.

One lovely summer's day in 1968, shortly after we had bought it, as we were walking down the little boreen from the cottage to the seashore Kay

113

and I began to talk about our lives. Quite suddenly—in the context of our good fortune, with the house in Howth, the cottage, the good money we were earning, and our happy life-style—she began to talk about children. I knew that as a side-effect of her TB treatment she was unable to have children of her own. (Again there is the recurring connection with Éamonn Andrews. The same thing happened to Gráinne.) This was not earth-shattering for me, nor even all that important. But of course it had been a source of tremendous interest and curiosity to everyone else. For the first four years of our marriage there was the usual Irish nudge-nudge in our direction, the constant smirks of 'Any news?' that developed into knowing looks. Kathleen suffered in silence. She always felt that people considered we were trying desperately for a family. Of course we were not. All young Irish couples will know what I mean.

On that lovely Donegal day with, it seemed, only the two of us in the world, Kathleen said that all the material success and all our enjoyment added up to nothing without a family with which to share it. She said she wanted to adopt a child.

My attitude to that was a floating 'of course!' If she wanted a child, then I would gladly go along with her. She had gone along with me in everything I wanted to do in my so-called brilliant career, even moving back to this goldfish bowl from London, where she had been so happy.

The procedure for adoption was long and, in my view, quite justified. The authorities at the adoption society where we had applied for our first daughter were extraordinarily good and kind to us. I have no complaints whatsoever about adoption procedures in Ireland. I think that the baby has to be protected absolutely. All the safeguards, hurdles, footnotes and stops they put along the way are absolutely above-board and necessary. But I suppose it was easier for me, because all along I had the attitude that this coming child was mainly Kathleen's, since it was she who wanted her so desperately. I attended all the interviews and counselling sessions with her, of course, but I really left all the preparations and all the nitty-gritty to her.

We had wanted to keep the adoption as quiet as possible, and had not mentioned it to anyone at all. We even went to collect Crona at dead of night. Everything went well, and we were creeping out the front door of the adoption agency with the baby in Kay's arms when we were hailed in surprise from the footpath outside. Paddy Sweeney, the son of Patsy the solicitor, my best friend in Dungloe, was walking by at that precise moment. Talk about keeping a secret!

My reaction to Crona's arrival was initially muted. I was pleased, of course, but not over the moon. (Sometimes I wish I was a more passionate man.) It was not long, of course, before Miss Crona Byrne wormed her

IRISH PRESS

☐ *Crona, Kathleen and Suzy in their younger years in the living room at home.*

IRISH PRESS

☐ *Proud Dada, aunty Clare, cousin Susan Ryan, Crona and Mum on the day of Suzy's confirmation in the Church at Sutton.*

□

conniving little way into my heart. She can still, in her late teens, wind me around her little finger. During the six-month period before her adoption was confirmed, for the reason I've already mentioned—the protection of the baby—I never once resented the sudden, no-warning visits made to us to check how we were coping. We were pretty lucky, I think, in that the procedures went smoothly, although we did have to go through the normal period of doubt before the final papers were signed and Crona Byrne was finally ours.

Kathleen has a method—not peculiar to her—of sidelining problems in her life. It is a blind, bone-headed refusal to face unpleasant possibilities head-on, in the hope that if she ignores them they will go away. She had a friend in London whose adopted child had been taken away because the natural mother had changed her mind about the adoption. So it was naturally her greatest fear in the six-month period after the arrival of first Crona and then Suzy that the same thing would happen to her.

But if it was, no-one would ever have known. She bought all around her: clothes, equipment—enough to outfit an orphanage. She was characteristically refusing to consider that anything could go wrong and that the babies might be taken back. She was daring anyone to do it. I saw my function as cautionary nag. Day after day during those periods, as she became more and more immersed in the girls and as the piles of clothes mounted up, I reminded her monotonously that Crona was not ours, then that Suzy was not ours. I was not popular. Nevertheless I did have the effect, however transitory, of forcing her at least to consider the worst, and she now says I was right. Because from time to time she did face the worst. She did decide that if it happened, she would be brave. If the baby was to be taken away, then Kathleen would buy her enough clothes and equipment and everything she could possibly want for years to come. She would send her child back out to the world with everything she could have given her.

So for Kathleen, and even for cold-hearted me, it was a wonderful moment when the papers were finally signed for Crona. Kathleen had always wanted a daughter: there had never been any question of applying to adopt a boy. And then when it came to Suzy's turn, and Crona decided that she would like a sister (it was she also who named her new sister), Kay was delighted, because she too wanted another girl.

We could not go together to collect Suzy. I was in my office one day and the telephone rang. It was Kay with the breathless announcement: 'She's arrived!'

There was a particularly moving moment when Suzy's papers were signed. We all went in to this room to appear in front of the adoption board, presided over by a judge. Crona insisted on carrying Suzy—not too easy a

☐

feat, because she was a tiny little girl and Suzy was a big, pudgy, happy and heavy armful. Carefully she carried her new sister all the way across the big room right up in front of the judge. And the judge and the board made a great fuss of her, oohing and aahing over what she wore and saying what a great little girl she was. Then the judge looked Kathleen straight in the eye. She has never forgotten the words: 'Suzy is yours now. And no-one—but *no-one*—can ever take her away from you.'

Crona was baptised in University Church in Stephen's Green, and Suzy in the chapel of the little convent beside us in Howth. At that second ceremony, various people stood up one by one and mentioned their wishes for the baby. I remember Pan Collins, my long-time colleague and researcher from the 'Late Late', who quoted from the Bible (Psalm 23, verse 4): '*Yea, though I walk through the valley of the shadow of death, I will fear no evil: for thou art with me; thy rod and thy staff comfort me.*'

The sight of that little girl being put under such protection, with her sister and Kay there in the little church, and all now part of my family and under my own protection, brought more than a lump to my throat. There has never been a feeling in me that Crona and Suzy were anything less than entirely our own children.

Neither Crona nor Suzy has shown the slightest inclination towards musical careers, although Suzy has kept up her piano lessons. That harp has been lying around our house for ever, and neither of them is in the remotest way interested in touching it. As for me, it was probably far better that I had daughters, because I wonder how I might have managed should a son have asked me to take him to football matches, to play ball with him, or to take him fishing.

I suppose I could have taught him about cars or bicycles or motorbikes. Or microphones . . .

The study of gene inheritance must be fascinating. There was one occasion when Crona and Kathleen were driving along together in the car and Crona suddenly announced that she would like to pursue a particular career when she grew up. It gave Kay quite a start, because it was a career that had been pursued by her natural mother, a fact Crona could not possibly have known.

Both Kay and I believe that we have taken them on for whatever they are and for whatever they want to be themselves. Occasionally their very individuality and the unexpectedness of their behaviour make us stop and think. In a way there is one great advantage to the adoption of children over having them the natural way. Every day is a fascinating adventure, as the layers of the surprise packages you have brought into your home are peeled away one by one and you begin to see what lies underneath.

☐

I understand why Kay decided to put her career on hold and to stay at home with her children. Once, she spoke to another woman who, knowing that we had gone through the whole adoption procedure, was asking her advice. The woman was saying how she was really anxious to give a child a home. 'We have a nice home and plenty of money,' she said. 'We could afford to pay someone to look after it.'

Well, to Kathleen that way of thinking is absolutely impossible. She could not understand why someone would want to adopt a child as a sort of charitable act. The same way of thinking informed her decision about sending the children to boarding schools. She did make an effort for Crona's sake, because she was keen to go; but her attitude is that, since adopted children are 'brought in' to a family, they should be given every security and every chance at family love.

She believes I am totally indulgent with the girls. I must say I do not agree. I can get very annoyed and can shout and roar with the best of them. But without giving them the impression that money grows on trees, I have provided everything I believe they should have in the way of opportunities.

Like all fathers of my generation, I can only wonder where the time has gone. I look at my daughters and see that they are young women. I can remember snatches of time when they were toddlers: nothing terribly significant, but the time sped out of control somewhere along the line and I lost it. I remember one day an old consul here at the American Embassy, John Beitz, saying to me, 'The time goes so quickly from the time they are in prams to the time they walk out the door to get married, and you must value the time.'

Maybe it was because of this advice that I have one very vivid picture every time I think of Crona. She was about 11 and already tall. One glorious summer afternoon I walked with her up our driveway to the gate. She was wearing shorts and a tee-shirt and a pair of those brown Clark's sandals that all parents buy and that all children hate, and her hair was in pigtails. She was going down the road to visit a friend, and from the gate set off, while I stood watching her, a sturdy little figure of independence. But there was a dog of which she was nervous in a house a few hundred yards away, and I watched the swinging, independent little stride faltering a little as she got closer to it. She hesitated just before she got to the danger zone and gave a quick look back at where I stood: just checking; Dad's there, everything will be okay . . . then she straightened her shoulders and walked resolutely on. It was one of those moments that you know for certain are for conscious storage.

I know that other fathers like me, who have had such busy careers, sometimes mourn that irrecoverable time. But looking back, I truly believe

□

that our children have been with both of us a great deal. I did try to get them interested in a whole host of things, like photography, or even stamp-collecting, in which I could get involved in tandem with them, but they are both very independent by nature and do their own thing. They were never the clinging type, but always had their own friends and activities. They have been to a lot of theatre and cinema with us, on outings and on holidays abroad. We have spent a great deal of time with them in Donegal. They have been to London, to the ballet and the shows. (I thought that I had gone too far on the day one of them stepped onto an aircraft and said disparagingly: 'No movie!') Crona has been a regular attender and companion at the 'Late Late Show', where she has met the most interesting and stimulating of people.

I do not want to give the impression that everything in the Byrne household is totally rosy and that we are all sweetness and light all the time. With three women in residence, there are plenty of doors slammed! And there have been many threats and counter-threats. But ours is a good, family-oriented household, a haven for me against all the tensions and the stresses of the outside world. All day long at work and in public there are people talking to me and at me. I have to make decisions all the time. There is always someone asking me for something, or trying to carve a slice out of me. When I am on the radio or television I am performing, and the concentration involved in that alone is heavy and very demanding, without the other work I do every day. I am not complaining about this: it is what I have chosen for myself. I still enjoy my career; but as I get older, I get tireder. And as I get tireder, I appreciate my home more. There are few men I know whose wives get up as early as mine does just so that I can have a good breakfast. Six o'clock on a January morning is a very bleak time of day.

And somewhere along the line, Kathleen decided that radio and television would not intrude into our lives at home. Not that we do not listen or watch, but there is little angst-ridden discussion about our careers and the latest outrages, tittle-tattle or scandal within the walls of Montrose. So when I get home, I hardly open my mouth. I sink into quietness. I listen to Suzy and Crona as they pour out all their doings of the day: I regard that as necessary for them. Sometimes it is pleasurable; often I am very tired and I have to force my mind not to wander. Occasionally, Kay and I will have a decision to make and we have to discuss it. But usually I just mooch around, reading, or watching television, or doing my own thing.

I used to sit back and marvel at the incessant talk, discussion and chatter that went on between Pan Collins and her husband, Kevin. Each read voraciously. Each had an elephantine memory. Each could not wait to

☐

discuss and debate with the other the discoveries of the day. The communication style between Kay and me could not be more different. In the last few years of Kathleen's mother's life, she spread her living around her daughters' families. She told everyone that the thing that astounded her each time she spent her three or four months in Howth with us was how absolutely quiet and silent I was. Gaybo the ghost.

I have often been asked if Kathleen feels threatened by the women who write to me professing undying love and so on, and occasionally she is asked directly if she worries about what I might get up to when I am away from her. She has a perfectly valid answer to that, which is that she can easily turn the tables. She is alone here while I am gone, is she not? And she too goes off on little trips. (She has been known to say that relationships thrive on small separations.)

There is one incident she uses as an example. We were at an exhibition and were being dogged by a very attractive young woman who kept trying to talk to me while ignoring the presence of Kathleen, Crona, and Suzy. I could not seem to shake her off, and Kathleen was getting more and more upset. When she was really at the end of her tether, she stepped menacingly towards our uninvited shadow. She did not need to say anything. An angry Kathleen Watkins is a most formidable sight. The young lady backed off. But a few days later, on a weekend, the same young lady turned up at our front gate, looking in at the house. Kathleen went up to her. The young lady had, she claimed, let her dog off the lead and he was now missing. Had we seen it? Kay says she could only laugh . . .

She has always been the keystone of our marriage. By the time we did get married, she was willing, even anxious, to let her career take a back seat to her commitment to our relationship. I think this is one of the reasons our marriage has worked. If she had been very ambitious in show business in those early years, I think it would probably have been a disaster. I am not being coy when I say that I believe that Kay is a far better person than I am. On a superficial level, if you can call it superficial, she is much more refined than I am, and she would have a refining influence on me, certainly on the children. She is desperately loyal to old friends. And she does not like show-offs or people parading what they have. She would prefer to have a few pals around a table for a meal than to go to a big fancy party.

And while Kathleen denies desperately that she cares what anyone thinks, I think that deep down she does care a lot. Underneath the self-sufficient shell she affects, she is quite sensitive. She has better taste than I have, and higher principles; but the reverse of that is that she can be, at times, rather unyielding and inflexible, unbending in certain ways. She is inclined to be stubborn and to believe that there is only one way to do a

☐

thing, and that is the Watkins way. Any other way is wrong and less than sufficient. This, naturally, causes flare-ups with our daughters. All children suffer from their parents' autocracy and think that their parents are old-fashioned and know nothing. Ours are no exception.

With all that she has given me, I sometimes wonder what it is I give in return. I asked her recently, and she could not immediately answer. I have been racking my brains. I know I can certainly make her laugh, especially when I get totally and completely exasperated and drive myself into a terrible temper. She suddenly sees the funny side of my total inability to get myself out of this state. But now that I think of it, this is something that again she gives me rather than the other way around. I do not think she would consider me particularly to be an affectionate man—she says that I touch other people and am more affectionate with other people on a day-to-day basis than I am with her—and I think that is probably true. I have certainly tried to give her security.

There have been difficulties with regard to my public profile. While she does not resent my being criticised professionally, and is not over-protective, she does resent, more and more, the constant invasion of our family privacy. I must say I can see her point, for instance when there is a constant stream of people parading down our driveway in Howth on a Saturday morning to deliver requests or opinions or letters, simply because they cannot be bothered posting them.

When she was younger, she would suffer in silence and ferment away quietly, but in latter years she has become more assertive, especially with the 'pokers': the people who emphasise every syllable of whatever grievance they have against Gay Byrne, Mike Murphy, the Catholic Church, the media, RTE, and the world in general, with a stabbing forefinger: the 'and-you-can-tell-Gay-Byrne-from-me . . .' people. Once or twice I have seen her retaliate with a forefinger of her own: 'Why-don't-you-tell-him-yourself!' Then there are the crow-pluckers, the 'I-have-a-crow-to-pluck-with-your-husband' brigade. She is now inclined to retaliate with: 'Go pluck it with my husband then and don't bother me!'

It is the public who put the bread on the table, and while she does accept that and tells others that I am 'marvellous' with the public, she still believes that I am far too tolerant. I think she gets annoyed for two reasons. One is the public's expectations of her. She cannot see why she, as an independent person, should be expected always to be 'sweetie-pie' to everyone. If she gets rotten potatoes in a shop, she feels, why should she not complain like anyone else, without being labelled as Miss Hoity-toity, throwing her weight around because of who she is? The other is, I think, the application to others of her own register of good manners and behaviour. I keep telling

□

her that other people have not got her high standards, yet she cannot accept that people can be so demanding and intrusive—even to the extent of drawing up a chair at a restaurant table to join us, uninvited, on some of the rare occasions we go out to eat.

Now that the children are more or less reared, she is increasing her involvement in her own career. She jumped at the chance of doing her own television series, 'Faces and Places', when it was offered to her by producer Justin Nelson. And it was a great boost to her when it was decided to continue the series after its first season. I think that the success of that programme lies in its simplicity, and Kathleen's success in it lies in the fact that she was not trying to prove anything nor to do anything special. She is very gentle with the people she meets. Almost by accident, the programme did what a good many people in Ireland think RTE should be doing anyway, that is, going to Carrick-on-Shannon and showing it as a beautiful place with blue skies and boats and lovely people. That is what she was doing, and that is all she was doing.

With hindsight, although she does not regret it, she believes now that she probably immersed herself too much in family life in Howth, perhaps somewhat neglecting her own development as a person. She would love to have been a producer-director in television, and has a good visual sense. My own view is that she would make a great late-night radio broadcaster: she has a lovely mellow tone of voice.

But with hindsight, I am selfishly glad she devoted so many of her most productive years to me and the girls. I really do not know how those showbiz marriages work. By the time we got married, Kathleen had already got showbiz out of her system. She wanted a break. She had done all the tours, been on television, been on radio. She even gave up the harp (which I have always thought was a great pity). And then when the children came along, she very definitely decided that she wanted to be at home with them during their formative years. Their memories of home will always include a welcoming mother after school and a warm room (which we call the snug) heated on cold afternoons and evenings with a solid-fuel stove and set aside specifically for them so they could do their homework in peace.

I have huge sympathy for the man who finds himself caught up in an uncontrollable, passionate attraction for 'another woman'. In our business, such a real dilemma (as opposed to a passing, one-night-stand type of affair, which is really not worth talking about) is called a 'turtle' (as in rhyming slang for turtle dove). I have seen men in this situation behave like cornered rats. They get extremely impatient and short-tempered with their wives and families and with all who restrain them in the attainment of what they want above and beyond all else.

☐

Genuine turtles are probably far more common than we realise in this country, despite all the publicity, salacious, 'psychological' or otherwise. Men do not confide in one another in the way that women do, so the confessions are not widespread, and I am firmly convinced that in Ireland, up to recently, because of our puritanical upbringing and the religious obsession with sexual matters, very many men mistook lust for love and got married just so they could get into bed with a woman. I am sure that this is equally true for very many women. There was little emphasis on companionship or friendship in the relationships between the sexes. After a relatively short time, when the lustre of unaccustomed sexual activity began to dim, many a person found that he or she was trapped. It has been a cause of dreadful sorrow and frustration over the years for young men and women who then found no escape.

This feeling of desperation within marriage is not something I have discovered recently or through the confidences poured out to me on the radio programme. When we were growing up on the South Circular Road, we were all aware of so many appallingly unhappy marriages all around us. People of my mother and father's generation and older were frequently acknowledged to be trapped in the kind of situation in which they could—and did—brandish hatchets at one another. Neighbours were frequently involved in keeping the peace. Neighbours would know the signs of a build-up of tension and would move in to keep the warriors apart until they simmered down. Even at the age of 14 and 15, I used to watch this and wonder, asking myself why on earth people who so obviously were unsuited and incompatible ever got married in the first place.

So I do have great sympathy for people who turn turtle after marriage. I am very grateful that my own marriage is sound enough to have withstood any onslaughts. I too could have been that soldier.

CHAPTER 7
THE BETRAYAL

I t is difficult to write about Russell Murphy. He was one of my closest friends, a father-figure; yet he embezzled all of my life's savings. He also used a power of attorney to borrow money for himself, using my investments as collateral. After he died, I found that not only was all my money gone but I was in serious debt.

I have been in two minds about writing the story at all, because I know that some people will be critical of me for its inclusion on the basis that it might appear to be mean-minded both to the dead and to Russell's family and colleagues, who might be hurt and offended. Some of my own family and friends believe I should just forget about the whole episode and move on with the rest of my life. I have thought about this a lot, but have decided to tell the story, because of all the things that have ever happened in my life it is the one episode that inevitably I am asked about by everyone I meet. And to tell the story of Gay Byrne and not to include it would seem to me a distortion.

In so far as it may open wounds for Russell's family and friends, I am sorry about this, but I must point out that my family and I have to live with the results of what he did to us for the rest of our lives—and unfortunately his family also have to deal with the consequences. They have to cope with it as best they can, as we have to as best we can. Russell did what he did and there is no way around that.

Some time in 1959, Éamonn Andrews was making one of his regular visits to my mother. I was absent in Granada at the time, doing well, career-building, on the commuting trail between Dublin and Manchester. In the course of conversation, Éamonn asked Ma how much I was earning, and was absolutely amazed to hear that it was about a hundred pounds a week, plus air fares, hotels, and all expenses—a fortune in those days. And for a red-raw rookie!

He rang me the following week to congratulate me, and warned me to make sure that my tax payments were up to date, that if I did not take things in hand I might find myself paying tax in both jurisdictions. He told me that I should contact an accountant, the best in Ireland according to him, called Russell Murphy. 'He might not take you on,' he said; 'he is very fussy, but he has a great fascination with people in show business, and he just might.' He

THE STAR

☐ *The magic moment as Frank O'Reilly, Chancellor of the University, handed me the scroll certifying my honorary doctorate of Trinity College, Dublin.*

RTE

☐ *Doctors all! James Dooge, myself, Hugh Leonard, Maureen Potter, William Bermingham and, in the distance, Feargal Quinn.*

G.A. DUNCAN

☐ *There was this girl I'd heard about who lived in Saggart who had red hair and played the harp...*

THE STAR

☐ *Kathleen enjoying the conferring ceremony at Trinity College.*

JIM O'KELLY/SUNDAY INDEPENDENT

Crona, Kathleen and Suzy but a short step from where we live, with my beloved Baily Green and Lighthouse in the background.

☐ *Pan Collins and I in typically busy form amidst the chaos of the Toy Show.*

☐ *A surprise presentation on the 25th anniversary Late Late Show wheeled on, to my utter astonishment, by Maura Connolly.*

RTE

☐ *Terry Wogan brought with him to the Late Late Show his collection of hilariously rude letters which listeners have sent him down through the years.*

RTE

☐ *David Frost always comes totally prepared for an interview and always manages to be outstandingly funny.*

RTE

☐ *Eamonn Andrews catches me unawares. You can see the suspicious look on my face and my tentative stance.*

☐ *After David Niven, Douglas Fairbanks must be the epitome of showbiz aristocracy and wealthy charm.*

☐ *Peter Ustinov is quite simply the perfect talk show guest and it was a pleasure and a privilege to welcome Fred Astaire to our studio.*

RTE

☐ *Big Jack and the Irish team just before their record-breaking dash to Europe.*

RTE

☐ *An hilarious Maureen Potter Show Christmas Special with Chris Curran, Danny Cummins and Maureen Toal in great form.*

☐ On the Late Late Show we regularly chance the impossible. A small section of
the Georgian State dancers doing their thing.

☐ The audience is an essential ingredient for the success of every show.

☐

mentioned that Russell acted for people like Siobhán McKenna and T. P. McKenna, both highly respected actors. And he gave me permission to use his own name, which he felt might be an entrée, since Russell had advised him once or twice when he needed special help in Ireland. So, I rang this august person and made an appointment to see him.

The office was in an old building opposite the Moira Hotel in Trinity Street, at the top of a dark staircase. Russell's secretary occupied a tiny cubbyhole-room looking out into Trinity Street, and in his own dim office he himself sat under a large Seán O'Sullivan painting of his father, the late Henry M. Murphy, who had founded the firm. Tall and angular, very thin, with striking dark eyes, he rose to greet me from behind his big mahogany desk, which was scrupulously tidy. He was smoking, using a cigarette-holder, and there were other holders ranged in precise symmetry in front of him on the desk. He was almost a chain-smoker, although not quite; and each time he lit a fresh cigarette he always inserted it into a fresh holder, as the holder he had used for the previous one was too warm for his fastidious taste.

His entire demeanour was awesome. His papers were held together neatly under paperweights. Another, smaller desk held his two telephones, and the only other furniture in the room was a mahogany bookcase holding his accountancy books. The carpeted atmosphere was hushed and discreet and somehow timeless. The view through the window, which overlooked the rear of Andrew Street post office, was not an inspiring one, but one I was to get to know well. Russell Murphy agreed to take me on as a client. It was a sort of favour to Éamonn.

From then on, Russell handled all my financial affairs. I supplied whatever it was he said he needed in the way of information on my earnings. And from the very beginning, any time he asked for cheques to pay the Revenue Commissioners or anyone else who needed money from me, I sent them, always crossed, payable to Henry M. Murphy and Co., for onward payment.

We gradually became close personal friends. After the first few years, we began to talk to one another about subjects more intimate than the one of money. He seemed to delight in taking me under his wing, and, after we got engaged, I brought Kathleen in to meet him. They formed a bond of mutual admiration and liking.

Right from the day I first met him I was included in his theatrical sweep. Always the one for the grand gesture, as his contribution to the Dublin Theatre Festival he would block-book numbers of seats at various venues. Then his secretary would send out a form, one to each of his favourite clients. We would tick off the shows we wished to see, send the form back

☐

to her, and receive the tickets for our chosen shows by return. He was very much associated in those early days of the festival with its first director, Brendan Smith. He was also involved in an honorary, advisory capacity, as financial consultant, in the formation of the Film Finance Corporation, a lending agency that invested up to ten per cent of the finance in three or four movies before the formation of the National Film Board.

He led a very quiet life, almost reclusive, but T. P. McKenna believes that Russell was an actor manqué, and I would concur with that. Ulick O'Connor, with whom he went to school in St Mary's (and who had a lucky escape when Russell refused to handle his money) remembers him playing a 'very distinguished' Bassanio in a school production of *The Merchant of Venice*. He was certainly very taken with actors, and although he believed that they were a nuisance to any accountant, since by their very nature and the nature of their profession they were unreliable and incapable of looking after themselves, he seemed to feel it was almost a duty to take them by the hand and to look after them. He could not have made much money out of them, but in return for this favour he had the opportunity to live their lives vicariously.

Around the period of our engagement and wedding, he became, I thought, unusually concerned that I was quite sure I was making the right decision in marrying Kathleen. I knew, however, that the concern was genuine. I had already known that he was very unhappily married, and that there were a lot of rows at home—it was common knowledge among the clients who knew him well—but since we were by then very close, he began to confide in me. (I must stress here that anything I'm about to say about Russell Murphy's private life is what *he* told *me* through the years. I have not checked it with anyone else, except in the course of ordinary observation. But upon his death we all discovered that he'd been a consummate liar: indeed, it's hard not to believe that his entire life was a lie. However, until that sad time I had no real reason to doubt what he said.)

That he was unhappily married was a truth simply accepted by everyone who knew him. In his youth he had been a well-known athlete. He met a girl called Marie Fawcett, the daughter of a judge, stunningly beautiful and the toast of Dublin society. He fell passionately in love, and did all in his considerable power to make her his own. She fell under his spell, and married him. He told me very specifically that within two weeks of getting married, he realised he had made a dreadful mistake.

He and Marie had three children, whom he adored: Henry, Frank, and Paula. However, as far as I could see he avoided being at home as much as possible, burying himself in his work. He arrived at his office every morning, straight from seven o'clock Mass in Clarendon Street church. He stayed in the office all day, with just a cup of tea and a sandwich at his desk at midday, provided by his secretary. He worked as late as possible into the evenings, because it was clear from what he said that the first row of every evening began as soon as his foot hit his front doorstep. He liked to meet clients after the normal office hours usually kept by accountants. I would meet him at about six o'clock, and we would eat sandwiches in the Moira or in the old Jury's Hotel across the road. Then, after our meeting, quite frequently he went back to the office. It was only in later years that I heard that he had been christened 'the Mad Monk' by Tony O'Reilly.

After Kathleen and I were married and moved to London, the contact between Russell and me was of necessity mostly by telephone and letter. Everything was meticulously tabulated, in that every letter was replied to and every reminder accounted for. Even if you sent him a brief scribbled note, there was always an immediate acknowledgment. It seemed to me that as far as he was concerned there was only one way to do things, and that was the correct, long-winded, troublesome way. There were no short-cuts. The old-fashioned ways were best.

When I told him, from London, that we were moving back home, he was not at all sure that it was the right decision. His advice would have been to stay in London with the BBC. Based on financial considerations alone, the advice was the best. I would probably have become a millionaire if I had taken it. But as I have already mentioned, I was coming home for other reasons.

After we had settled in the flat in Elgin Road, we invited Russell and Marie to visit us. It was really a big deal to have Russell accept our invitation, and we behaved as if we were expecting royalty. We invited Al and Frances along to spread the responsibility of entertainment, and Kathleen pulled out all the stops at the cooker. We lit a fire and put candles around the place and ensured that the wines were good. But we need not have bothered, because as soon as I opened the front door to our guests of honour, I knew that we were all doomed. They stood there, reeking of a recent dreadful row, the kind of vibe instantly recognisable to the married. Quite clearly, Marie had been forced—yet again—to come and meet another of Russell's clients, and she did not want to be either with him or with them.

The evening was a fiasco, although at the beginning, for a while, there was some semblance of festivity. Russell loved to stand theatrically, the centre of attention, posing with one hand in his pocket and the other carelessly handling his long cigarette-holder, like a player in a particularly sophisticated piece by Noël Coward. But Russell consumed a fair amount of drink fairly fast, and quite early on his posturing and pleasantry

127

□

disappeared. He adopted a demeanour of deep camouflage, pretending to bend his full attention towards everything everyone else was saying, affecting to ignore Marie. The atmosphere was deteriorating by the minute, and it was excruciatingly upsetting to the rest of us.

The situation got totally out of hand, and quite unable to cope, I went over to Al, asking desperately for advice about what I should do. Kay and I were not socially adroit or experienced enough at that time to be worldly or casual about this dreadful situation. Al's advice was that there was nothing I could do, so we all simply had to sit it out, writhing in our embarrassment.

Next day, always a man for the grand gesture, Russell sent an apologetic bouquet of flowers to Kathleen.

It is only fair to say that a return visit by us to them turned out quite differently. They had a large, lovely house of some opulence in Temple Villas, near Milltown Bridge, complete with tennis court. Naturally we were dreading the occasion, but we need not have worried. It was a Sunday afternoon. Henry, Frank and Paula were there, and we all played tennis. We even had a sing-song, and all in all it was very jolly.

Over the years, we continued to see each other socially. Russell would come out to Howth, walk around our house making what he called his 'tour of inspection', have a meal, a few drinks, and then leave. (I always felt he was uneasy on those occasions. And he always maintained that he socialised only under duress.)

His business advice contined to be solid—and cautious. I was always being offered 'opportunities' to go into one busines or another, in partnership with a great many people: anything from shops selling showbiz souvenirs, to recording studios. All I had to do was to buy a trawler in Donegal, and someone else would worry about the running of it; or I could buy forestry land and leave it to my business partner to plant the trees. Again and again the idea of buying a pub would come up. Russell always cautioned that this would have been a disaster. The first thing necessary for an absentee owner of a pub is the appointment of a manager or a foreman and barmen, and since the owner will never be there, this is almost an open invitation to fiddle the cash. Quite clearly, there is no way you can run a business while you are elsewhere engaged. CRM pooh-poohed all business approaches to me. Continue to do what I was good at, I was instructed, and he would see to everything else. Like minding the money.

My accountant's reputation grew and continued to be flawless. He lectured in university and was teaching a new generation of young people to follow him into his profession. He also ran a sort of unofficial careers guidance service. Young people who were worried about their future, or

☐

who did not know which career might suit them, came to him, and he always gave good advice. His clients were envied. If you were with Russell Murphy, you were in good hands and you were obviously a person of substance. Henry M. Murphy and Co. was *the* office to be with. Only the best qualified to be taken on as clients. Telegraphic address: 'Integrity, Dublin'!

His private life tortured him more and more, however. It had always been his intention, I knew, to live at home only so long as the children were dependent. When they grew up and began to make lives for themselves, he moved away from home at the earliest opportunity, taking a succession of small apartments, in Merrion Avenue, in Kildare Street, in Burlington Road, and in Clyde Road.

He claimed not to be able to cook so much as a boiled egg or a piece of toast for himself, and told me often, with a sort of perverse relish, that his secretary had to write out the instructions on how to make a cup of tea. She would shop for him, and at the beginning of each week would make sure there was a sufficiency of eggs, bread, milk and tea in his apartment to supply the week's breakfast needs. He dined out. He hated to dine alone, and had a small circle of privileged clients, business associates and friends, whom he invited to dine with him, people like Brian Farrell, the professor and television presenter of 'Today Tonight', and Justice Séamus Henchy. I was one of the privileged, and was never allowed to pay, although I did try on numerous occasions. I always presumed he paid for his other companions as well. Different restaurants received his patronage from time to time. For periods, perhaps as long as six months, he would eat only at the Bailey in Duke Street, or at the Lord Edward, opposite Christ Church. Then something would happen, he would have a row with the waiter or the proprietor, and he would move on to somewhere else.

He was great fun as a dinner companion, with a fund of sometimes scandalous stories. He read widely, and was always reading several books at once. He loved discussing the latest play, or theatre in general. He loved to hear about all the latest scandals in Montrose, who was doing what to whom. I always sensed that suppressed longing in him to be a performer. Indeed once, many years ago, Fred O'Donovan, who was doing a lot of sponsored programmes at the time from the recording studios he operated with Éamonn, auditioned Russell. Fred believed that, with his deep, sonorous voice and impressive personality, Russell could have been the Jack de Manio of Ireland. (De Manio, a household name for years both in Britain and Ireland, hosted an early morning radio show for the BBC.) I had used Russell myself several times on the television programme 'Top of the Pops', where he was one of a panel of people invited to come on to give

☐

opinions on the latest pop records. The jury was always predictable. It would consist of someone who knew pop music very well; a glamorous blonde woman; and someone who was outside the pop scene altogether, someone to give stature to the jury and to the programme. Russell fulfilled this function very well. He would sit there on the set, elegant and sardonic, holding his cigarette-holder, quoting various scribes to support his opinions on the pop music he had just heard. He was always pithy and amusing, and created a very good reaction. The Jack de Manio idea came to nothing, but Russell was attracted to it—very attracted.

Later, I began to realise that there was another, darker side to this man. He was a binge drinker.

He had a special arrangement with the Moira Hotel, where the staff all knew and respected him. As I ate my sandwiches with him there during our business sessions, I saw that they watched him. Everything was fine so long as he drank pints of Guinness; but as soon as he asked for a brandy, everyone went on full alert, and it was advisable for any companions with whom he might have been drinking to make themselves scarce, because as soon as he started to drink brandy he would continue until he was paralytic. If he was still on the premises, the staff at the Moira would simply cart him upstairs to one of the bedrooms and leave him to sleep it off. If the batter had taken place elsewhere in town and he was found wandering the night-time streets after closing, he would be picked up by the taxi-drivers, all of whom knew him well. They would deliver him back to the Moira, where the staff would again take care of him. There was never any problem about the bills: they were always later discreetly paid.

The extraordinary thing was that he seemed actually to plan these batters. He would telephone his clients, or have his secretary do so, to cancel his appointments for a set number of days. That way, he never let anyone down. Then, when he was recovering from the binge, he would clean himself up and arrive back in the office as though he had never been absent, and would apply himself to his work as assiduously as before.

Everyone, certainly all his friends, knew about these little perambulations on the wild side. They were just taken as small blips in an otherwise straight line of righteousness. The Moira staff seemed to believe that such venting and release was essential for the health of a fine mind and artistic temperament, and was only to be expected. And no-one seemed to suffer, except, presumably, Russell himself.

What most of us did not know, however, was how he behaved every year in Lourdes. Every year, with a friend of his, Russell travelled to Lourdes, where the two men acted as *brancardiers*: volunteers who wheel and carry the sick within the precincts of the grotto. We all knew how fastidious

☐ *Early specials – Me with Granny Connors on the first of our All Itinerant Shows when, to the consternation of the Itinerant Settlement Committee, we announced that we did not want any members of the Committee on the show, only itinerants. They were quite taken aback.*

☐ *One of our first Late Late Special Tribute Shows. This time to Mícheál Mac Liammóir. Hilton was there, of course, for the cutting of the cake and the entire studio was filled with friends and admirers.*

□

Russell was, how he detested anything as distasteful as illness. He could not bear dirt, or smells, or blood. So all of us who knew him well thought what a wonderful, self-sacrificing gesture it was for him to perform this service for the unfortunate and really ill people who had been brought to Lourdes. And to be charitable, perhaps his original motives were spiritual and high-minded. But the truth, which we did not learn until much later, was that each year, as soon as he arrived in Lourdes, he began to drink, and was sozzled for the entire fortnight. At the end of the trip he would come home, demurring graciously if anyone said what a wonderful gesture he was making or how wonderfully Christian he was.

One evening in 1975 I was in his office. It was around a quarter past six, and I was picking him up in my car. We were scheduled to eat in the Lord Edward. Russell never drove a car: he used taxis, and in the later years took on a car with a chauffeur.

I had begun to notice that his appearance was changing, at first subtly and then dramatically. He was growing his hair longer and more theatrically, and I realised it was being styled. Someone was caring for it. His dress style had also been changing. For as long as I'd known him his suits were always dull and of sombre black material. I knew that every six months or so his secretary phoned Des Williams of Menswear in Westmoreland Street, and another dull, black, sombre suit would be delivered—the measurements never changed; there was no need for Russell to attend for a fitting. His shirts had always been Van Heusen, with starched detachable collars. But now, in 1975, the shirts and ties were brighter. The suits were stylish and of lighter hue; the shoes and socks, I realised, were becoming almost flash. The new, elegant, well-dressed and well-coiffed, cared-for Russell Murphy had been slowly emerging over a period. I had noticed also that he was beginning to take frequent business trips abroad: to London—where I knew he stayed at the Westbury, in which Kathleen and I had honeymooned—and farther afield, to Zürich and Geneva. He mentioned once or twice that a lot of these trips were in connection with work he was doing for the banker Jocelyn Hambro. I was impressed. Even I had heard of Jocelyn Hambro, and I knew that this was a big international banking business. During this period Russell even made one or two trips to New York.

That evening, in his office, I knew there was something on his mind. He was uncharacteristically preoccupied. He excused himself briefly to go upstairs to his little bathroom, and when he came back he said he had something to tell me. He said he could not face me any more without telling me that he was having an affair with Bronwyn Conroy. He thought I ought to know.

□

Bronwyn is a well-known and well-liked personality in Dublin, with her own beautician's business. She had been another client of Russell's, and as the years passed they had simply grown closer to one another. I think Russell's agitation that evening was because he expected me to be shocked at his surprise announcement. My reaction was entirely the opposite one. I knew how lonely and austere his personal life had been, and as far as I was concerned he deserved such a lucky break. So I merely asked him how they had met and a little bit about her. Then I wished him well. And I told him—and meant it—that after all the years of unhappiness I was delighted that a little sunshine had come into his life.

I eventually met Bronwyn. For years and years, since the 'Gay Byrne Show' started on radio, we broadcast the Christmas Eve programme from Grafton Street. At the end of the programme, the tradition was that the whole crew who had worked on it would retire together to Champers in Chatham Street for a Christmas drink. Then Kathleen, Crona and Suzy would come in to meet me and, en famille, we would all go down to Trinity Street to wish 'Happy Christmas' to Uncle Russell and to exchange presents with him. Needless to say, even though it was Christmas Eve he would be work-ing. From the time Bronwyn and Russell became a couple, she would occasionally be present at these Christmas Eve pleasantries.

She certainly had an impact on Russell's social life. Amazingly, he began willingly to visit people. They came to visit us in Howth once or twice, and once we were guests with them for dinner in Joe Malone's house in Foxrock. (Joe, well known in the tourist industry, is Bronwyn's brother-in-law.) Bronwyn was also instrumental, I am sure, in Russell's cutting down drastically on his drinking. The batters were far less frequent, and certainly less violent. I have the impression that he may have got drunk in her presence once or twice and she let it be known that she would not tolerate it again. As far as I could see, the relationship between them was steady and—again, as far as anyone can tell about others—satisfactory and joyful. I was really happy that my friend, after so much heartache, had at last found happiness.

Our friendship prospered, and so, I thought, did my affairs. They continued to be meticulously documented. He sent me bills for his services—small bills, not at all excessive. He claimed that in fact they were so small that his colleagues often suggested that he should send food parcels as well, to make his service more comprehensive!

I did not lodge my RTE cheques with him, but he regularly checked my bank balance. If there was a surplus he would advise me not to leave it lying there but to send it to him so that he could invest it for productive purposes. Over the years it amounted to a lot of money. As far as I knew, it was being

☐

put into a pension fund for me, or was used to buy property. This property was to be my golden handshake, my pension and my redundancy money (to none of which I am entitled from RTE: I am not a member of the staff of RTE and never was; I am a self-employed contract person.)

When my tax bills were due, Russell informed me how much was needed and I sent the cheques, always crossed, payable to Henry M. Murphy and Co., in the amounts requested, ten thousand or twenty thousand or whatever it was. I would receive an immediate acknowledgment. Quite why I always made the cheques payable to the firm I do not know—in fact I never questioned the procedure. After all, I was with the best office in the country.

I saw annual accounts. Conor Dignam, or one of Russell's other colleagues, would show the sheets to me and would explain what they were all about. I understood the gist. I knew that at one time or another (needless to say, not all together) I owned a shop in George's Street, which was bought and sold; then another in Dawson Street; a house in Fitzwilliam Square; at one time or another an apartment in a block in Clyde Road, bought for about £65,000 in the name of a small shelf company of mine. I never questioned any of these deals: Russell knew best.

On occasion a courier would arrive at Montrose with papers for me to sign in a hurry. The courier would wait while I signed and would then depart immediately, taking them back to Trinity Street. This frequently happened, and did not seem remarkable to me. I trusted Russell completely, and gave these documents only the most cursory of readings.

The fateful one, giving him power of attorney, was signed during a week when the entire office was up in a heap preparing the 'Late Late' toy show. Russell rang me in the 'Late Late' office, saying, 'I'm doing a little deal on your behalf, and I'm sending out some documents by courier. Now don't concern yourself with them: you'll see where to sign; but be sure to do it right away. I'll tell the courier to wait and to bring them back to me as fast as possible.' The courier duly arrived a few mintues later and stood in front of my desk while I signed where Russell had indicated with an X. The courier took them and went away, and I resumed my work. It was as simple as that.

I can honestly say that I was under the impression that he was authorised to sign for me for this one deal alone. But even later, when the words 'power of attorney' were mentioned—as they must have been—they caused no alarm. Russell was my most trustworthy friend, with only my interests at heart.

One evening, in the early years of our association, while we were walking back along Dame Street after dinner in the Lord Edward, Russell pointed

☐

at the old Hibernian Insurance Chambers and remarked that he had bought the building. He had applied for planning permission to convert it into offices. The planning permission had been turned down, he told me, which meant that he had suffered a big financial loss. He remarked wryly, as he frequently did, that he was a past master at looking after other people's affairs but an amateur at looking after his own.

In the summer of 1983, Kathleen's sister Clare was told that Russell was seriously ill. Kathleen, who by then was extremely fond of him, was very upset. She rang him and said she wanted to talk to him very seriously and very soon. To her astonishment, he arrived in Howth within half an hour. (In the light of subsequent events, his alacrity is understandable. He thought the game was up.)

She told him what she had heard. He stood up from where he was sitting and flew into a rage quite out of proportion to the issue. It was all rumours, he said, put out by his enemies to undermine confidence in his business, the sale of which, he said, he was in the process of negotiating. He ordered her to put those thoughts instantly from her mind. There was no truth whatsoever in those rumours. In fact, by then he had already had a lung removed in London and had sworn all his staff to secrecy about it.

The following Christmas Eve, at about lunchtime, we went as usual to his office. As we got to the building, he was just walking into Trinity Street from Dame Street. He opened his office front door and we all went up the stairs. Suddenly, I realised he was breathless. He had always been very fit, but his sides were heaving five minutes after we all sat down. I mentioned it to him, but he again denied that there was anything wrong.

In January, I went to see him in his apartment in Wellington Road. He told me that the doctors had said that he would not see Easter. He had lung cancer, and there was no hope. He told me that he already had a permanent nurse with him in the apartment. All the rumours had been accurate, and the trips he had been taking back and forth to London were not, as heretofore, for business or pleasure, but for treatment and surgery. I started to weep. He told me to stop it as it would do no good. Then he asked me to visit him as often as I could.

But a sort of battle began in this regard. I would telephone him and say I would be around to see him at six o'clock. He would say that there was no need to come and I was not to. I would go anyway. Sometimes he would see me and sometimes he would not. On one or two occasions the nurse would not allow me to come in as he was not very well. On others, she would call in from the door: 'Gay's here—do you want to see him?' His reply was invariably a stream of abuse. As long as the abuse continued, I knew I was welcome, so I would brush in past her.

He was often, understandably, in very bad form. He had been told that he would probably die from a blood clot as a result of the cancer. He asked irascibly why I kept coming to see him, and ordered that I should stop coming. I took no notice of his orders and continued to visit him. I told him I wanted Crona to come to say goodbye to him, as she was his goddaughter, and that Kathleen was very anxious to say goodbye as well. He would not have it. He said he was not having even the members of his own family in to say goodbye. He got tetchy and said he suspected that the only reason I was coming to see him was that I was worried that my affairs were not in order.

Nothing could have been further from my mind, but I went along with what I thought was the spirit of the conversation, bantering in the old, sardonic Russell Murphy manner. I asked him if I *should* be worried. He assured me that everything was in order. 'If anyone's affairs are in order, dear boy, they are yours . . .'

I visited him for the last time two days before he died. It was a Tuesday evening. He had what he called wonderful news. He had made his peace with Marie and was going to Marie's house to die. He said that if I wished to see him again I could call to her house the following Thursday. I said I would. He seemed content and as relaxed as he could have been expected to be.

Just before I left him, I asked him if there was anything he wished to tell me, to get off his mind. (I meant anything of a spiritual nature.) He retorted that he had two confessors, Father Paul Lavelle, a man I knew because he had been a guest on the 'Late Late Show', and the parish priest of Beechwood Avenue church. He had consulted both of them at considerable length, and both had, he said, envied him his faith. His last words to me were, 'I know where *I'm* going.' Then he added that he would see me on Thursday in Marie's house in 'the Lane'.

On Thursday morning Conor Dignam rang me. Russell had died during the night. He had been in the bathroom and had got sick and had called the nurse. She went for help, but by the time she returned he was dead. The doctors who had told him that he would not see Easter had been deadly accurate.

There was a news item in the *Irish Times* the following day, of which the third-last paragraph read: 'The dedication apparent in his work and cultural interests was also evident in his personal life. He was a sincere and dedicated Christian.' Underneath, Hugh Leonard's appreciation began: 'He was the kindest man I ever met . . .' and continued with personal glimpses of Russell's kindness: 'his idea of a holiday was to take a mortally ill friend to Lourdes . . .'

□

And a day later Brian Farrell's appreciation was published: 'Much remained hidden in a decent sense of reticence that spurned unsought familiarity. The rarely mentioned athletic background and continuing interest in rugby, the pilgrimages to care for the sick in Lourdes, the critical but appreciative awareness of broadcasting skills, the discriminating passion for the theatre, the tolerance to those in trouble and the generosity to those in need were less evident.'

The funeral was from Beechwood Avenue church to Dean's Grange cemetery. It was a bright, cold spring day with that keen Irish wind that seems to gust hard around the porches of churches during funerals. The former Taoiseach Jack Lynch was there, Tánaiste Dick Spring was there, and so were the Attorney General, Peter Sutherland, the Chief Justice, Tom O'Higgins, the President of the High Court, Tom Finlay, and Justices Dónal Barrington, Declan Costello, Brian Walsh, and Seán Gannon. Actors such as Siobhán McKenna, Cyril Cusack, Godfrey Quigley, David Kelly, T. P. McKenna, Ronnie Walsh, and members of the RTE Repertory Company, were also there.

The lessons were read movingly by Brian Farrell and Mike Burns of the RTE newsroom. Industry and banking were represented by their top men, including Don Carroll, Michael Killeen, and Michael Dargan. The 'small man' was represented by columnist John Healy, another of Russell's clients, who now thanks his 'very good guardian angel' that he did not write a tribute to the great man, and who nevertheless has no complaints against him.

I made what my mother would have called a 'show' of myself. I had cried the night Russell told me he was going to die, but my tears in the church were uncontrollable, particularly when the celebrant eulogised him. He read what he said was a favourite poem of Russell's:

> We shall do much in the years to come,
> But what have we done today?
> We shall give our goods in a generous sum,
> But what did we give today?
> We shall lift the heart and dry the tear,
> We shall plant true peace in the place of fear,
> We shall speak the works of love and cheer—
> But what did we speak today?

□

We shall be so kind in the afterwhile,
But what have we been today?
We shall bring each lonely life a smile,
But what have we brought today?
We shall give to peace a grand new birth
And to steadfast faith a deeper worth;
We shall feed the hungering souls of earth—
But whom have we fed today?

We shall reap such peace in the by and by,
But what have we sown today?
We shall build up mansions in the sky,
But what have we built today?
'Tis sweet in idle dreams to bask,
But here and now do we do our task?
Yes, this is the thing my soul must ask:
'What have I done today?'

There was not a dry eye in the church. I did not cry like that for my mother or my father. Later on, I did not cry that way for Éamonn Andrews, who more deserved my tears. I was weeping, I suppose, for the end of an era. Russell was more than a good friend to me, I thought. He was my guide. If ever I rang him and said I had a problem, he saw me as soon as he could and would discuss the problem impartially. I was afraid that, alone, I would get lost.

His generosity in life was legendary. No child could have had a better, more attentive godfather than Crona. And because Suzy's godfather, Larry Cassidy, had died, Russell adopted her as well. No birthday was ever forgotten, nor were Christmas or Easter. The Easter egg or the birthday or Christmas gifts always arrived on time, delivered to the door. And they were always expensive, and most carefully chosen. Oddly enough, in the way that such precedents get established in friendships, he never gave Kathleen or me a gift, nor did we expect it; but we always made sure to give him something small by way of remembrance on his birthday and at Christmas.

There was a running gag for years between us, whereby he always sent me the same birthday card, then I crossed out the dedication and sent the card back to *him* on *his* birthday. The very same birthday card flew between us as each birthday came round.

☐ *Fergal O'Connor, renowned for his total honesty and many controversial statements made on the Late Late Show when such talk was neither popular nor profitable.*

☐ *The extraordinarily robust Sean Keating. This was the very first Late Late Birthday Tribute we ever made.*

☐ *Seamus Kelly of The Irish Times and, of course, Milo O'Shea on the set.*

After the committal at Dean's Grange, his close friends and relatives all went back to Marie's house in the Lane, where she was the soul of hospitality. I was still very shaken but gave myself a swift kick and forced myself to rally and to chat over the tea and sandwiches. I went over to where Conor Dignam was standing with two of Russell's accountant colleagues. I said something trite, like 'It's a sad day for all of us . . .' Then: 'I suppose there will be some major changes in the office?' They looked at one another, and even at the time I thought their reaction was a little uncomfortable. They sort of sniggered. Then one of them said: 'Yes, you could say there will be some changes.'

The Sunday after Easter, it was a sunny morning and I was taking my usual walk around the hill. My mind was preoccupied with piddling detail. I was due to fly out to Luxembourg the following Tuesday to do the commentary on the Eurovision song contest. But the radio show was coming from the RDS in Ballsbridge that day. I was worried about missing the flight, and was planning the fastest route from the RDS to the airport.

Just after I got back home, the telephone rang. It was Conor Dignam. He said he had to see me urgently. I knew he lived in Malahide, which is not too far away, so I invited him to come straight over. I was not in the least worried: I merely assumed that there was some minor problem with Russell's will, and perhaps I was needed as an additional executor or something. Advice from an old friend, maybe.

Kathleen was lying out in the sun on the patio. I knew Conor was not exactly sure where the house was, so I went up to the main road to intercept him. I was there for quite a while, and began to wonder. Perhaps it was something more serious than just a glitch in the will?

When Conor arrived, I got into his car and we drove together down the road and to our gate, chatting about the weather and this and that. I showed him into our dining-room, which is small and sunny and very quiet, with windows on two sides, one side facing out over the sea. That early afternoon, the water shone below the cliff, and the sea-birds wheeled in the fresh breeze. Conor sat in business-like fashion at one end of our dining-table and I sat at the other. He spread out a number of files. By this time, although he had not said anything, I was sure there was something on his mind other than asking me for help with Russell's estate.

One by one he opened the files, asking me if its contents meant anything to me, pointing to the familiars: George's Street, Dawson Street, and so on. I said yes, I was familiar with them all. I didn't know anything about them in detail but I knew they'd been mentioned, as it were, in dispatches.

He closed the files briskly with little snapping sounds, one after the other, and said: 'I'm sorry to have to tell you this, but it's all gone.'

☐

I just looked at him. 'What do you mean?'

He told me succinctly what he meant. Russell had been 'on the fiddle'. He had been on the fiddle for eight years, and there was at least one-and-a-half million pounds missing out of the files of a number of clients, and unfortunately for me, I was one of them.

I asked if he was sure. Had they checked everywhere? Was there not simply a problem with mislaid files, money somewhere that no-one knew anything about? I remembered the trips to Zürich. Had they checked if Russell had a Swiss bank account? Conor replied that they had searched everywhere they could think of, and nowhere could the money be found. He told me that some time before Christmas, a few months before he died, Russell had come up with an extraordinary scheme. He came into the office and asked the other accountants in the company, including Conor, to buy him out for a million pounds, on condition that they did not examine the books. They thought this offer was, to say the least, unorthodox. Nice one, Russell, but no thanks.

They already knew he was ill, and while they thought he was very courageous, struggling in to the office, they declined his offer. They said they would have to see his books. After a long argument, said Conor, Russell agreed to let them see the books. But when they did see them, there was no money to be seen. They refused to buy him out. And in the three weeks since his death, they had been through the books again with a fine-tooth comb. The money was just gone.

I think I thanked Conor as I walked him to his car. He apologised over and over again. He said that he and the others in the firm were just as bewildered as I was—and that they had not been paid for several weeks since the balloon went up. He said he would have come up to tell me some time before but that his wife had urged him 'for God's sake' to let us get over Easter with some semblance of normality. Eventually, still apologising, he got into his car and drove away. Still it had not sunk in. I thought it might be the sort of black joke that Russell would play, and that the money would turn up labelled *Gotcha!*

I walked slowly back down the driveway and went out to the patio where Kathleen was sitting in the sun. I told her. Russell was on the fiddle. No apartments, no nest-egg, no pension, no security. She sat bolt upright. 'Nonsense!' she said. Somehow, I got through the rest of the day.

On the Monday morning I drove into the studios at my usual time, but I just had to talk to someone. At a quarter past eight, an unprecedented hour, I rang Maura Connolly, my Special Assistant on the 'Late Late Show', at her home, which is just down the road from RTE in Donnybrook.

'I have something dreadful to tell you; can you make it in fast?'

□

'Are the children okay; is Kathleen okay?'

'They're okay—it's Russell.'

She knew, of course, that Russell was dead. She asked no further questions, and arrived at Montrose within a few minutes, by half-past eight. I was already in the radio studio, in the preparation phase for the radio show. Outside, in the control room there was the usual calm bustle, telephone lines being tested, discs being lined up. I had tried to concentrate on the newspapers and the day's batch of letters spread out on my desk in front of me, but I found it very difficult. When Maura arrived, pushing in the heavy soundproofed door between the control room and the inner studio, she sat down facing me.

As succinctly, as quickly and as calmly as I could, I told her what had happened. At the time, I did not know how bad things were, just that they were very bad indeed.

I had made the right decision in calling on her. She was exactly the right person in the right place. She made instant decisions, like whom I needed to call. In some areas, her list of contacts and friends is better than mine. She said the right things, such as that the whole affair simply had to be placed at the back of my mind for the next two hours, since I had to get through the radio programme. She made arrangements to meet me after the programme to talk again, and said the only way such a problem could be faced was piece by piece, a small piece at a time. She was immensely practical.

The problem was that I had a show to keep on the road, and I felt, rightly or wrongly, that I could not let anyone see how badly this was affecting me. Because she works so closely with me, and has done for years, and because I would trust her with my life, Maura now knows more about the detail of the 'CRM affair' (the mental shorthand I now use to describe it) and more about how badly affected I was, and still am, then almost anyone else, even Kay. Although Kay obviously saw me at my lowest, I did try to maintain a certain area of tranquillity in our lives where she was concerned, because she herself was so affected and involved.

Ten days later, it was Maura who put a few things in perspective, like pounding into me that I still had my health and strength. She even said something that at first I thought was off the wall. 'Thank God', she said, 'that Russell Murphy died when he did.' I looked at her as if she had two heads. 'No,' she insisted, 'just think: if he had lived for another ten years, you would have been ten years worse off and would not have had the same health and strength.' I saw the logic, and held onto that for a while.

I know that in my memory I have got events and dates out of sequence—perhaps I have ranged them in order of importance. There were some

□

shining moments that stand out in relief, like the day I got a telephone call from Patsy Sweeney, who had taken a lift down to Dublin all the way from Donegal and who wanted to meet me in a pub in Donnybrook. He came to show his friendship, and, in addition, he offered me cash. There and then, he offered to go next door to the Donnybrook bank; if cash was what I needed, as far as he was concerned I could have whatever he had. Another person, who is not wealthy, came to me and offered me ten thousand pounds, which he said he could get together. I did not accept either offer, but the gestures like that at a time like that are what you remember.

So I was not panicking just yet. I still believed that some day soon there would be a telephone call, ringing with Russell's hollow laugh.

On the Tuesday, I did the show in the RDS and went to the airport for my flight to Luxembourg. The song that year was written by Johnny Logan and sung by Linda Martin, and we all set out together. I could see that the others—John Caden and Mary Martin from the radio show, Ian McGarry and Charlie Byrne from television, and even Larry Gogan, who was doing the radio commentary—were looking at me a little strangely. I suppose I was behaving oddly, preoccupied, making calls from the public telephone outside the departure gate just before boarding. One of those was to a very good friend, and it is a measure of my state of mind at the time that, although I did not give any details as to why I wanted them, I asked for prayers.

Throughout the days in Luxembourg, instead of carousing with the rest of the gang I was fairly constantly in my room, trying to deal with long-distance telephone calls, trying to find out exactly what the situation was. Although I had now, on the surface, accepted what had happened, there was still an air of unreality about the whole thing. I was walking and talking and eating, and so was everyone else, as if the world had not stopped. The only person I confided in was our television Head of Sound, Charlie Byrne, who was most sympathetic and supportive, although I could only give him a very rough idea of what was troubling me.

I got through the ghastly week and the Eurovision song contest somehow, and flew back to Dublin via London. Terry Wogan, who had been handling the commentary for the BBC, was on the plane to London with us. There was a brief moment when we were alone at London airport, and I remember saying to him: 'For God's sake, will you make sure that whoever is looking after your money, please make sure they're looking after it properly.' He said, 'Well, thank you for that splendid piece of advice!' (He must have thought I had really got a touch of the avunculars, or had been drinking.) I repeated that, whoever he had looking after the pennies for him, would he, for the love of God, make sure he was on top of the situation

☐

himself. Terry gave me one of those funny looks as though he did not quite clearly understand what I was talking about. Subsequently, when the full story became public, he realised what it was I had been talking to him about at the airport, and he wrote me a very kind and supportive note. On the day, at the airport, he thought I'd gone a bit bonkers, and had no idea what I was getting at.

All through that period, I was reviewing the four o'clock march-past, that awful four-o'clock-in-the-morning parade of 'if onlys' and 'whys' that tramp across your ceiling in front of your staring eyes. The worst part of the whole thing was the complete untouchability of Russell Murphy.

The newspapers began to get the word. People began to come at me out of the woodwork, waving pieces of paper. I owed them £7,000 for this, £490 for that, £250, £1,600—the figures were endless: bills for hire of limousines and purchase of air tickets; bills for the decoration of an apartment that the tradespeople had thought was mine because Russell had signed on my behalf. Everyone had pieces of paper signed C. *Russell Murphy for Mr Gay Byrne*. They were people I'd never heard of and I knew nothing about them. Except that they had bills with my name on them, and they wanted money. Like, as soon as possible.

The tax cheques for the Revenue Commissioners, which I'd been paying to Henry M. Murphy & Co., had not all been passed on: he'd stolen those as well. The tax inspector completely accepted the situation and had evidence that the cheques had been paid to the company. Russell had cleverly contrived a long-running dispute with the inspector over my affairs—of which I was totally unaware—which meant that he would not have to pay much of my tax until the matter was resolved. He'd paid only nominal amounts on account. My tax affairs were ten years in disarray.

The tax inspector was sympathetic, but made sure I understood the position. After all, Russell Murphy was *my* accountant, not theirs, my responsibility, not theirs. So please, could I get up to date as soon as possible?

For someone who had never been in debt in his life, and never been even in the red in the bank, this was a devastating situation. I owed a lot of people an awful lot of money, and what I thought I had saved was also gone. And there were more interesting revelations with each day's post.

Suddenly, I could not remember having seen the deeds of the house. I did not have a notion where they were. Jack Maloney, the solicitor who had negotiated the purchase, was dead. I knew I had sent them to him about five years prior to Russell's death, and found a letter from him to Russell in which he had requested them for some reason for review. No-one could find them: they were not at home, not among my papers at Henry M. Murphy and Co.

☐

I found the man who had taken over Jack Maloney's practice. He searched and could find nothing. I rang everyone who I knew had had any dealings with Russell or with his company. No luck. This time the penny had really dropped. I faced blackness. Not only everything I had worked for, but my home . . . I rang almost every bank in town. No.

Then, on an off-chance, I rang a bank with which I had never had any dealings at all but that I recalled Russell mentioning. A man said he had been expecting my call. His bank did have the deeds of my house. He said it had all been confidential up to then, but since the story had broken anyway and was all over the papers, he could tell me. He said he had good news and bad news. The bad news was that Russell had taken out a loan of £65,000 on the deeds of my house. The good news was that from two years previously he had begun to pay some of it back in dribs and drabs.

This good man from this good bank would not tell me how much was outstanding. All he would say was that the loan was now 'manageable'. (Mind you, he didn't say whether it was manageable for them or for me!) He asked me to write him a letter setting out my side of the story. I wrote the letter and delivered it. The man from the bank rang me at the 'Late Late' office and told me that the debt had been written off. I could come down to collect the deeds of the house any time I liked, on condition that I never revealed either his own name or that of his bank.

I think I simply said 'Thank you'. I told Maura Connolly. I saved the information for Kathleen until I got home that evening. The situation called for a few tears of relief.

Throughout those dreadful days, the one bright spot was that at least Russell had not got his hands on our cottage in Donegal. Until the debt on the house was so kindly cancelled, it was the only thing that we still owned, even though the debts far outstripped its value. I have a theory about why he did not bother with that little place. He and Marie came to visit us in it shortly after we bought it. They drove up in Marie's little sports car and arrived, cranky and in foul humour, clearly having had a blazing row. It was a day of dreadful weather, stormy and cold. The cottage looked awful; we had as yet done nothing at all with it. He hated the hotel in the town where they stayed, hated the weather, hated Dungloe, hated everything about Donegal, and could not wait to get out of the place. His memory of Dan Jock's was that it was a tiny, horrible little place in a horrible part of the country, was worth about five hundred pounds and therefore not worth his while bothering with. I firmly believe that this is the only reason he did not purloin it as well as everything else.

There were a number of side-shocks for me during the whole matter. For instance, like every ordinary Joe in the country I had thought that a crossed

◻

cheque could be lodged only to the payee's account, or cashed by him in a bank where he is known. Well, yes. Unless you're *very* well known, like Russell Murphy, in which case the answer is no.

One of his scams was a beauty. On some pretext or other, he persuaded Kathleen and me to resign as directors of a small company we had, called Omnico Ltd, which owned an apartment. He nominated two of his staff to take our places as directors. He then raised a loan from Bank of Ireland Finance for £50,000 on the title deeds of the apartment. He then got one of his nominee directors to endorse the cheque. It was then lodged directly to his account.

Now you see it, now you don't.

He was a founder-member of Bank of Ireland Finance, and a director of both the Bank of Ireland and Bank of Ireland Finance. In fact, he was a member of the Court of the Bank of Ireland—a distinction granted only to the most trustworthy. He managed to move the money he had raised on loan in such a way that it bypassed all the normal checking procedures that apply to any ordinary punter. It was all done on a first-name basis and a 'Don't worry about that, I'll take care of it . . .' Fortunately, over the following two years and with much negotiation, we reached an amicable settlement with the Bank of Ireland on the matter.

Day followed day and weeks blurred into months. I doubt if very many of the people I work with either on the radio or the television team knew just what I was going through. I am a private person and was not in the habit of confiding in people. Sometimes I envy the women I see around me who seem to me able to talk their troubles out of their systems. Apart from those at home, I spoke at length only to Maura and to Al.

As I said at the beginning of this chapter, I am telling this story of Russell Murphy only because it is the story that most people have asked me about in the years since his death. He seems in death to have a fascination for people: who he was, why he did what he did, how he did it, and how he got away with it for so long. It's a rattling good yarn. And I hasten to add that I fully realise that no-one—not *anyone*—goes through life without getting some kick in the mouth from fate, or life, or God, or whoever arranges these things. And in a long list of set-backs that can happen to people, including cancer, heart attack, prolonged illness, marriage break-up or unhappiness, sick children, awful accidents, terrible physical disabilities—everyone can add his or her personal list of horrors— in that long list, if I had a choice of set-back to happen to me, then brother, I'd much prefer Russell Murphy's swindle that any of the others mentioned.

Why did Russell do it, and where did all the money go? No-one will ever know the full story. He was acting for a lot of people, not only for me; and a lot of people lost money.

It was Laurence Crowley, appointed as administrator to Russell's estate, who unravelled most of the skeins. It was he who found that Russell embezzled approximately one-and-a-half million pounds in all—and before his death, shredded every piece of paper that might have given some indication of how the money was spent. The best guess is that the money went simply on Russell's high living in the years before he became ill. Some of it was undoubtedly spent on the secret operations and medical treatment he had in London before his illness became known, but most went to support his extravagant life-style.

He was drawing approximately £35,000 a year from Henry M. Murphy and Co. In the years of his renaissance, he was spending close to £100,000 a year, with the jetting to London and Zürich and New York, the best hotels, chauffeur-driven cars, the best opera seats, expensive gifts. While it was going on, I thought it was wonderful: Russell discovering sex and love and romance late in life and having a ball. The love affair with Bronwyn was for real, but rumour has it that there were other lady friends in his later life. (It is perhaps worth saying that since his death, I have probably heard one thousand nine hundred and sixty-three rumours about Russell Murphy, what he was up to, who his friends were, with whom he had liaisons, the number of allegedly illegitimate children for whom he was responsible, and all sorts of combinations, permutations and derivations of those rumours. Whatever story it is you know about Russell Murphy, I can guarantee that I have heard it and have ten more to match it.) At the time, it never occurred to me to question where the money was coming from for all this extravagance. I just assumed that there were 'big deals' being done from which he earned a lot of money. And certainly where Bronwyn was concerned, she was a successful businesswoman in her own right and would have had her own money.

I believe that initially, way back around 1977, he got into trouble when the planning permission for the conversion of Hibernian Chambers was refused. He had gambled heavily and lost, and that period coincided with the start of his love affair with Bronwyn. He had borrowed money to buy the property. So he dipped in to survive that loss, and then began to rob all his Peters to pay his Pauls. The dipping started at the same time as his outgoings began steeply to climb. He also had to maintain his payments to Marie.

I think that, like many another, Russell thought that somewhere along the line it would all come right. He would pull off a huge coup, or be awarded a monster liquidation that would go on for years, or would use his

☐

considerable brain-power so that everything would slot neatly together again. No-one would ever be the wiser. What happened to him was lung cancer.

T. P. McKenna agrees with my theory that Russell always intended to make things right, though he is, I suppose, more charitable than I am (mind you, he was not caught by the swindle). He also believes that Russell, like many other people with cancer, had secondaries in the brain and was subject to false bursts of optimism and a sense of unreality.

But to me, the awful sin he committed was that he did not approach anyone when he found out he was going to die. He had a clear year's warning. If he had gone to his office colleagues, the Bank of Ireland, or the Institute of Chartered Accountants, I am quite sure they would have rallied around him to keep the lid on the pot in order to maintain the good name of the accountancy profession. That he did not do that was the real betrayal of those he called his friends. On the other hand, I know that in saying this I am just whipping the empty air. Russell had such a gargantuan, such a colossal ego that he could never have gone to his peers, those whom he taught and whom he allowed to attend at his court. In doing so he would have had to admit that they were his equals.

There is no point in pretending that I do not mourn what happened. Unlike Hugh Leonard, who is on record as saying that he intends to forget about it, I cannot sideline it. Unlike him, not only was I left with nothing, I had less than nothing, at the age of almost 50.

I saw Kathleen wandering around the house looking at the things she loved, and knew what she was thinking, that it was all going to go. That money came hard. There was a lot of gathering in it, a lot of driving through the night and gigging at venues where I did not want to be and driving myself through tiredness and beyond. There was a lot of conscious thrift and saving.

But even having said all that, the important point to remember is that if Russell had come to me and confessed that on a vagary, he had put all my money on a horse in the 3.30 at Leopardstown and that the horse had fallen at the first fence, I might have coped with it. What I could not cope with was that he sat for six or eight years in that little room in Trinity Street and quite clearly, meticulously and methodically planned and connived to defraud me, while all the time meeting me as my best friend and confidant, allaying my fears about my security. In case I have not already made that point clearly enough, this betrayal was more important than the money.

I have, unfortunately for me, inherited my mother's attitude to unnecessary extravagance. I carry her stern face around on my shoulder, asking reprovingly: 'You're spending how much money? On yourself? How

□

can you possibly justify that?' My mother never owed anyone anything. If you did not have the cash, you did not purchase. If you wanted something badly enough, you saved up for it. And that is the way I too have always handled my affairs. In fact, over the years, I have spent very little money on myself. There is nothing material that I want all that much. I have my bicycle and my car, and I am not particularly interested in clothes.

The loss of all I had worked for was a shock, the impact of which I will never be able adequately to describe. One curious side-effect was that for quite a long period I was not able to write by hand. Even to put my signature to a piece of paper was a great effort: the pen tended to slide downwards and off the page. I first noticed the effect soon after the initial shock. I have to type almost everything now. I could sign an autograph—just—before the pen began its wobbly downward slide, but there was no way I could write an ordinary letter. I have a thick welt in the side of my right index finger now, which has developed from the pressure of my thumbnail as I dig it in, trying to keep the renegade index finger steady on the pen. The pop psychiatrists have given me the pop answer: my brain, so punished for the devastating signatures I gave to Russell Murphy, refused to countenance any more foolish writing! Ho-hum!

I believe I can relate totally to the feelings of a man I admire greatly, John Stalker. In his book about his aborted investigation into the alleged shoot-to-kill policy within the RUC, he notes how extraordinary it is that the people whom you would normally expect to have courage and integrity, honesty, loyalty and principles, when the going got rough simply abandoned these virtues and ran. Likewise, all Russell Murphy's lofty friends in banking and accountancy simply disappeared into the undergrowth. 'Not I, Lord! Not I!' They didn't want to know.

I reserve particular anger for the Institute of Chartered Accountants, which has an impressive set of rules concerning obligations by members of the accountancy profession to the public. In the beginning, I had hoped that they might have done something to alleviate the suffering of those who had been defrauded by Russell Murphy. If Russell had been a lawyer, his victims would have been compensated by the Law Society from a special fund set up for such eventualities. And although I know that the institute has not got a similar fund (and they should have), I believe very strongly that Russell's professional organisation should have made some efforts to deal with the matter. That they did not do so is, to me, a source of resentment.

I know that there is someone out there who knows the whole story. And even those who know parts of it are not saying. I find this conspiracy of silence extraordinary.

☐

In the immediate aftermath of the whole affair, when I was agonising to her about the betrayal of the friendship and trust, Maura Connolly said something very telling. She said that her mother had always told her never to trust *anyone* in business where money was concerned. I now understand that sentiment only too well.

RTE was corporately very helpful to me at this time. The then Director-General, George Waters, and his successor, Vincent Finn, were the essence of kindness and concern. There was very little they could actually do, but in so far as they were able, I was offered all available advice from the financial and legal departments and I was steered in the right direction.

Derek Quinlan was then a partner in Woods and Co., chartered accountants (he has since left to set up his own firm), and he took me on. His was the task of unravelling, as far as it could be unravelled, the whole sorry mess, in order to find out where we stood when the bubble burst. A daunting task. He coped amazingly well, and still handles my affairs.

One of the many ironies in this whole episode is that in my naïve arrogance, it was always my proud boast that I could recognise a chancer or a shyster and a swindler coming at me on a dark night in thick fog, using what Hemingway called 'my built-in long-distance shit-detector'. One of the great disparagements of myself now is that the person I trusted most turned out to be the greatest swindler of all.

Perhaps a better consequence is that I find myself now to be, strangely, a more generous person, more conscious of other people and their disappointments. Up to Easter 1984 I do not believe I was all that sympathetic to people. My attitude was callous: why did they not simply get on with it? That, too, was a throw-back to the tough upbringing of my mother. She was tough on herself and expected others to behave likewise. 'Carry-on' and self-pity was not be countenanced. It was simply self-indulgence and 'looking for notice'.

Kay is very concerned that I am driving myself as hard as I am since the Russell Murphy affair in an effort to replace what Russell took. That might have been a first reaction, but I have calmed down. That money has just gone, and that is all. I am turning down far more jobs than I am accepting. I do not sell myself or my services cheaply, but the great cry in the office now is 'no' to *everything*. Kay had grave reservations, I know, about the court actions I was contemplating in an effort to recover some of the money. Her attitude was simply, 'Why don't you just walk away? It's a chapter in your life, it's over and done with. You're only causing distress to yourself by prolonging the agony.' She sees my efforts at salvage as a constant tearing of scabs off wounds.

Perhaps to preserve her own sanity, I feel that she has adopted a blanked-

□

out, studied indifference to the whole thing, the same sort of posture she affected towards the possibility that one of the children might have been taken away before the adoption was confirmed. If you pretend the bad thing does not exist, then it might go away. In the same vein, she seems firmly to have resolved that life is worth living and that we are to go about with our friends and enjoy it.

But I am very grateful that never once, either immediately, when we thought even our house was gone, or during the long messy years afterwards, did she utter a word of recrimination, although she must have been sorely tempted. After all, it was her life savings and future too. She never once said, 'You're a bloody eejit. Why did you allow that to happen? Why did you not keep a closer eye on your own affairs?'

She did not need to ask it. I have scourged myself with that question often enough.

Kathleen was never a hoarder like me, and has a far more adventurous personality. While she would have been devastated if we had lost the house in Howth, she would not have been in the least perturbed if the cottage in Donegal had gone. And even if 'Onslow' had been lost, she claims that she would have little difficulty in pulling up all roots and heading out to Australia to start again. I'm not so sure I would feel the same.

When the story of the extent of the swindle hit the media, Olivia O'Leary of 'Today Tonight' did an across-the-line interview in London with T. P. McKenna. And to her incredulous question about how none of Russell's friends ever had the slightest suspicion about him, the actor named a number of those friends and people with whom he dealt, including Brian Farrell, Justice Henchy, Hugh Leonard, and Douglas Gageby, and asked: 'When you take that group, and throw in Gay Byrne, would you accuse them of being naïve and ingenuous men?' Laurence Crowley, that much-respected man of finance who was appointed administrator for the Russell Murphy estate, told me at one stage that Russell was perhaps the only man he could think of for whom he would sign a bundle of papers without question, such was the respect he had for him.

In finishing about Russell, I would like to emphasise that my view of him is my own. Hugh Leonard was more succinct about him: he said Russell was a swindler, and he swindled those he professed to love the most. The story of Russell's personal life as told in this chapter is as told by him to me, and it is as I observed it during the years that I knew him.

Poor Russell—I wonder did he ever know what havoc he caused in others' lives?

CHAPTER 8
THE 'LATE LATE'

■

I met a woman recently who said to me, 'I used to feel so sorry for my mother when she used to say that the "Late Late Show" was the highlight of her week. Now I find I'm at the stage in life when the "Late Late Show" is the highlight of *my* week!' I arrive in to the 'Late Late' office from the Radio Centre at 11.25 on Monday mornings, and I expect everyone to drop whatever they are doing. This post-mortem and planning meeting is to start at 11.30, and if I can make it on time, so can they.

There is bartering and selling and criticism at this meeting. The guest list for the show, which is sometimes not finalised until hours before air-time, is the culmination of a communal effort by all of those who work on it, but the final decision is always mine. I operate largely on hunches, and have generally found it to be true (although, to be fair, not always) that if I allow my instincts to be overridden, no matter how attractive the proposition appears on sight or to its proposer, I will regret it on the night.

If the previous week's show was good, we say so; if it was not, we say so too, and those who were responsible for the items that died hear about them in no uncertain terms; but that is the end of it. There is no carry-over. Our method of rating audience sizes is by scientific sampling, which results in a scale called TAM (television audience measurement) ratings. I keep a close eye on the TAMs If there is a very good show against us on another channel and we have slipped a little, then I do not worry too much. But if there seems to be no good reason for our slippage, other than our own bad planning or programming, then I want to know why.

We never lack for PR companies pushing products, or publishers pushing books, but I believe that balance is very, very important within each show, or, even more importantly, over each 'term' of the show. We should get the proper mix of light and heavy items, and if, for instance, the North of Ireland situation gets out of hand, as it seemed to do early in 1988, then I will be in two minds whether or not to do something on it. On the one hand, perhaps we could contribute to the debate. On the other hand, should the audience not be given a respite from the constant battering from television news bulletins and current affairs programmes and from the newspapers?

RTE

☐ *Rejoicing for the 21st Anniversary of RTE Television. Memories of programmes long gone and forgotten with Justin Keating, Michael O'Hehir, Kay Toal, Brendan O'Reilly and a rather morose Charles Mitchel – he must have got some bad news. Together with the first three continuity girls on Bealach a Seacht, Maire O'Sullivan, Kathleen Watkins and Nuala Donnelly.*

RTE

☐ *Memories of Radio Éireann, with Joe Linnane giving us a memorial tinkle on the piano as he was wont to do.*

□

On that subject, I would love to have a crack at interviewing the President of Sinn Féin, Gerry Adams, either on the radio programme or on the 'Late Late Show'. I would like to try to travel the labyrinthine canals of his mind to try to find out what makes him tick. When being interviewed in the newspapers (and on radio and television, until the British government recently banned him) he never gives answers to questions, merely statements—and is always talking in the context of the latest atrocity. I am not suggesting that I would achieve any more than anyone else, but I would really like to have a go. (Of course, under the present legislation I have two chances to interview Gerry Adams: none and none. Overall, I am against section 31 of the Broadcasting Act.)

I will always have my own ideas about prospective items, and there will be some that for one reason or another are already agreed and in train. At the Monday meeting, the pushing starts for the open slots. The researchers vie with one another to get projects and guests on the show. They have to sell very hard to me, except in very obvious cases of big stars who we know will deliver. Brigid Ruane, for instance, pushed and pushed to get Fr Bernard Lynch onto the show—he was the priest who was helping AIDS victims in the United States, and was subsequently involved in a court case in New York. Somehow I felt that the AIDS coverage on television had zoomed out of all proportion and that viewers would find it a big turn-off. But Brigid, who is a most persistent woman, kept on at it, and Bernard Lynch proved to be a very good guest. (He also won his case; the allegations against him were untrue.)

In a similar manner, the Dubliners special, which proved to be one of our all-time greats, was pushed and pushed by John McHugh. I was inclined to keep it to the original suggestion, which was a half-hour segment. Gradually it became an hour, then ninety minutes, then one of the outstanding successes of the past five years.

I like to have a group of researchers within which each has different special interests. For instance, when June Levine joined us from the *Irish Independent* many years ago, her drive for feminism was, to my then-untutored mind, too radical by far. And she made no secret of the fact that part of her reason for joining us was to inject a more enlightened view of women into the air waves. But we got on well personally, and as June nagged and nagged, pushing me and the show an inch at a time, we began to move, beginning to encompass the feminist viewpoint as well as all the others.

I suppose June had an uphill struggle with me. She has said that at the time she met me I tended, along with a million other Irishmen, to classify women under one of two headings, 'mothers' and 'others'. I honestly

□

believe that if it *was* true (and if it was, it was simply that I had not thought enough about the subject), she could no longer say it of me. By the time she left the show, to write her best-seller *Sisters*, she had had a significant impact on opening up our attitudes.

I believe that one of the great strengths of the 'Late Late Show' has been its willingness to deal with new, even frightening, ideas. I have tried to be willing to deal with them as well, and in doing so I have developed my own attitudes. Although I might put up quite a fight and force people to justify ideas or opinions, the day I do not listen and learn is the day I should give up. The analogy has been made that I am like an editor of a magazine, around whom all these eager-beaver reporters hustle to get their stories in. The researchers have to compete also with Maura, who contributes her own ideas, and with everyone else who attends the meeting: the Production Assistant, who at the moment happens to be Róisín Harkin, the director, Anita Notaro, and everyone on the team.

I am not so sure which is pulling which, society, or television in general and the 'Late Late Show'. Certainly we reflect what people are ready to talk about, sometimes slightly in advance of public discussion. We would never impose a discussion on a society that is not ready for it, because it would be fruitless to do so. It has been said of me—and I agree that it is one of my strengths—that I have very good timing, in knowing when exactly the boundaries are ready to be pushed out another half-inch. The cynics opine that this is simply bandwagoning. Naturally, I disagree strongly. I read a great deal, and from time to time I can instinctively identify a matter of national or international, social or cultural importance that I would file away in a quiet part of my brain, where it would steam away, occasionally coming to the surface, when I could put faces on it to facilitate discussion. Even in the teeth of great reservations or absolute opposition from the team around me, I insist that it is a subject we are going to run.

Every time I am asked about this aspect of myself and my work, I think about the discussion we had in March 1967 about the ban on Catholics attending Trinity College. Those taking part were Joe Foyle, David Thornley, Jim Lydon, Fr Paddy Brophy, Vincent Grogan, and Diarmuid Moore, all informed, articulate Catholics. The discussion was intelligent, but it became clear quite early on that in the opinion of most of the panellists—and the studio audience too—the ban was outmoded and basically nonsensical. What was memorable about this discussion was the public reaction afterwards. Some very critical things had been said about the Catholic hierarchy, albeit in a controlled and considered manner. The reaction might have been expected to roll up in the usual manner—we were biased against the clergy, slanted, and so on—but it did not. What had

155

happened was that, just at the right time, we had voiced what most people felt in their hearts to be true, had aired the subject and had made it a matter for informed discussion.

On the other hand, I found during several discussion programmes on the Irish language that this is a subject that will never be laid to rest peacefully. I believe that Irish should be preserved, and so do we all. But I object to fanaticism on this score, as on any other, and for some reason the Irish enthusiasts are among the most fanatical of any group in this country. The reaction was vitriolic after the first major debate, in 1965, in which two of the chief protagonists were Dónal Ó Móráin and the actor Joe Lynch; but as an example of hatred, one woman's sentiments are hard to beat. She wrote to me after one of our 'soap-box' debating programmes in 1972, on which we had allowed Mrs Joan O'Brien, President of the Language Freedom Movement, her allotted few minutes on behalf of her cause, and then threw the debate open to the audience and to three panellists from the pro-language lobby. I had been ill for a short time previously, and this was known. My friend wrote: ' . . . Far from people engaging in prayers for your good health, we should all be asking God to send you multiple cancer so that you will soon be removed for ever from our sight.'

But this being Ireland, and morals being identified largely with s-e-x, it is the sexual issues that receive most attention. The late Oliver Flanagan's well-repeated maxim that there was no sex in Ireland before television can be laughed at in these more open days, but there is a germ of truth in it. There was sex, but no discussion of it—that is absolutely true; and the journalist Colm Tóibín, writing in a special issue of the *Crane Bag* devoted to 'the media and popular culture' in 1984, speculated that without television in general and the 'Late Late' in particular, it would have been entirely possible for many people to have lived and died in Ireland in the twentieth century without ever having heard any discussion on sex. A slight exaggeration, but that is what the man said . . .

I have visibly lost my patience with guests very few times. Once, alas, was with the late columnist John Feeney, during the early days of the 'Late Late', when he was a student activist and was in the news all the time for demonstrating at the gates of Clonliffe College. We had him on a panel alongside a priest. In the course of the interview, John announced firmly that he knew positively that the Archbishop of Dublin, John Charles McQuaid, had shares in the condom company, Durex! This was too much for me, and I lost the rag. I said to him that it was more than even I could take . . . Immediately, the reverend father sitting alongside Feeney, who I would have thought would be staunch in defence of his prelate, had a go at me for attacking his fellow-panellist. This totally flummoxed me,

□

whereupon the audience, scenting blood, of course joined in. The show that night ended, to put it mildly, in high confusion. The upshot of the story is that about a week later I received a letter from John Charles, in his own neat handwriting, which I still have, thanking me for my defence of his honour. And after he died, his brother gave me Dr McQuaid's gold pince-nez (which I also still have) in recognition of that defence so many years previously.

I confess to a great regard for the late archbishop. It is generally recognised in Dublin that, although he was a tough man on the morals, nevertheless behind the scenes he was a most charitable and saintly individual. For instance, the story goes that not far from his palace in Drumcondra lived a woman—call her Mrs Murphy—who supported her six children by practising the oldest profession in the world. The archbishop came to hear of her, and sent the parish priest to see her to ask her to desist. She sent the parish priest packing.

So Dr McQuaid allowed a decent interval to pass, then sent the PP along to the house again. This time the message was that there was a certain gentleman, a man of means, who knew of her plight with her six children and who wished to supply enough money weekly to support them without any monetary input from their mother. The emolument was dependent on Mrs Murphy's retirement from the oldest profession in the world. Mrs Murphy agreed, and the money was hand-delivered every week by the PP.

But it began to get in on her, this wondering about who this gentleman was and why he was supporting her. She began pestering the PP, and this poor man was heartily sick of her. He begged the archbishop to let him reveal the source of the money. Eventually Dr McQuaid agreed, but said he would tell her himself, over tea at the palace on a certain Sunday afternoon.

The great day dawned, and Mrs Murphy and her six children were packed into the PP's car. They were ushered, wondering, into the arch-bishop's formal dining-room. In honour of the occasion, the great man had ordered rashers and chips for tea . . . Things were going very well, when suddenly one of the six children began to whine: 'Ma! There's a fucking rind on this rasher . . .' Without blinking an eyelid, His Grace turned to the housekeeper, who was pouring out the tea: 'Would you cut the fucking rind off his rasher, please?' (No, I'm not sure I believe it either.)

People tend to blame television alone for the changes in morality, whereas there have been a number of other equally powerful influences, such as better education for all and increasing opportunities for people to broaden their minds with foreign travel. There are aircraft taking off from our airports in this era at a rate that no-one could have foreseen twenty-

☐

seven years ago. In the last fifty years the rate of acceleration of change in the world in general has speeded up dramatically. Due to the invention of the microchip and the mushrooming development of sophisticated technology, the social changes that have taken place in this period have been greater than in all the previous history of the planet. Ireland cannot resist that change any more than any other country in the so-called developed world. As well as television, all of these other factors are adding to the sum of our general experience and attitudes.

As a controversial topic, sex is evergreen, but there are other subjects that I believe are equally difficult to discuss, because they are so emotive, such as death or suicide. We have not shirked those either. Divorce was a subject we covered in the early seventies, long before there was any major open discussion about it in this country. The first time was the programme on which Fr Fergal O'Connor, God bless him, turned out to be completely and sanely pro-divorce, and on which he announced, and in my opinion proved his case, that there was no valid reason why the Roman Catholic Church should object to divorce.

As I have been the host since the show's inception, I am in a good position to have seen the societal changes we have reflected over the years. There is now open discussion both on radio and television of subjects like child sexual abuse and marital infidelity, both of which would have been totally taboo as topics for discussion twenty years ago. But I am not sure that their incidence is all that more prevalent. If you like, we have alerted people to what is going on. (I had thought that in its twenty-seven years, the 'Late Late' must have covered every subject under the sun, until I saw John Silkin's talk show on morning television on which he had a group of men discussing their own sexual impotence. Are we yet at the stage where a group of Irishmen would appear on the 'Late Late' for such a discussion?)

We have had homosexuals and a courageous lesbian, Joanie Sheeran, who as far back as eight years ago spoke frankly about her problems. We have had lesbian nuns, transsexuals and bi-sexuals; we have discussed divorce and abortion and curious religions, the clergy, hare-coursing— even politics and politicians. One year we gave our soap-box to the terrier of Baggot Street, Vincent Browne, and urged him to rant against politicians as he wished. He wished. And he was very good, the instigator of a very lively debate.

I think that the main change in attitudes has been that at last, people will accept that discussion on subjects such as those that come within the ambit of sexual mores is actually possible without too much danger to our sainted society. For instance, when we had a pseudonymous woman we called Eilís on the radio programme, who talked very frankly about her affair with a

□

married man, the initial reaction was not from the outraged Catholic mothers-of-seven but from other thoughtful women who had been through the same thing themselves or who were worried about their own husbands. Very, very few said we should not have interviewed Eilís at all, which would certainly have been the overwhelming reaction eighteen years ago when we started the programme, on the grounds that just by hearing her filthy, depraved voice the youth and holy people of Ireland would rush out to corrupt themselves in similar fashion.

There are undoubtedly deep pockets of conservatism and resistance to all this openness. Some of the resisters have very genuine fears, and I have great respect for them, because I do not believe that all the changes in our society are for the better. What I do believe is for the better is that there is this new willingness at least to hear the other guy out—if not always to listen: the two things are not synonymous. And there is a new perspective on what is truly important and what is not.

Radio and television over the past twenty-five years have made it easier for people to realise the normality of their reactions and their situations, and they are prepared to talk about it—or at least to write to Gay Byrne about it or to Marian Finucane or any of the clones of the 'Late Late Show' or the 'Gay Byrne Show'.

I do not believe, for instance, that the Bishop and the Nightie incident could happen today. This episode, which has gone down in history and folklore and to which I refer for the benefit of those who are not old enough to have seen it, happened because we had decided in February 1966 to include, as one of the lighter items on the show, a pastiche of a quiz that was popular at the time on other channels, in which husbands and wives were asked the same questions while out of earshot of one another but within earshot of the audience. The object of this exercise was to see how much their answers tallied with each other, to what extent they knew each other's thoughts and attitudes or to what extent they would find they did not understand each other at all. The questions were pretty harmless—or so I thought.

Two of the volunteers for the quiz, a Mr and Mrs Fox, were asked individually what colour nightdress had been worn by Mrs Fox on their wedding night. Neither could really remember, and Mrs Fox ventured, in all innocence and good humour, that perhaps she had worn none at all . . . The audience laughed delightedly, and that, I thought, was that.

You can imagine my astonishment when, after the show, I was told there was a most urgent phone call for me from a reporter in the *Sunday Press*, who wanted to know if I had any statement to make in answer to the strong attack made on the programme by the Bishop of Clonfert, Dr Thomas

159

Ryan. I knew of no attack, and knew only slightly of the Bishop of Clonfert, and I asked for further details. The *Sunday Press* had them, in the form of a most forthright denouncement of the 'Late Late Show', which had been provided to them by telephone by the bishop's secretary, and which denouncement he intended to make the subject of his sermon in Loughrea Cathedral the following morning. Further, the *Sunday Press* was going to give its full front page over to the bishop's statement, and make it the major story of the day. I was so surprised that I had to ask the reporter which part of the show had so affected His Lordship, and I was told it was the section of the programme that featured the husband-and-wife quiz; they had their front page made up and were able to give me full details of it.

The *Sunday Press* plans for such a big story made everybody surprised, except presumably the bishop and his secretary, and I went home that night not a little convinced that the whole thing was some huge gag being perpetrated by someone just to see what my reaction would be. But not so. The next morning Kathleen and I went to ten o'clock Mass in University Church in Stephen's Green, and coming out we bought both Sunday papers. There it all was. They differed little in their coverage of the story, and it was obviously the most serious thing to happen in the country in decades. I remember as we drove up Dawson Street on the way back home that we were overtaken by an old friend of ours, Fr Brendan Heffernan. He had seen us coming out of Mass and had read the newspapers; he raced after us to offer his condolences, and I was somewhat relieved to find that he had seen the show and was as much at a loss as I was to know what all the fuss was about. I say I was relieved, because I was beginning to think I was going a bit mad.

That morning Al was having a few friends round for drinks, and he had asked us to drop in. When we got there, Gunnar Rugheimer, the Controller of Programmes, was also there, and was in rollicking good form about the whole saga. He thought it was intensely funny, and another indication of the quaintness of the Irish mind. Everyone present had a good laugh about the whole thing; but by the next day, after the story had gone out on both the radio and television news bulletins on the Sunday, the atmosphere had changed somewhat, and the laughter died down a little.

On the Monday I was told that the Controller of Programmes and the Director-General wanted to see me. They had obtained a transcript of the whole programme and had examined it minutely—that is to say, they had had typed every word spoken by everybody on the show from beginning to end. I was forced to admit as I looked at the transcript that in the light of the bishop's criticism it was quite the most filthy, double-meaning and suggestive programme that had ever been transmitted anywhere in the

☐ Colin McStay and Louise Browne are alive and
well, thanks to advances in medical science. John
Caden, Northern Bank officials and myself
counting some of the astonishing £1.25 million
donated to the Colin McStay fund (above) while
Louise Browne seems unperturbed by all the fuss
in the Late Late studio.

world. Right from the moment I came on and said, 'Good evening, ladies and gentlemen, welcome to the "Late Late Show!"' one could sense an evil glint in my eye and a knowing, suggestive smirk about my mouth. The further in we got the worse it became, and, of course, in cold print, taken out of context, the husband-and-wife encounter was sheer dirt from beginning to end. Again, bearing in mind what the bishop had seen in the programme, my final 'Good night and God bless' was pornography rampant. One didn't need to hear the actual words: one knew instantly what was in my mind.

Both the Controller and the Director-General were agitated and wanted to get out a statement. Why they wanted to do this was never very clear to me, but I got the distinct impression that there was a bad case of the screaming funks going around, and everybody was catching it fast. I believed then, and I still hold the belief, that the bishop should have been told by the DG that we had thought about the show and that we had come to the conclusion that there was nothing wrong with it; therefore we were making no apology for it. But this is not what happened. Having run up and down the corridor a few times with draft statements, the Controller and I sat down and wrote something to the effect that we now realised 'that part of last week's programme was embarrassing to a section of our viewers and we should like to say we are sorry about this.' And that became the official statement in reply to the objection. I was quite appalled at how so many people in responsible positions must have known that they were right but allowed themselves to be placed in a one-down situation—and I include myself in that criticism.

But that was not the end of it. The wolves were out on the rampage and saw a field-day being presented to them on a plate. Every good soul in search of a bandwagon to clamber onto realised that his day had come, and thousands must have been hurt in the scramble to get on board.

The *Irish Times* on the Monday was toffee-nosed and amusing, and right. Its leading article was headed—predictably— 'The Bishop and the Nightie'. It ended off by saying: 'While feeling that His Lordship was killing a fly with a sledgehammer . . . the Bishop in this case may find that, as our music-hall correspondent tells us, Saturday night's joke is one of the staples of vaudeville and may have bored more viewers than it offended. A lapse of taste has been treated as if it were an outrage to morals.'

The bishop was quoted in Monday's *Evening Herald* as saying that he had been 'inundated with calls to congratulate him on his stand in speaking out against an objectionable show.' He added that he had seen the show on a few previous occasions 'but could not see anything then which could be regarded as morally objectionable.' He said he was not a great television fan,

☐

and added that he mostly watched news and sporting items, and one or two other programmes, such as 'Tolka Row', for relaxation.

Loughrea Town Commissioners got in on the act in their weekly meeting on the following Wednesday (surprise, surprise: they just happened to live around the corner from the bishop). 'A dirty programme that should be abolished altogether' was how one speaker put it when the commissioners were discussing a vote of congratulation to the bishop on his stand. 'It's time to nip this thing in the bud, and His Lordship deserves the support of the people in this matter,' said Mr Devine. The Mayo GAA Board joined with the Meath Vocational Education Committee in passing resolutions condemning the show. The letters pages of the evening papers were full of controversy, and of course the *Irish Catholic* was not behind the door in pointing out just why they supported the bishop against those who were abusing him for his action. By the time the *Irish Catholic* got to it, however, what had happened on the 'Late Late Show' had become, not just a quick question on a superficial quiz 'but a public discussion of bedroom relations between married couples'! (The exclamation mark is mine.) Further, thundered the *Irish Catholic*, 'what is important is that a person with authority and courage has drawn public attention in an arresting manner to the growing tendency to play down the grave implications of the Sixth and Ninth Commandments and the unworthy part that Telefís Éireann, deliberately or unthinkingly, is taking in that process.' Dear Lord, I thought—what, little old us doing all *that*?

There was much more, and it went on for quite some time. The newspapers loved it and kept coming back for more bites of the cherry. But eventually the point of overkill was reached, and the turn came in the public reaction.

The outpourings of outraged self-righteousness eventually became so overpowering that a lot of people, all of a sudden and all at the same time, decided that they'd had it and that this nonsense had gone on quite long enough. The point was made, somewhere along the line, that if the bishop had wanted to make the front-page headlines in the Sunday papers, there was surely a sufficient number of real and important questions to be tackled in our society that were much more worthy of his attention. And anyway, when all was said and done, what precisely was wrong with a husband and wife describing a nightie with good humour on an adult programme, designed for adults, late on Saturday night? Perhaps, it was suggested, His Lordship was slightly out of touch with how real people lived? Gradually a lot of people came to the conclusion that never had so much fuss been made about so little by so few—and never had it all been exaggerated to such nonsensical lengths. The tide of criticism turned, basic good humour

□

took over, and the incident became the subject of jokes for many years afterwards.

However, for me, one of the most telling and truthful points was made in a letter to one of the evening papers. It said: 'The worst aspect of this squalid little affair is that Gay Byrne, knowing that his conscience was clear, should have apologised in public.' That was the one lesson that I took from the entire episode.

The Bishop—who had not at the time realised the implications of his action in issuing the hasty statement, which could and in my opinion should have been held on his behalf until the more clear-thinking light of the following morning—was deeply embarrassed; and months later he sent an emissary to Kathleen's brother, Jimmy Watkins, who is a vet, asking for a meeting with his representative in Bewley's café. When Jimmy went along, the representative, a clerical gentleman, asked him to convey His Lordship's regrets to me over the entire incident. Decent man.

Poor Tom Ryan! Clearly, a bunch of the boys had been tippling a few in the back room that Saturday night, which, God knows, they were perfectly entitled to do. But Tom failed to build in protection for himself in the event of having one over the eight, and thus found himself embroiled in something that was to cause him the most acute embarrassment for the remainder of his life.

It has dogged my days for twenty years also, to the point of boredom; and the only reason I tell the story here again (and believe me, this is a very shortened version of it!) is because I know the younger generation will find it hard to believe that such an incredible fuss could have been made about so little. The hypocrisy, the cant, the posturing, the lies of that period are beyond credence, but the whole ridiculous incident is a historic marker of how seriously Irish people took their telly in those days. They've improved!

The year 1966 was a vintage one for controversy of this nature. The Bishop and the Nightie affair had just calmed down when Brian Trevaskis, a very bright young Trinity student and part-time playwright, who had been invited onto the show to discuss the craft of play-writing with Wesley Burrows, attacked Galway Cathedral as a 'ghastly monstrosity' and referred to the Bishop of Galway, Dr Michael Browne, as a moron. He went on to include in his sweeping condemnations the Archbishop of Dublin, the Christian Brothers, the clerics who got rid of the novelist John McGahern from his teaching post, even the Irish language. We were off again.

This time the bishop, in the person of Dr Michael Browne, issued a dignified statement, restrained in the circumstances, more hurt than angry. But this did not appease the legions who were out for blood. There were county council denunciations and floods of letters to all the papers, and the usual hysterical telephone calls.

Eventually the Director-General, Kevin McCourt, tired of the fuss, issued a statement of his own, which began: 'The "Late Late Show" is unscripted and unrehearsed. In any other form it would fail in its purpose as a spontaneous television programme of discussion and entertainment. Those invited to take part are chosen in the belief that they will contribute in a fair-minded way to the enjoyment and interest of the programme; their opinions do not necessarily have to be popular opinions.' The statement then apologised to Dr Browne and to the Archbishop of Dublin for 'disparaging remarks' and 'unkind references', and ended: 'The producer-compère of the show is fully aware of my concern that standards of taste and courtesy are maintained at all times.'

I was, and am; and this particular controversy might have stopped right there if Mr Trevaskis had not announced that he wanted to come on the show the following Saturday to apologise. We knew that viewers wanted to see him again, but, taking no chances, we lined up a 'balancing' panel of heavyweights, which included Conor Cruise O'Brien, Vincent Grogan, later to become Supreme Knight of Columbanus, and Seán Whelan, another prominent Catholic layman.

Trevaskis did not disappoint those who wanted more fireworks. He apologised all right, saying he should not have called the Bishop a moron, allowing that it was an 'obscene and indecent' word. Then he broadened his 'apology' to include an attack on a society that would discriminate against an unmarried mother and her child, concluding his impassioned oration by asking if the Bishop of Galway knew the meaning of the word 'moron', since he doubted if he knew the meaning of the word 'Christianity'.

I leave the rest to your imagination. In retrospect, those turbulent programmes were not the norm, but they are undoubtedly the ones with which the programme earned its stripes. This was when television was young in Ireland, in the era of student unrest, the Beatles, Vatican Two, apocalyptic assassinations in the United States, flower power, and rapidly increasing prosperity in Ireland. It is far more difficult now to imagine what a storm could be raised by a single remark. And one of the constraints under which we all operate in these areas nowadays is that we are all, in radio and television, pulling out of the same pot. There are more and more of us, and the pot is not getting any bigger. I suspect that boredom will set in soon. There are too many programmes on radio and television *doing the same thing*.

But the demand for tickets for the 'Late Late' has never slackened, and

□

the TAMs are still very high. The latest figures would indicate that in the season beginning 1987, of the thirty television programmes with the highest viewing figures, twenty-two of those were 'Late Late' shows, eight were episodes of 'Glenroe', one was of the Rose of Tralee Festival, and one was a programme in the 'Saturday Live' series. I think one of the reasons for this is that the format is formatless, in a sense, able to accommodate anything that comes up. One week we can have Angela Rippon on with the Boomtown Rats and Richard Kiel, who played the steel-toothed villain in the James Bond film *Goldfinger*; the next, we can have a 'full-issue' programme on Irish or on the Catholic Church, the problems of itinerants, or, in our 'all-priests' show, rarely heard opinions on the laity from the other side of the altar-rails. The week after that we can have classical music and a few comedians. Undoubtedly, one of the show's attractions is that its content is never known in advance.

For instance, the Jimmy Magee special programme in 1989 was a great indication of just how quirky the 'Late Late' format is. It was extraordinary how many people who are not remotely interested in sport contacted us to say what a great show that was. We were flooded with congratulations, even from Channel-Four-land in Britain, where an edited version of the 'Late Late' is now broadcast weekly, from viewers who, up to the time they saw the show, had never heard of Jimmy Magee.

Of course every programme, particularly one with a single theme, is a great jump into the unknown. I could just as easily be writing about Great Disasters of our Time when referring to the Jimmy Magee special or the birthday tributes to Mícheál Mac Liammóir, or Hal Roach, or Peggy Dell, or Noel Purcell, or the Chieftains—or the Dubliners special, which went on to be an international hit in video . . . This leap into the unknown, in spite of the meticulous preparation and our years of experience, is the essence of the programme. I never really know until I am well into it each week whether we have a cracker or a dog.

I do not minimise the influence of television as a propaganda medium. The Provisional IRA has certainly recognised its uses and has used it to its own ends in a massive world-wide propaganda exercise, as indeed all terrorist organisations have tried to do. And I think that the overall influence of television in that sphere has been baneful.

I think as well that the medium has been instrumental in creating a very disturbing dissatisfaction and resentment amongst ordinary people, which has led to a rise in lawlessness and a general deterioration in honesty and ethics. With their own eyes, people can see the good, rich and wealthy life in a consumer society in which not they but only the top ten per cent can fully participate. When as a boy I used to go to Bray on the top of the bus,

☐

I could look into the rich houses and gardens of Foxrock and Bray and Westminster Lawns, a whole society away from my two-up-two-down in Rialto Street. But all I could see was the outside, and it never occurred to me to question how those people led their lives, what they ate, how they played, or how they got there in the first place. I never touched their lives in any real way.

What television has done is to bring a tangible realisation to ordinary people of what it means to live like that. 'Dallas' and 'Dynasty' are the extreme examples, so daft in many ways, but the overall picture from television is that the good life is possible for a few. More and more, people are taking it into their own hands to become one of the few, and if they are denied this, they revolt. I am convinced that this is what lies at the base of all the senseless vandalism of telephone kiosks and bus shelters, cars, trees, and buildings. If they cannot—or are not allowed to—remedy their own state, people try to get at the only physical things they can get at, to cause problems for those who seem to have no problems. In that context too the influence of television has been baneful.

On the other hand, when you consider that twenty-five years ago many people were living in little whitewashed cottages on the sides of mountains in Ireland, remote from the rest of the world, the beneficial difference that television has made to their lives is unquantifiable. One Saturday afternoon recently I was watching Seán Kelly cycling in an international race between Milan and San Remo, and international rugby from Twickenhan, as it happened. The people in those cottages now see forms and styles of life in the wild-life and travel programmes from the other end of the globe; they are as moved as the rest of the people in the world when they see the awful pictures from starving Ethiopia. They participate vicariously in the achievement of man walking on the moon or in the signing of an American-Soviet anti-nuclear treaty in Washington. They can see Andy kiss Fergie, and the naked, hating face of an IRA mob as it starts the frenzied killing of two British corporals.

Maybe, as de Valera would undoubtedly have thought, they might have been happier if they were left in their glorious isolation with their paraffin lamps and their pampooties. But I believe that for most people, television has brought great enrichment and education.

The 'Late Late Show' has come a long way from the initial vision of Tom McGrath, who saw it as being representative of an Irish family living-room into which people could drop for a chat. In the early days we always had a panel, which Tom thought should also be representative of types who could be easily identified. Our first panel was supposed to be thus representative. Professor Liam Ó Briain was the fatherly one; the beautiful

☐

Verona Mullen was everyone's younger sister or cousin or girl-next-door; and Danny Cummins was the scamp, the rake, guaranteed to stir things up.

The whole thing was to appear totally spontaneous, and therefore there was very little research. I was expected to ask the sort of questions that any ordinary member of the public would ask if they had just met someone for the first time at a party. If someone's main reason for living was kite-flying, I was to find out why, asking all the silly, uninformed questions that anyone would ask to keep a bright conversation going. Tom planted people in the audience, and I never knew who they were or where they were sitting or if they would interrupt or not. It kept me on my toes, and the whole concept seemed to work very well.

Our guests on our very first show, on 6 July 1962, were Count Cyril McCormack, Ken Gray of the *Irish Times*, George Hodnett, now an occasional music reviewer for the same newspaper, and the sports broadcaster and fencer Harry Thuillier. The show was to be a summer 'filler', but it was so successful with the public that it was decided to keep it running in the regular schedules. Our panellists changed; but the pair most easily remembered by most people from those early days were Dennis Franks and Ulick O'Connor, who, when on together, knocked sparks off one another. For a while it became almost immaterial what guests we had, as the whole nation tuned in to see what row they would have tonight. It is difficult to believe now that in all they were only on together on six occasions. If you asked most people who remember the sparring, the estimate would be much higher.

Ulick is outspoken Ulick, and always will be. Dennis Franks was an actor of Polish-Jewish extraction who was suggested as a panellist by Pan Collins, who had first brought him on as a guest, having known him through her former job as a film publicist. He was a very gentle man in reality, homosexual, almost timid, who would not sleep in a room without a light. Tom McGrath had various categories and lists of people under which he placed people, and Dennis was first suggested as a guest under the column headed 'kooky'. He turned out to be a very good guest, and his name was readily accepted when he was later suggested as a possible panellist.

The animosity between himself and Ulick was immediate and, to be fair to Ulick, I think mainly engendered by Dennis, who could not bear to be in the hospitality room, in the make-up room or in any room at all with his fellow-panellist. Franks was very easily insulted, and always rose to Ulick's bait. He started to write pained letters to the papers about his treatment at Ulick's hands, and organised his friends to write too.

Ulick, whose animosity was not real but a performance, got his own back on two occasions. On the first, when Dennis was left temporarily without

G.A. DUNCAN

☐ *John Huston never looked any different in the entire course of his life but my goodness what a young Gaybo! And even younger, with a delightful visit from Bob Hope.*

a seat, he said: 'I'll just stand here behind Ulick.' 'Not behind *me* you won't!' retorted Mr O'Connor.

The second occasion was their last appearance together on the show. Ulick went out and bought a single rose and had it delivered to Dennis at the studio before air-time with a little card: *'From an admirer in Rathgar'*. Dennis was thrilled. 'You have to present it to me on-air, Byrne,' he said to me. The show opened, and I gave him the rose: 'There you are, Dennis, from an admirer in Rathgar ...' The audience applauded, and Ulick muttered something under his breath. Sensing an insult, Dennis rounded on him. 'Are you saying that this is spurious?' he demanded. 'No,' said Ulick, all big-eyed, 'I'm your greatest admirer!' and produced the receipt from the florist.

Poor Dennis. Their 'feud' was our gain, and it was really a lively series. It is unfortunate but true that television thrives on controversy. What happened to Ulick and Dennis as a panel pair was that they became victims of their own success: there was so much controversy about *them* and what *they* would do next on the show that the rest of the guest-list became irrelevant. And gradually, prospective guests started to decline our invitations to the show, because they did not want to be merely cannon-fodder for these two. People did not mind guesting on the show even in a hard-hitting interview, but they did not want to get lost in the middle as Ulick and Dennis performed their own show on the side.

Adrian Cronin came into the director's box after brief stints put in by directors Burt Budin, Louis Lentin, Denis O'Grady, and Don Lennox, although to place him there was an unorthodox move. He was Head of Light Entertainment in RTE, and therefore he was my boss. Yet I was producer of the 'Late Late Show'; and while he was director in the gallery during transmission, he was technically my subordinate. It is a most unusual arrangement in television, since the producer is the one who decides what happens on-air. When I am on-air as host, as producer I am in complete charge of the floor, doing my own timings from my own wrist-watch. There are very few programmes anywhere in the world that follow this arrangement—and yet it appears to have worked very well during the last twenty-seven years without any resentment from directors or pro-duction assistants or anyone else.

Adrian and I knew each other so well that we never had to work out any of the normal technical signals used in television studios. He has always said that he knew from my body language when I was getting tired of an interview and was about to wind it up, or when I was about to stand up from the desk and move into the audience, or when I was about to go for a phone call; or, indeed, when I was in particularly good form—or otherwise! He

□

says it has to do with the way I scratch my nose or pull my ear-lobe or even straighten my back. He has rarely been wrong. With one hand tied behind his back and in the depths of illness, he is the best and sharpest and most tasteful director of a live show like the 'Late Late' anywhere in the world. He is extraordinarily good, patient and kind with artistes, and they appreciate and respond to him. And he is hugely popular with crews.

Audiences take on mob coloration as soon as they take their places. It is an amazing thing, but four out of five weeks the audience will be bright, happy and cheerful, co-operative, anxious to respond and to have a good time. That remaining week, regular as clockwork, they will sit like a big, dead, lumpy suet pudding, a communal black hole, absorbing all effort and giving nothing back. They refuse to be amused or even interested, but sit like a hanging jury, daring me and those in the hot seats to entertain them. On those nights, I try with them for a while, but when it is evident that they will not be shifted I shuffle them off the deck and play the television audience.

I never use a 'warm-up' man. These are characters, usually second-string comedians, who go onto the set about ten minutes before the show starts, to settle the audience down, to tell a few jokes, get them giggling, get some sense of what they are like. He explains the equipment, tells them what is expected of them, and then gets off to let the host get on with it. I think that Irish audiences are too sophisticated for that kind of treatment, and, with Irish begrudgery, would probably resent it anyway. Dammit, they came all the way from Ballina or Wexford or Mullingar to see the 'Late Late' and Gaybo (and themselves), and they are not going to be fobbed off. So I go out before the show and warm them up myself. The great advantage of this is that I can sense what they are going to be like. I never cease to be amazed at the unanimity of their response, good or bad. I believe that the ideal studio audience size for a show like the 'Late Late' is about 350, but we can only fit 120, and we have to be contented with that. Most of those 120 people are there for one purpose and one only: to be seen. They want to wave to their mammies and daddies and all the folks back home, even if back home is only two hundred yards down the road.

They are difficult to control and quite difficult to 'play', because, for technical reasons, they are quite far from the 'action' on the set. During most of the show they are calculating, 'Are we on?', watching the monitors for a glimpse of themselves. In addition they are filled with disappointment at the smallness of the studio, with wonder at the hugeness of the cameras and the length of the boom microphone, and are extremely susceptible to distraction. But now and then a total silence descends, and that is the harbinger of a successful interview or item. It is quite rare.

☐

There have been some particular moments on individual shows, only a very few, that shine head and shoulders above the rest, when the audience and I were grabbed utterly unexpectedly. One such happened with the American singer Don McLean. He came on the show in January 1981. He was performing in the National Stadium that night, and I did not know an awful lot about him. I was told he would come after the show, arriving at eleven, and therefore I would not have all that much time with him. When he came in, my impression of him was that he was a pale, pimply little fellow with a guitar, and I thought he gave a pleasant, if undistinguished, interview. The show was nearly over, and I asked him to sing. He said he would sing 'The Mountains of Mourne'.

Mother of all that's good and holy, I thought, *since I started compering concerts I've heard every strangulated double-herniad tenor in the world murdering 'The Mountains of Mourne', and do I really want to hear this yet again—from a little pale-faced American? It's going to be the greatest murder of them all . . .* But I smiled sweetly and nodded. I had no choice; he was a guest.

He took up his guitar and started singing. And suddenly it was one of those very rare, utterly outstanding moments that I can remember in the twenty-seven years of the 'Late Late Show'. The entire show crystallised and came to a standstill, and all concentration was on him, including mine. He galvanised us. He interpreted the song completely differently, and for the first time I—and, I believe, the audience—could divine what Percy French's intentions had been in writing it. Whereas I had always heard it sung as a come-all-ye, McLean recognised the desperation and sadness of generations of Irish emigrants who were thinking of home and writing inarticulately to their loved ones. It was brilliant and very special, and could never be repeated. Afterwards, the audience exploded in applause.

There have been only a few such moments, and they can never be planned. In the entire twenty-seven years of the show I can remember only five others when there was a similar galvanising and fusion of performer, audience, people at home, and everyone in studio. Liam Clancy did it with 'The Band Played Waltzing Matilda', and the others were Mary O'Hara, Burl Ives, Val Doonican, and the Italian tenor Mario Malagnini. Each performer might try to repeat the experience but would probably not be able to.

On the musical front we haven't done too badly. We've continued our efforts to feature on the show most kinds of music, although in this effort, as in most, it's impossible to please everyone. What is musical sweetness to one person is intolerable cacophony to another, but we try to promote the best of what is on offer in each category.

Chris de Burgh came to us at a time when he'd conquered Japan,

□

Germany, France and Ireland, but he hadn't had a biggie in the UK charts. It was at our instigation that he performed 'Lady in Red', which his record company had no intention of releasing in Britain. But when they saw him on the Channel Four 'Late Late Show' the following Monday, and saw the reaction which the song got from our studio audience, they decided to run with it and he had a most satisfying hit.

Sinéad O'Connor, bald pate glistening in the studio lights, converted a lot of Mums and Dads to her side, who previously might have had grave reservations about this young wan who shaved her head—what kind of girl did that? I found her a most attractive young person (I kept on trying to imagine what she'd look like with hair!) and she obviously came across as a sharp, alert, intelligent girl who knew precisely what she was about in the rough business she's in.

The first time Bono and U2 did the 'LLS', they sang a song dedicated to *me*—this was a *long* time ago! They insisted on coming to pay their tribute to the Dubliners on their tribute show; and then at Christmas 1988, when the world's media were hounding them for interviews, they came and did a forty to forty-five minute session, ending with a Christmas song, just sitting there on the panel with acoustic guitars. I thought they were splendid, and I was grateful to them.

I get particular personal satisfaction from our association over the past four years with the Lombard and Ulster Music Foundation Bursary Competition for classical music students. I think talent in that category should be nurtured and cosseted and encouraged and the £15,000 bursary (the most valuable in these islands) is an excellent way to do this. One might have reservations about some forms of sponsorship but this seems to me to be totally worthy.

Bob Geldof and the Boomtown Rats first appeared on the show when they were mere lads just out of short pants. Bob managed to scandalise everyone that night with his criticisms of his Catholic upbringing in Dublin, specifically of Blackrock College, and with his stated ambition, within a year, 'to get rich, get laid and get famous.' He managed to do all three in the time specified. And subsequently he went on to his astounding achievement on behalf of the starving millions in Ethiopia—more than all the spouting politicians in the world managed to do.

We first came across Hothouse Flowers when Liam Ó Maonlaí and Fiachna Ó Braonáin were invited on as buskers from Grafton Street on 25 November 1985. They were known as the Incomparable Benzini Brothers and I liked them straight away because of their style and rhythm, so much so that I invited them back on the show on the nearest available spot the following January. By the time they got back to us as the Hothouse Flowers they were international stars and it seemed like no time at all.

The list is long and we haven't space; the big bands and small, established performers and beginners, the comedians and jugglers and archers and acrobats—they've all passed through our 'LLS' studio, some instantly forgettable; others went on to make the grade. But they all experienced that studio audience, one of the most difficult anywhere; because there are only 120 of them and they are there to be distracted and it requires a special spark for any performer to grab their undivided attention and earn that special round of applause. But when it happens, it's impressive.

People are always asking who was the most impressive, the best, the funniest, the most embarrassing, the worst guest we ever had. Well, by far the most impressive to me, as I think everyone in the country must know, was Mother Teresa of Calcutta. I find it difficult adequately to describe the effect she had on me, as indeed she has on everyone. Interviewing her is like looking deep into a bowl of shining light. The audience that night was also deeply affected. Unbidden, during a commercial break, they passed around the only receptacle they could find, some lad's motorcycle crash-helmet, and filled it with money, engagement rings, everything they could donate; and for weeks afterwards it rolled in for her, tens of thousands of pounds, although we had not mentioned a word about money.

It was no secret that I was also very impressed with John Stalker, the 'honest cop' who, when it appeared he was getting too close to the uncomfortable truth about a shoot-to-kill policy in the North, was taken off the official inquiry. It is rare to come face to face with someone you know is completely incorruptible. It was a long interview, but I could feel that the audience was gripped.

On a different level, I was gripped, and very strongly, by the presence of Britt Ekland. As most people in the country know, I am susceptible to female pulchritude—feminists would call me patronising—and I have never in my life, before or since, met a woman like Britt Eklund from whose every pore oozed the aura of (sorry, Oliver! Rest in peace!) s-e-x.

It has been remarked by outsiders that when they open the door of the 'Late Late' office they are met by a sort of densely packed beehive, with me at the core, which is very difficult for them to penetrate. Yet compared with other programmes, especially cross-channel ones, there are relatively very few of us to get through the mountain of correspondence, planning and vetting that goes into both the radio and the television show. I expect a lot from people who work with me. As well as working with professional competence and enthusiasm, I expect my researchers and the others on the

□ *I'd love to see Sinead O'Connor with hair on because she's mighty attractive even without it!*

□ *Lydia Roche is one of those women who looks quite stunning on camera.*

△ *Nana Mouskouri is always very friendly and has a particularly soft spot for me and the Late Late Show.*

◁ *Audrey Hepburn, see on p. 79 why she's a favourite of mine!*

□ *And if I hadn't become a broadcaster I always think I would have been quite happy flying as a pilot for Aer Lingus and it would be difficult to imagine a more delightful captain than Grainne Cronin. She was on the Show on the occasion of her maiden flight as captain.*

programmes to respect confidentiality. There is a voracious and ceaseless newspaper appetite for tittle-tattle and trivia about me and the programmes, and I dislike any leakage. In my insurance days I developed a great respect for discretion and confidentiality, and I believe that very few businesses can operate without such principles being observed. I must say that I have never had many problems in that area. All my colleagues are and have always been very loyal. I think that they all enjoy their work and would not endanger the shows, so that that particular stricture is not very onerous. Although the application required from researchers is demanding, there is never any shortage of people who would like to work on what they consider to be the prestige show in the station.

I am also very protective of the 'Late Late', perhaps sometimes too unthinkingly protective. Uri and Irena Ustimenko came to Ireland from the Soviet Union. Uri was the TASS man here, a lovely man with very good English. He was popular at social gatherings, although everyone, of course, 'just knew', nudge-nudge, that he was a senior agent of the KGB. Pan Collins befriended him, and all the busybodies in town, some quite senior, *very* senior in certain circles, made it their business to tip me off that Pan and Uri were friendly and had actually been seen (horrors!) in public in the Gaiety Theatre. They wished to point out that Gay Byrne might allow himself to be used by subversive forces like Uri and Irena through the influence of Pan Collins. Did Gay Byrne realise who these people were and what they were up to? Should Gaybo allow the 'Late Late Show' to be used in this fashion?

I formally mentioned it to Pan, whose attitude quite rightly was that her friends were her own business, but that if I as a broadcaster felt I should not associate with certain people, then that was my own responsibility. Fair enough. I agreed that it was no busybody's business with whom I associated in my spare time, so when we in turn were asked, Gay Byrne and Kathleen Watkins accepted an invitation to dinner with the Ustimenkos. As I recall, Tim Pat Coogan, then editor of the *Irish Press*, was also invited with his wife, but they did not turn up that evening. That night, I did realise with a chill that while one of the Ustimenkos' two children was with them here in Ireland, the other was always in Russia, and when Uri went home for a visit, Irena and one child stayed here. The reverse was also true: if Irena went home, Uri stayed in Ireland. They were never allowed, as a family, to live here all at the same time. Pan has a very sad memory of the last time she saw Uri. He had been recalled to Russia, and came out to her flat to say goodbye to herself and Kevin. Her last sight of him was as he stumbled down her hallway, sobbing, blinded with copious tears and trying vainly to stem them with a huge handkerchief.

176

□

Many years later (in 1986) it was proposed that we do a 'Late Late Show', live, from Moscow. Leaving aside my grave reservations about taking the show *anywhere*, we started to make enquiries. We were promised full co-operation from the Soviet embassy in Dublin, and they in turn were promised full co-operation from the broadcasting authorities in Moscow. But I was unsure, so I decided that money would be well spent on a recce. Colette Farmer (of 'Roll it, Colette!' fame) and Claire Duignan (who was the show's director at the time) went to Moscow. I refused to commit myself until I had some idea of what we might be getting into.

It became apparent to Colette and Claire during the week in Moscow that there would be Difficulties. Our Russian broadcasting colleagues could not accept that we would choose the guests, not they; ditto the panel members; that the show would be live, not recorded, and that it would not be edited. And what they could not cope with, what they could not fathom, what they would not countenance, was the possibility that we would have two hundred people in the audience who could stand up and talk *and say anything they wanted to.*

The answer to that was 'nyet!'

That, pal, was just not on.

Recce money well spent: we shelved the idea.

Incidentally, I talked to Seán Bán Breathnach (SBB) recently on the 'Gay Byrne Show', and he told me an even more intriguing story. He was in Moscow covering the Olympic Games for Raidió na Gaeltachta, broadcasting reports home at least once a day. They'd been there a fortnight and had got to know their Russian technicians fairly well. One day they were having trouble with the machinery, and SBB said to his Irish friend: 'Níl fhios ag mo dhuine cad tá ar siúl in aon chor.' (Roughly: 'Yer man hasn't a bloody clue what's going on!') Whereupon the Russian technician pressed the talkback switch and said: 'Tá fhios ag mo dhuine gach aon rud atá ar siúl, a chara!' (Roughly: 'Yer man knows every word you're saying, pal, and so do I!') They'd appointed Irish-speaking technicians to man the 'SBB Show', just in case!

All of these things came to pass in the days before glasnost and perestroika and Mr Gorbachev.

Over the years I keep dinning into new researchers who fall in love with people's stories that it is not the story that is important but how the person will deliver it. There is no point at all in having the most heart-rending, poignant or dramatic story to tell if you cannot tell it in public, under lights, live on television. I keep on telling them that ours is a talk show, and if a guest cannot talk, then . . . This is why I try to insist, whenever possible, that researchers actually interview our guests in advance.

☐

Pan Collins was the original and only researcher for the 'Late Late Show' when it began. She says that when she first met me I was cocky, brash, and a mental lightweight (so what else is new?), but that over the years I have matured and developed. Pan and I had knock-down drag-out fights over the years, particularly about the toy show. But she was an extremely good researcher, and to this day, if anyone in our office needs to know anything in a hurry about any previous 'Late Late' during the past twenty-seven years, all that is necessary is a telephone call to Pan. She has an amazing memory for faces, names, and dates, and can recall instantly who was on which show and when and with whom—and very often what they said and what happened afterwards. She has everything filed in a series of plastic-covered folders she calls 'mind maps', a method of connective thinking that bypasses linear notes. She came across the method through a guest we had on the show, Tony Buzan, and has become an avid disciple of his. The method certainly works for her.

It was she who masterminded the time I was caught out by Éamonn Andrews. She and the other researchers cooked up their little scheme when I was still away on holidays, and by the time I got back fresh and ready for our tenth season, it was all ready. What they planned was a surprise celebration of the first ten years of the show and of my book *To Whom it Concerns*, which was published in September 1972.

Pan knew Richard Widmark was someone I was quite keen to interview, and it was known that he was in London filming for his television series 'Madigan'. I was told that he had agreed to come onto the show, but that unfortunately he could only come at the last moment, since his schedule was packed. She gave me the research material on Widmark, and I did not like it; to me it seemed like a lazy job, simply culled from library stock. I told Pan I wanted her to interview him. She explained how he was only flying in to Ireland late on Friday night.

'Well, get him at his hotel.'

'He's not staying in a hotel.'

'Where is he staying?'

(Thinking on her feet) 'He's down in Ballymore Eustace, with very good friends of his . . .'

'Well, get them on the telephone and arrange— '

'They only moved into that house a couple of weeks ago and the phone hasn't been connected yet.'

'Who are these people?'

'People named Cadwell.'

'Well, go to the airport and meet him. Get an interview. I don't care how you get one, just get one!'

☐

Pan went off, and on the Saturday handed me the results of her 'interview'. Apparently, Mr Widmark had come to Europe before the war on a holiday and had met members of the Hitler Youth. By the time Pan was finished with him, Mr Widmark had grown from these youthful beginnings into a right-wing hard-hat Nixon supporter who had maintained secret contacts with underground Nazism since the war. I was delighted. This was going to be a really meaty interview.

I started the warm-up to the show. The first item was to be with three journalists, whom I met briefly in the hospitality room with the panellists—all in on the act, of course. 'Mr Widmark' was to arrive late, when the show had already started, since he was travelling up from Ballymore Eustace, tearing himself away from a convivial dinner party thrown by his hosts, the genial and mysterious Cadwells.

Myles McWeeney and Oliver Donoghue, the other two researchers, were in the meantime stashed away in the Montrose Hotel with the real guests and, as I was doing the warm-up, were herding them safely in to RTE where I could not see them. Pan shepherded a tiptoeing Éamonn in behind our studio set.

I got the count-down, the opening credits rolled, and we were on-air. 'Ladies and gentlemen, welcome to the tenth season of the "Late Late Show" — 'but before I could say another word, Éamonn's amplified voice boomed out from behind: 'Gay, I liked your book, but I'm not too sure I liked what you said about my flat-footed walk!' And in comes Éamonn . . .

Many of our 'Late Late Show' researchers through the years have done pretty well after their graduation from our showbiz school. Pan Collins, undoubtedly the person most identified with the show—a wonderfully dedicated colleague, unfailingly devoted and loyal to Gaybo, and guaranteed at any time to produce the best ideas for guests and topics when the going got rough—stayed with us three years beyond her retirement date, and then took a job as account executive with Foreman Dove and took to the PR and advertising world with her customary and lifelong zest

Vincent Browne, always probing, testing, worrying and worrisome, now with the *Sunday Tribune*, brought a lively political mind to the show. Dana Hearne is now married to a university professor in Canada. Myles McWeeney is now with the *Irish Independent*: his was the idea for our first court-case 'Late Late Show' about Ireland's entry into the Common Market. Oliver Donoghue, now with the ICTU, was the man who thought up our first all-itinerant show, amongst many others.

John Caden graduated from the 'Late Late Show' office to take over as producer on the 'Gay Byrne Show', and then 'Morning Ireland'. John McHugh and Coleman Hutchinson graduated to the big time in London and are now most successfully freelancing as researchers amongst the television companies of the UK. They found, to their astonishment, that the name of RTE (and, specifically, the 'Late Late Show') is so highly rated in London that their involvement with it for some years guaranteed an immediate berth on similar shows on British television.

All of these people—and there were many more—made no small contribution to the success of the show over the past twenty-seven years; and as the one constant North Star amongst them, I owe them a debt of gratitude.

Some guests refuse point-blank to be interviewed in advance. We were having Dr Jonathan Miller on recently, and he sent a polite but firm message that while he would come on, he would not be researched. The message ended with the perfectly sensible words, 'Gay knows me and knows I will deliver.' He did, of course.

In very deep contrast, the worst interview of my life, I think, was with the actor Dermot Kelly. Dermot was a little character actor who appeared in a very successful ITV comedy series with the comedian Arthur Haines. He was filling the sort of character role, the Irish fall-guy, for which people like Milo O'Shea became famous. This was in the days when television was young and not many Irish actors had made the breakthrough into the big time of British television. So Dermot Kelly was a Star, and we were lucky to have him—and that was only because he was home on holiday.

On the same night, we had Marie Keane, a wonderful dramatic actress but loved the length and breadth of the country as Mrs Kennedy of Castlerosse. I should have been more alert, because when I met Marie just before the show, she said to me with what I thought at the time was an odd emphasis: 'Have you *met* Dermot Kelly?'

'No—why?'

'Uh-oh,' she answered, looking worried.

I had not got the time to probe further. Unfortunately for me.

After Marie's interview the great moment arrived, and Dermot arrived on set to a great reception from the studio audience. He sat down.

Me: 'It must be fantastic to be such a wonderful success over in Britain, appearing with Arthur Haines . . .'

Him (looking off into the distance): ' 'S all right!'

Me: 'It must be marvellous to have made that breakthrough, being Irish in Britain and all of that . . .'

Him (shrugging): ' 'S all right!'

Me: 'Yes, but it must be marvellous to be playing opposite a man like Arthur Haines; he's a great comedian . . .'

Him (sniffing): 'Ah, 's all right!'

☐

I thought to myself with an inner grin, *Now I know what he's at; I understand it perfectly and he's doing it beautifully. He's doing the Milo O'Shea, making me sweat, and then he'll break out with 'Aha! Had you worried!'—and then we can start the interview.*

So I proceeded with the straight feeds to his never-varying answers. The audience started to cough and shuffle. I thought, *He's taking it too far; his timing's off, he shouldn't wear out the gag—but maybe I have it wrong, maybe it's a different gag from Milo's . . .*

As we continued until after the fourteenth ' 'S all right', the awful realisation dawned that this was it. This was not a gag, and there was to be no dénouement. This was what constituted Dermot Kelly's real personality. Marie Keane, trouper that she is, jumped in to my rescue and, with a fund of theatrical anecdotes, conducted the rest of his slot with me over his unseeing, uncaring little body. I shudder to think what would have happened to the show if Kelly had been the first on. This disaster demonstrates why I insist on prior interviews with scheduled guests. Dermot Kelly was a hoot on television. But Marie Keane was the only one in the studio that night who knew his real form, and no-one had thought to ask her.

For the record, the most embarrassing moments have been those when first a baby elephant and then a pair of performing seals from a circus did what these animals always do in television studios, necessitating armies of attendants with brushes and aerosol deodorants. In addition, the seals actually lolloped off their appointed spots on the set and zoomed all around the studio, under the audience seats, while their frantic trainers tried to capture them, helped by our security staff, researchers, and all the rest of us.

We had a lovely security man in RTE called Vincent Brien. One very, very wet night, everyone was gathered under the colonnade, sheltering, bunched together, after the 'Late Late Show'. Suddenly there were screams from across the way, from behind bushes in front of the old Montrose House. Vincent bombed over, just in time to prevent a man sticking a knife into another man. Man A had been minding his own business, having a peaceful pint and watching the 'Late Late' on a set above the bar in his local, when he had seen live on television, in an audience reaction shot, the smirking face of his wife sitting beside Man B. This was not the only such episode. I don't know how many marriages may have been damaged in this way; but after his appearance on the show as a guest, Dominic Behan was almost stabbed by a man who had a grudge against him, in the lobby of the television building. He was saved by the same Vincent Brien.

The show can be dangerous for guests in another way. The footballer George Best was on in 1980. He arrived late, straight from some function

□

he was attending, and so had not had a chance to meet any of the other guests before the show, one of whom was the actress Sinéad Cusack. Sinéad's interview was over and she was sitting demurely in one of the panel seats when he arrived on the set. Although they had never clapped eyes on one another before this, within two minutes of his arrival on the set I knew they were in trouble: the electricity between them was palpable. He just looked over to where she was sitting and—*ping!*

Subsequently they had a very passionate affair, which, of course, was gleefully followed—and probably wrecked—by the English tabloids at the time.

On 3 October 1981, Best came on the show again, this time with his wife, Angie. He was now, he promised everyone, a reformed character: sober, industrious, and penitent. They were promoting Best's book, the manuscript of which had been typed for him by Angie. He had written about the affair with Sinéad in it, and there was a photograph of him with her, with a caption underneath that averred that Sinéad was 'one of the women he had truly loved'. On the show, during the course of the interview, Best and Angie were talking absolutely frankly about his past and his problems with alcoholism, and she was saying that she had given him the ultimatum that if he went back on the drink she was gone. Towards the end of their slot I said facetiously, in the spirit of the interview—or so I thought—that she had to be careful about him on the 'Late Late', because of course it was on our show that he had met Sinéad—

Angie froze. (Remember, she had actually typed the manuscript of the book, the affair was noted in black and white and recorded in the photograph . . .) I recognised the *faux pas*, but it was too late to do anything about it. I stumbled on, but George had frozen too, and the interview died a death. Afterwards, in the hospitality suite, Angie attacked me furiously. I am no shrinking violet when defending myself, but I was genuinely nonplussed, and told her so. She was not appeased and would not forgive me, and I had to apologise abjectly. Normally I would not do so if I felt I was in the right, but she was clearly very genuinely hurt and angry, and because she was such a decent person I did the generous thing. But for the life of me I still cannot understand it.

I had a similar situation with the singer-actress Dory Previn, who was also promoting a book, in which she wrote movingly about the distress caused to her by her abortion. It was at about the time that abortion was becoming a very hot issue in this country, and I asked her, gently, I thought, if she had anything to say that might illuminate the subject from her personal experience, since it would be very interesting to people in Ireland in light of the current concerns. She too was furious and went cold.

IRISH PRESS

☐ *Adeveen O'Driscoll, Cathy Moore, John Caden and I before we took the Radio Show to Australia in 1987.*

RTE GUIDE

☐ *That Monday morning feeling – rise and shine.*

It is an odd thing, I now find, that people are prepared to put in print things they will not discuss. But these situations are the exception rather than the rule. Our guests are usually very pleased with their appearances. Take Whitley Strieber, who appeared on the show in May 1987. Whitley had been visited, he claimed, by little chaps from another planet—and of course had written a book about them. When Whitley wrote his book he immediately hired a 'media adviser' in New York. These guys are *de rigueur* nowadays. They are supposed to know every radio and television programme in the land and overseas—which will be the most effective from a publicity point of view, and which the trickiest.

When Whitley was invited on to the 'Late late Show', he called his media adviser, and the guy flipped! He told poor Whitley that the 'Late Late Show' in Dublin, Ireland, was the Trickiest Show in the West, and Whitley would be mocked, reviled, and made a laughing-stock by the audience . . .

Whitley, who seemed to me to be a calm, pleasant sort of chap, was a very nervous man when he sat in front of me. But after the show, he thanked us for looking after him. He said he had been treated courteously and with great consideration, that he had been given more time than on most other shows, and that his story had been treated with respect. In short, he was delighted with the 'Late Late Show' . . . And he was going back to New York to fire his 'media adviser'!

My personal favourite, over the years, is still the 'Liberties Special' (we had an all-Cork, an all-Derry and an all-Galway one too). There was something about it, perhaps because I am from Dublin, perhaps because I identify so strongly with the stand-up comics like Al Banim and the solid-working pros like Joe Cuddy.

My second-favourite was the Hal Roach birthday special, because of the way Hal blossomed with the appreciation he saw beaming at him from every quarter. He always felt, I believe, that he was never appreciated in his own country. It seemed to him, I think, that he was much more successful and far more popular outside Ireland than he was at home with his own people. But the good-will messages to him poured in that night from all over the country, and left him, and us, in no doubt of his popularity. Unfortunately for him, he was off to America the next day. Otherwise, on the strength of that one show he could have packed any theatre in the country for a month!

There were two most frightening episodes. One was when I was sure that an amateur stuntman who was doing a fall from the top of the (very high) administration block outside the studio had miscalculated his distances and was going to be splattered all over the tarmacadam. I believe that my heart actually stopped as I watched him fall.

The other episode involved my own very reluctant co-operation. We had a woman on from a circus whose act was to hoist someone sitting in a tiny chair that was attached to the top of a thirty-foot pole, which she balanced on her forehead. You are way ahead of me . . .

First, she had her partner sit in the chair and he was hoisted aloft. Everyone duly impressed, much applause. Then she asked for a volunteer from the audience, and people scattered for cover. There were no takers. Then she turned to me, the audience started to applaud, and there was not a single thing I could do about it if I wanted to retain my self-respect. I learned the true definition of terror as she hoisted me up on the little chair until my head was brushing right against the light-grid above the set. She had warned me not to try to balance myself, simply to relax and 'sit normally'. Of course you cannot sit normally; at the end of a thirty-foot pole, balanced on top of someone's head, it is extremely difficult to sit normally. There is nothing to hold on to and nothing to see beneath you, because you are balancing on a single pole, which in turn is balancing on her head. But the more I tried instinctively to correct, as one would on a motorbike or on an unsteady rocking-chair, the more work she had to do to compensate and to correct my corrections. It was an extremely terrifying experience. I do not honestly know how I got through the rest of that show.

I agree with an assessment made many years ago that the 'Late Late Show' is the town hall of the air. There are Ye Current Entertainments, and then, when we are discussing any current topic of note or controversy, I am a kind of chairman, running a debate in as fair a manner as possible, where there are special interests and Joe Soap and opponents and experts and as many sides as we can fit in. The object is to allow in as many points of view as possible. We draw no conclusions; we leave that to the punters in the pubs and living-rooms up and down the country.

From the very beginning, we were ruthless about telephone calls. No greetings. No requests. No grannies who are 105. When a call is made when we are on the air it is taken by a researcher, who will try to identify the single point to be made by the caller. That is all we want, because that is all we have time for. The problem is that the on-air discussion continues and by the time I get to that call the caller will have forgotten his point, or changed it while listening to the discussion. There is no way to deal with this except to let them straight through, and that would be chaotic.

My favourite telephone call of all time came in from a 10-year-old Dub, and I think it probably deserves to be included in some anthology or other of Dublin humour. We had the Scottish comedian Billy Connolly on the show one night, and he went into one of his very funny stream-of-consciousness routines in which, off the top of his head, he looked straight

☐

at me and the other people in the chairs: 'Did you ever wonder when people are talking about religion and faith and God, if Jesus Christ came back on earth today and he walked up to you, what would you say to him?' And we all went into a tail-spin, and none of us could think of what we might say to Jesus Christ if we met him tomorrow.

The telephone call came through from the 10-year-old Dub. 'Would you tell Mr Connolly that I know what I'd say to Jesus. I'd go up to Jesus and I'd hand him the Bible and I'd say to him: "Jesus Christ! This—is—your—life!"'

CHAPTER 9
THESE WE HAVE LOVED

■

I predicted years ago that people would stop getting so het up about this new machine called television, and I was right. They have subsided somewhat, although of course not altogether. I still get tons of letters written-more-in-sorrow-than-in-anger about the 'immense responsibility' I have in wielding such a 'powerful weapon', and really looking forward to the day I have to answer to God for how I have misused it: all the innocent young people whose lives I have blighted by the mention of s-e-x, and the great silent majorities of Mass-going Christians I have scandalised by bringing on apostates and foreigners. On the other hand, I know that part of what I am paid for is to act as a national target, a person whom a great number of people thoroughly detest. If they did not have me to detest, or Charlie Haughey or Dick Spring or whoever is currently fashionable in the hate stakes, they would find someone.

I know television is a powerful medium, but I have always thought that its power is exaggerated. It has been my experience that the public at large are not idiots and can spot phoneys instantly. It is never the public at large that objects to programmes, it is usually well-organised, well-drilled groups that act in concert.

A great example of this was the time Adrian gave an off-the-cuff comment to someone from the *RTE Guide* who was planning to do a page on our coming back into the schedule after the summer holidays. He revealed that we had organised an appearance by a pair of lesbian nuns.

These two nuns had already revealed their 'secret' in public, had gone into print about it elsewhere, and were serious women. But when the item was announced in the *Guide*, there was a deluge of the most obscene letters, telegrams and telephone calls to us, individually and collectively. There were committees formed and prayer vigils held, and it became a hysterical topic for the letters columns of the newspapers. Remember, all of this was on the basis, not of a programme or an item they had *seen* but on something that had only been mentioned in the *RTE Guide*. Some callers were quite honest, saying that they had been contacted and told to organise a pyramid group: each person who phoned was to get ten more people to phone.

☐

I would not budge an inch, and to give RTE its due the station did not either. I had contacted a priest, Fr Raphael Gallagher, a theologian, and an Irish nun, Sr Maura from the Daughters of Sion in Balinter, Navan, whom I have known for twenty years and for whom I have an inordinate respect and liking. They were to join the panel with our two lesbian nuns. On the night in question there were people down at the RTE gate with placards, and there were people praying around the building and showering us with holy water.

People frequently ask me how I keep my nerve in the face of such intimidation. The truth is, I am not intimidated. For instance, before this show many of the half-mad hysterical callers to our office concluded their rantings by telling us that everyone—but *everyone*—in RTE is a long-haired weirdo, a drug addict, and a communist agent paid directly from Moscow, is in favour of divorce, contraception, and abortion, is an adulterer, has herpes and AIDS, is a poof and a lesbian. It is a familiar litany—and might have been very depressing had I not tuned in to 'The Secret Diaries of Adrian Mole' on ITV that week. In the episode, Adrian was complaining to his granddad that his poems had once again been rejected by the BBC. His granddad advised him not to worry about being turned down by the BBC, because, he said, it was a well-known fact that everyone—but *everyone*—in the BBC is a long-haired weirdo, a drug addict, and a communist agent paid directly from Moscow . . .

Anyway, I deliberately left the nuns' item to the last half-hour of the show, and as a result, we got the highest TAM rating achieved by *any* show in RTE in the history of the station. It exceeded even the rating for the Pope's visit to Ireland, ending up with an average TAM rating of 76 over the entire two hours, which means that the actual rating for most of it would have been 80. This gives the lie to the people who complain that *if they had only known in advance* what was objectionable/filthy/immoral they might have had time to lock up their impressionable 19-year-olds . . . (And at eleven o'clock, just before the item, I actually warned them that if they were worried about this item they should switch off.) This TAM rating shows that people stayed glued to their sets. Even the ones who sent us Mass cards as a comfort for us when we are in Hell . . .

The ladies came on, the item went smoothly, and at the end, everyone looked at everyone else: 'Is that what all the fuss was about?' 'Yes, that was what all the fuss was about—*we* didn't make the fuss!' And not a bleep out of any of them afterwards . . .

I believe that this was one of the instances when we tapped in to the vigilant army, those people poised permanently on the knife-edge of hysteria, just waiting for something to happen on television about which

☐

to go bananas. Submarines under the Irish sea, s-e-x, hormones in meat—you name it, they are ready.

Not as bad as the lesbian nuns, but quite bad, was the reaction to the night we decided to have the statue-breakers on. There had been an epidemic of mass sightings of miraculously moving statues around the country, seen at more than thirty locations, attended nightly by thousands of people. These two men, who belonged to a self-styled true Christian sect, objected to the idolatry, and attacked with hammers and hatchets the main statue, the mammy of moving statues, the one in Ballinspittle. The news got out that they were to be on the 'Late Late'.

For some reason a campaign began about having these guys on television. It was going to be an affront to the Catholic Church, and would corrupt the morals of the young, etc. It was perfectly clear to me that they were a pair of misguided noodleheads who had got a great deal of newspaper publicity, very little of which gave any answers to the question of why they did the dirty deed in the first place. I just wanted to find that out. In spite of the reservations of many people, we went ahead with the item, and, as in the case of the lesbian nuns, it ran smoothly; and I believe that everyone in the country watching that night saw these people for what they were, a pair of violent, misguided clowns. What they badly needed and deserved was a swift toe up their rear ends and a warning not to step out of line again—or else. Having been identified on the 'Late Late Show', that's precisely what they got. They've not been heard of from that day to this and the statues of Ireland are safe—as long as they don't move.

On the other hand, there was plenty of follow-up to our AIDS programme, which handled the whole subject, particularly the transmission of the disease and prevention of that transmission, with complete frankness, including a lecture by me on the use of a condom. I think it was probably the first time that an Irish television programme had shown these items and had demonstrated their use, and I feared that there might be an outcry. But the reaction afterwards showed a maturity that gave me hope. There were the usual crowd— 'I was watching with my 19-year-old son,' etc. (the poor young innocent)—but they were outnumbered three to one by the letters that outlined the trouble they had taken to ensure that their 14-year-old daughters had watched, or by those who wrote to say how much they appreciated such a candid approach and the fair way the subject was handled.

For some guests, we will move heaven and earth to attract them on, as far as our resources allow. Our budget is minuscule, and we rely on Irish connections, international good will, or just plain chutzpah, the hardest of hard Jewish neck, as defined by one of the easiest guests we have ever had, Sammy

Cahn. Sammy is the antithesis of Dermot Kelly. All you need with Sammy is to have a list of song titles, to mention them one by one, and Sammy is up and running—leaving you very little space to interject a single word.

Sammy writes wonderful songs ('Pocketful of Miracles', 'Love and Marriage', 'Three Coins in the Fountain', 'All the Way') but sings like a crow and plays the piano like a one-armed gorilla. Sammy's definition of chutzpah is the day he went in to see Mario Lanza with his new song, which, he just knew, would be right for the tenor, who was at the time an international megastar. He handed the sheet-music to the great man, who said, 'I don't take songs from the dots—I like to *hear* songs.'

So there and then, Sammy, the one-armed gorilla, sat at the piano and cawed 'Be My Love' for Mario Lanza. 'Now *that*', said Sammy triumphantly, 'is *chutzpah!*'

It is a great relief to the brain to know that you have an old pro like Sammy on the show, where you know that all you have to do is press the right button and sit back to enjoy the ride.

Des O'Connor is like Sammy. There are five points for Des. The night he was nearly fired off his own show; how all the slagging of him from Morecambe and Wise came about; his new wife and baby ('The wife now has a baby—at long last she has somebody her own age to play with'); his singing career; and golf. He is such a pro that it is unlikely you will get to the golf.

Peter Ustinov is another such old reliable. In fact, it has come to my attention that Ustinov is like a one-person public relations firm for the 'Late Late', in that he tells all and sundry all over the world about us and how we are the greatest. He has an endless fund of stories and anecdotes, complete with totally accurate ethnic accents. My favourite is about the time he was invited to Ireland a number of years ago as part of a Bord Fáilte incentive group tour. The group was being shepherded around by Tom Sheehy, and the tour started in Dublin. There were several Americans and people of other nationalities in the group, including a tiny Japanese man who was the Professor of Celtic Studies in Tokyo University.

In they go to Mulligan's in Poolbeg Street. Tom goes into his spiel: 'Now this, ladies and gentlemen, is a very famous pub indeed; this is the pub where James Joyce is reputed to have written many of his best stories, especially those in the *Dubliners* series. And if you look over there at that little table there, you'll see a little blob of ink in the middle of that table, and that is reputed to be the very table where James Joyce was sitting when his pen gave trouble and in his temper he blotted the ink. And that ink is there ever since. That ink, there now' (pause for dramatic effect) '*belonged actually to James Joyce—*'

RTE

☐ *Taken after the Late Late one night when we were about to lose Colman Hutchinson to STV in Southampton and Mary O'Sullivan to the Clothes Show. This includes general studio crew, sound, cameras, technicians as well as our own programme team.*

IRISH PRESS

☐ *With Christopher Reeve (Superman), and Jane Seymour in action for Group W in Philadelphia.*

□

The little Japanese interrupted. 'Iss not so!' Stunned silence from rest of company, all heads swivel towards Japanese. 'Iss not collect! This pub not James Joyce pub. James Joyce pub, other pub' (he points down the Liffey) ' —this pub, Oriver St John Gogarty!'

Thereafter, poor Tom Sheehy, no matter where he went, to whatever church, cathedral, or castle, would stand in front of his group: 'Now these Doric columns, ladies and gentlemen, date from— ' (nodding over his shoulder towards the Japanese man) 'now correct me if I'm wrong— '

Unlike Sammy Cahn, Des O'Connor, or Peter Ustinov, some guests have to be handled very carefully. Fred Astaire was due to do a movie here called *The Purple Taxi* with Peter Ustinov. He had a sister, Adele, who lives in Lismore, and a daughter, Ava, who has a holiday home in Schull; and needless to remark, over the years the 'Late Late' had made contact with the two of them in an effort to snag him, but without success. He was aging gracefully, but I believe he mourned his lost agility and was not anxious to be reminded of it.

While on holiday, Kay and I happened to be driving in west Cork, and just for the hell of it I decided to pay a call on Ava and her husband, the artist Richard McKenzie. Ava was sympathetic and helpful, but she could not guarantee anything about her father. But we got on very well together, and irrespective of Fred we became friendly, and the McKenzies returned the call, visiting us in Howth.

Fred arrived to do the movie. He was staying in the old Hibernian Hotel in Dawson Street, where Ava remembers coming down one of the dark corridors towards his room on one occasion. His door was open and the television was on, showing some old black-and-white musical movie. All on his own, his back to the door, Fred was swaying and doing a little one-two to the music, far away in some happier, younger place . . . She broke in gently and put a bit of pressure on him to do the 'Late Late Show'. He was most reluctant, but finally agreed. I had to go and see him a few times, and realised that he would not be a sparkling guest, but Fred Astaire was Fred Astaire, and we were going to have him.

There were two preconditions. One was that I would not ask him to perform, which was understandable; but the second astonished me. By chance, Bill Harpur, the man responsible for the movies on RTE, had a feast of old Fred Astaire movies available on the shelf. There was an Astaire season scheduled, and for once, we could have any clip we wanted. I told Fred this, and asked him which clips he would favour. He answered that he did not mind, with one exception. There were to be no clips shown on the 'Late Late Show' featuring him with Ginger Rogers. Her alone; him alone; him with anyone else—but *not* him with Ginger.

☐

There had always been rumours in show business about enmity between Fred and Ginger, always discounted by both of them. Now here was Fred seeming to confirm it. I asked him in a circuitous way why he did not want the clips used. And several times he said: 'Well, you know Ginger was just a can-can dancer when I met her . . .' Obviously he had his own little scale of excellence, and can-can was nowhere near the top. All these years later, he would not allow it to contaminate his own memory.

He was well received on the show, and naturally running through the whole item was the unspoken request for him to do a little warble. During the day of the show his attitude had appeared to soften somewhat and he seemed to be a little more relaxed. My hopes had risen. I was not going to break my word about asking him to sing, but maybe some way around it could be found, leaving us both with honour intact. The pianist Jim Doherty and a small combo were on semi-standby on the set.

I finished the interview, and then I said: 'There is a man over here who is one of Ireland's greatest piano-players, and he is one of your greatest fans and he knows all your numbers, and he would just like to shake your hand.' Fred rose obligingly and walked across to Jim and shook his hand. It was one of those moments that you have to grab or lose. It was the moment when, if he had been at all inclined, he could have said, 'Do you know "Cheek-to-Cheek" in E flat?' Or I could have said something, despite my promise to Ava; or Jim could have said something. None of us said anything, and the moment passed. I was sad. Should I have done the killer thing and forced the situation?

Charm goes a long way on television. Like everyone else in the world, I fell completely under David Niven's spell. He was one of life's natural charmers, with impeccable manners. He could not come to Dublin, so in December 1975 I went over to London to interview him in the BBC's automated Henry Wood Studio.

David was one of those inveterate, incurable gigglers who, even when they are telling the same story for the umpteenth time, still find it excruciatingly funny and make you giggle too. Life to him was one long giggle. Some people use drugs or alcohol to escape the awfulness of the world. I am firmly convinced that he consciously used humour. Even when in the last stages of the dreadful, wasting motor neurone disease, of which he died, humour was what sustained him.

About three weeks before he died, he was standing at the front gate of his house in Gstaad, in Switzerland, and a neighbour passed by: 'Morning, Niven! How are you?'

By this stage, David's speech had slowed, and movement was very difficult. But he answered as cheerfully as he could: 'Oh, I'm not bad, thank you, but I have motor neurone disease . . .'

'Oh, really?' said the neighbour with interest. 'I've just bought a new BMW myself.' And walked on.

David thought this was the funniest, most hilarious thing he had ever heard.

He also had that capacity, which I always believe is the essence of charm, to make you believe that while you were with him, you were the most important person in his life. So it was a dream interview, gliding along on feathery, timeless wheels. One of the film clips I played in was from his Oscar-winning performance in the movie *Separate Tables* with Deborah Kerr. Watching it, his eyes filled: 'All that time ago—I have never seen that scene, you know; or if I did, I don't remember it.'

I wish he was around so I could interview him again and again. And someone, somewhere has a tape of that interview. It has disappeared out of the RTE archives.

Sometimes, the behind-the-scenes show is more entertaining, and often more bizarre, than what appears on screen. Another big international star, Peter Sellers, had moved to Ireland to live in the penthouse suite of Castletown House during the filming of the movie *Hoffman*, which starred Sinéad Cusack. Our researcher Tony Boland, who lived near there, had made all the preliminary overtures to try to get him to come on the 'Late Late Show', and found that he was quite amenable. I went out to Castletown to talk to him and to finalise the arrangements, and found him to be thoroughly charming, a gentle fellow. Out of the blue, a day or two later, he telephoned, inviting me to dinner at Castletown. Kathleen and I arrived at the appointed time, knocked on the correct door, and waited for an answer.

We waited. And waited.

Finally, Sellers himself opened the door. He was completely, egg-shiny bald. He had shaved every single rib of hair off his head. He smiled beatifically and invited us in. It became one of those whatever-you-do-don't-mention-the-war situations. Oh please, dear God, don't let me look at the head . . .

His wife, Miranda, was nowhere in sight. Sellers told us that she was getting ready upstairs. He footled around, ambling amiably in the vastness of the room we were in, chatting now and then when he felt the urge. We sat, waxwork dummies, trying to pretend that this was the sort of occasion with which we were completely at ease.

He mentioned casually that he had been in touch with his mother earlier that day. We knew his mother was long since dead. He mentioned that

□

Miranda was delayed upstairs because she had lost 'the key to the cutlery box' and he was was helping her to find it. He produced a sort of talisman in the shape of a cross on the end of a chain, swinging it to and fro like a pendulum six inches from the floor, remarking that his mother was going to help him to find this key, and the thing on the end of the chain would point to its exact location. For a moment, I wondered were we included in a sort of Goon gag.

Then a huge man arrived in to join our happy little gang. He was at last six feet six inches tall, and Sellers introduced him as his valet. Afterwards, we discovered that the 'valet' was in fact a psychiatric nurse. In the course of that day this man had gone off to do something, leaving his charge to his own devices, one of which devices was a Philishave, which he promptly used to defoliate his head.

Strangely enough, the small dinner party went off happily enough. Even Miranda, when she eventually joined us, seemed to have a good time. Sellers told funny stories and, pate shining in the candlelight, was a charming host. The dinner party was on a Thursday night, and the following Saturday morning, the morning of the show, I got a call from the minder to say that Mr Sellers would be along, as agreed, to do the 'Late Late' that night, but on no account was anything to be said by anyone, including the other guests, about the hair. So I telephoned the other guests, Éamonn Andrews and Jackie McGowran (sad to think that all three are now dead), to say, 'Whatever-you-do-don't-mention-the-hair!' I also warned all the staff.

Everything went fine. All three were in the hospitality suite before the show, chatting, cracking jokes, getting on well together. No-one said a word about the hair, and everyone kept their eyes firmly below eye-level. The show began. Éamonn came on and did his stint, Jack came on and did his, and both were well received by the audience. Then: 'Ladies and gentlemen, would you welcome, please, Peter Sellers!'

On comes Sellers, with all of his head and half of his face hidden underneath a huge German war helmet. He wore it during the entire show, its poll gleaming under the lights, while we all tried valiantly not to mention it. No-one had told the audience not to mention it, however, and finally one of them ventured to ask him: 'Mr Sellers, why are you wearing the helmet?'

'Why not?' answered Mr Sellers with his nicest smile. End of query. End of story.

I think I have the self-preserving facility, as do a lot of very busy journalists and others who meet and deal with hundreds if not thousands of people every year, of allowing my conscious brain to remain stocked only

□

to a certain level of recognition of people I have met and interviewed. I know that physically the memory is supposed to be limitless, but I certainly have cordoned off only a certain area for names and faces.

For instance, once I had as a guest the very pleasant and very British actor Michael York. He was so pleasant, in fact, that once home after the show, I mentioned to Kathleen that he was one of the nicest people we had ever had on. But only three years later, Pan Collins watched in horror from her recuperative couch as, Michael York having come on, hand outstretched, 'Hello, Gay, nice to see you,' I blithely informed the audience that although we had not had the pleasure of Mr York's company previously, his face would no doubt be familiar to them. It certainly was not familiar to me.

On the other hand, there are some nights I would like to forget but cannot. They provide stories on which to dine out; but while they are in progress you begin to wonder why you ever voluntarily agreed to become a broadcaster.

One such show happened on 20 November 1982. We knew that R. D. Laing, the noted Scottish psychiatrist, was in town. He had given a lecture to Ivor Browne and his colleagues in the Eastern Health Board the previous Wednesday night. We did know that he had started this lecture with an open whiskey bottle in his hand, and had slugged from it throughout the lecture until it was almost gone. We did know that some doctors had left in disgust.

But as part of her research, Mary O'Sullivan had interviewed him on tape in his hotel, and because she had met him in the morning she had found him to be quite cogent. We decided to risk having him on, but realised that to keep him cogent it would be necessary to arrange for him to be 'minded' throughout the Saturday. This we did, arranging for two stalwarts to watch what the great man put in his mouth.

Adrian Cronin was going through reception at about nine o'clock that Saturday night, on his way upstairs to the gallery to start the count-down to the show, and he saw three people coming across the car park, footless, like a re-run from the Three Stooges. He turned back down the stairs and he said to the commissionaire: 'Do you see those three guys coming across the car park? If they are trying to get in to the 'Late Late', even if they have tickets, no way, no way are they to be let past this desk. Call the police if you have to, if they get obstreperous.' Then he continued on his way. He was just getting to the door of the gallery when the breathless commissionaire came running up: 'Mr Cronin, Mr Cronin, they're your *guests* for the show. That's Dr Laing and his friends . . .'

It so happened that Ivor Browne was in the reception area. He was not there for the 'Late Late': he had a book that he had borrowed from Laing

□

and simply wanted to return it. Knowing that Laing was booked for the show, Ivor knew he would be going through reception at about this time and was waiting for him.

Adrian by this time was knocking at my dressing-room door: 'Get out here, fast . . .' I come out into the corridor. 'What's going on?'

I look up the corridor. Maura is on one side of Laing, huge Ivor on the other, each holding an arm, all three bouncing like some ghastly misshapen beach-ball from one wall to the other. It is now ten past nine, and Laing is first on the show.

As they continue their bouncing progress towards me, Ivor shakes his head. His meaning is clear. There was just no way this guy could be allowed on. I venture a stupid question directly to the drooping, sagging figure in front of me. Has he been drinking, I want to know.

He swivels his too-heavy head on his neck in an effort to find where the question had come from. He considers his answer: 'I migh' have had *one* . . .' (he ponders, lost in deep thought) 'or maybe *two* . . .'

Ivor shakes his head again: 'Minimum of a bottle,' he mouths at me. Then, like the good man he is, he volunteers to try to sober up the bleary Laing with coffee and fresh air and psychiatry or whatever it takes, but advises me not to count on anything.

Meanwhile, up in make-up, sipping a quiet gin-and-tonic, secure in the knowledge that she is the second interviewee and will not be needed until about ten past ten, sits the second guest, Viv Nicholson, the English-woman of 'Spend, Spend, Spend' fame, who won a fortune on the pools and who went to pieces as a result. Someone rushes in to make-up, yanks the protective overall from around her shoulders, and frog-marches her down to the studio. She is now the lead item.

The unfortunate woman is in such a state of shock that her interview dies. Into a break. What's the word? They all shake their heads; no, no.

Get Emmylou Harris on fast, sing the song, get her off. Into a break. What's the word? They all shake their heads; no, no.

Next item; more music; frantically get the piano where it's supposed to be and move the drums; dammit. Into a break. What's the word? No.

Ulick O'Connor . . . He's finished. *Now* what's the word?

There is an added complication in that the former American presidential candidate George McGovern is in the line-up, but the deal with him was that he had to be on at precisely eleven o'clock and off at precisely 11.25. He is guest of honour at a dinner that evening at a venue outside Dublin and has to get back to it. We are sworn to stick to his timetable. If Laing cannot be interviewed, there is a huge, yawning, terrifying gap before eleven o'clock.

197

□

Finally, Ivor sends a message that Laing is probably as good as he will ever be, and that he, Ivor, will come on with him as a security precaution, because he would probably be able to answer some of the questions. A most generous act of charity.

They arrive on the set. It is obvious to a one-eyed Martian that Laing is still three sheets in the wind, and needless to say, the switchboard lights up immediately with every self-righteous ex-bibber in Ireland demanding to know what had RTE and Gay Byrne and the 'Late Late Show' come to.

Although Laing achieves the stringing together of words in some sort of order, he is desperately, painfully slow, and Ulick, who has moved to one of the panel seats, can contain himself no longer. 'Why are you drunk?' he demands to know, with all the finesse and tact that only Ulick can muster on such occasions. I decide to row in—after all, Ulick is a guest too—and I repeat the question. 'Yes—why *are* you drunk?'

Laing sways backwards and forwards in the chair with attempted outrage, an attempt that fails miserably as he tries to click his fingers for emphasis: 'You . . . jusht wan' shomeone to . . . talk *fasht*— '(failed click, failed click) 'I *conshider*' (he attempts to click again and misses) '*wha*' I am going to shay . . .'

With that, one of the two minders we had assigned for the day in an effort to prevent this sort of thing interjects from the audience. They had been separated from their new buddy when Ivor took over, and are seated in the audience. How dare I insult such an eminent professor in such a manner!

'All I want to find out is why such an eminent psychiatrist, who has known for three weeks that he is to come on the show, would jeopardise his appearance by drinking so much— '

'Dhrink! *Dhrink!*' Such an unfair, such an appalling slander . . .

Ulick decides to defend me and attacks them, and as usual will not shut up, and they shout back, and the whole show starts to go down the tubes. Meanwhile George McGovern has arrived . . .

Next day, and for days afterwards, the abuse flew. From the initial self-righteousness about allowing someone like that on the air, the invective swung 180 degrees towards yours truly. I got abuse from journalists, and from every drunk in the business. The most charitable thing I was called was a prig.

The following Monday I had to be in the Burlington Hotel in the late morning, in connection with the Housewife of the Year competition. There was a woman seated in the lobby clutching a letter. She called me over: 'Funny I should run into you this morning, I was just going up to Montrose with a message for you!'

I thanked her, and went upstairs to the meeting. In the room I opened

RTE

☐ *Mary O'Sullivan and I having a ball on the Toy Show.*

RTE

☐ *Maura Connolly (during her long-haired period) and June Levine with Ms Lilian Carter, mother of the President.*

the letter, to find that it was a long tirade of abuse, calling me names, castigating me for my treatment of the unfortunate Dr Laing. I was a cur, ill-mannered and obnoxious, and it was time I learned my place; also, how dare I suggest that the man was drunk? So I came back down in the lift and I asked one of the waiters in the lobby who she was. 'Don't know,' said the waiter, 'but she's in here most mornings. Drinks like a fish—she's on her sixth gin-and-tonic.' It was about noon.

But the most amazing memory I have about the whole episode is that while we were all in the hospitality suite after the show, all the best of friends, although still trying to pour coffee into our eminent psychiatrist, I went up to him and said quietly, 'Look, all I wanted to know was why you were drinking. Knowing your high reputation and that you were coming on to a public show, why did you do it?'

And he said, interestedly: 'I think tha's a very . . . fair question! A very *jushtifiable* question.' He focused unsteadily: 'And, indeed, if I had had time I migh' have given you a ver' *intereshting* answer . . .'

Several years later we had him on again, and he was perfectly fine, played the piano, sang and all. In the words of Synge's Pegeen Mike, ' 'Tis true for Father Reilly that all drink's a curse.'

Laing got on because of the special circumstances and the hole in the show before George McGovern arrived; but, like every other live show, we have had occasion not to allow people on the air because they were so much the worse for wear. One or two drinks before an appearance can calm natural nerves, but that would be about the limit of safety. One who is a law unto himself in this regard, however, is Oliver Reed. If you invite Oliver on to your show, you take the consequences. I was reminiscing about Oliver recently with Des O'Connor, who has his own show in Britain and who had more or less the same experience as I had.

Oliver Reed does not come on to a show, he makes an entrance. In my case, I took one look into his eyes and realised there was nobody home. But in the course of his discursive interview, he insisted on proving that he was not drunk. He took an ordinary kitchen chair and performed a very impressive circus trick, standing on it on his hands, feet straight up in the air, holding the position for quite a considerable period. He got a wonderful round of applause. Coming back down, he miscalculated, and it looked as though he was going to break his back. Susan George, who was also on the show, shot forward instinctively to help him, and she stumbled and fell. He fell on top of her—deliberately, I am quite convinced, because once on top of her he stayed on top of her, quite at home and obviously loving every moment of it.

As it became clearer and clearer just how thoroughly he was enjoying

□

himself and that he had no intention whatsoever of getting off Susan George, the rest of us stood around helplessly, saying ineffectual things like 'Come on, Oliver, be a good egg!' and 'Get up off Susan, willya?' —or things equally asinine. We eventually hauled him off, and the interview continued.

My Oliver Reed experience was not as bad as the one suffered by poor old Des O'Connor, who, also on seeing Reed's eyes, knew instantly that he was in trouble. Hoping to make the most of the situation, he decided to abandon his research and to ask the most banal questions he could think of, so that Reed would not make a show of them all. Reed managed it anyhow.

'I believe you have a tattoo on your bum?' asks Des.

'Not only that, but I'll show you,' answers our Oliver, and before anyone can stop him he has lowered his trousers and displayed the tattoo, which was not on his bum at all but somewhere much more private. That, at least, has never happened on the 'Late Late Show' . . .

Then there was the night we had a celebration of the centenary of the Irish Rugby Football Union. Such glitz! Photographs of Lansdowne team of nineteen-oh-dot and—oh joy!—the Wanderers team of nineteen hundred and thirty-tumty. And just imagine, folks: who was in that picture but the father of someone on the Wanderers team of nineteen hundred and six! If you can have an exaltation of larks (or a fluff of radio announcers), this was a constipation of a 'Late Late Show'. To be charitable, maybe my memory of it is coloured by my own stunning lack of interest in rugby football, or any ball game, but God, how they all competed with each other in a miniature Olympics of boredom!

For having gone through that, I think God should reward me by giving me my allotted time with my two fantasy interviewees, Ms Jane Fonda and/or Ms Meryl Streep. And not for the reasons you think, gentle reader. I would genuinely like to find out more about either or both of them. On the other hand, wouldn't everybody?

Maybe I should hang on until this dream becomes reality. But if I am spurned, as no doubt I will be, I cannot see myself at the helm of the 'Late Late Show' beyond 1992. Thirty years of the same show should be enough for anyone; and even if RTE decides to continue the show I may take myself off it at that point—maybe!

At the time of the station's (and the 'Late Late Show's') twenty-fifth birthday, I was genuinely depressed to think that the biggest names in RTE television were *still* Gay Byrne, Mike Murphy, and Brian Farrell. I thought that was a sad reflection on the corporation, an admission that there had been no really persistent and vital effort made to find and groom new

□

presenters, new stars, new identities. I know there is a major difference between good, competent, efficient, workmanlike broadcasters on the one hand, and marketable, saleable broadcasters on the other, and I know the latter do not come by the front door every day. But I still thought it was bad that we did not have a stable of new people, that the place was still stuck with Gaybo and Micky. And I said so at the time.

I have to admit that in the past four years the situation has changed dramatically. Shay Healy, Ronan Collins, Bibi Baskin, Gerry Ryan, Marty Whelan, Derek Davis—there are at least a dozen relatively new names in the presenter category who can handle any show the station cares to throw their way and they will come up smiling. Which is as it should be.

CHAPTER 10
NEW BEGINNINGS – ALMOST

■

Another of the questions I am frequently asked is why I never settled in America when I did try it, those few summers in the eighties.

I was still going through the deepest, darkest throes of the CRM affair when we broke up for the 'Late Late' summer recess in 1984. I had been in New York during the season to host RTE's NATAS (National Academy of Television and Screen) annual presentation at the Lincoln Centre. This was a showcase for the best RTE had to offer, and the hope was that we would make sales. The presentation, apparently, including my own contribution, went down well.

Because I had to be there, we did the 'Late Late' out of New York, from the CBS studios on 47th Street, live as usual, via satellite, although it was a little strange to be broadcasting it in the middle of the afternoon. Obviously, during that type of mission at that level one meets people, and I met plenty of them, but I was genuinely unaware that some of them were making strenuous efforts to view recordings of the 'Late Late Show'.

Later that season, some members of NATAS were doing what they call a reciprocal 'off-shore trip' to Ireland, so RTE had to reciprocate the hospitality it had received while in New York. In true Irish style, the hospitality was lavish (and very alcoholic!). The delegates were taken to Ashford Castle and to the medieval banquet at Bunratty and all the usual spots and ended up at a farewell drinks party at the Shelbourne Hotel, to which I went along.

Bill Baker, the boss of the Westinghouse television divison, Group W, which has twenty television stations and as many radio stations across the States on its books, approached me there and asked casually if I had ever thought of working in America. Unthinkingly, I said, 'Well, yes, it would be nice,' or something equally inane. He went on, flatteringly, to say that he had seen more than thirty 'Late Lates' and how impressive I had been at the NATAS presentation and all the rest of it, and I nodded pleasantly. In the course of the conversation he said that the buzz in the States was that 'talk shows' were dead except for Johnny Carson. He said that he thought the buzz was correct, but that the decline of the talk show was only temporary, and that there would be a renaissance. I agreed politely, wasn't that interesting, etc., but really I did not take it very seriously. I had had many abortive offers in the past, and I had learned not to take anything very seriously.

So, off I went on my summer holidays. One day, I had to be in Montrose for something—I forget what—and as I pulled in to the car park I saw Dick Hill. Dick flagged me down, relief all over his face: 'Thank God I've found you, we were desperately worried you might be in Donegal. Can you come to lunch right now in Restaurant na Mara in Dún Laoghaire with Niall McCarthy and me and a few people from Westinghouse who want to meet us?'

We went out to the restaurant and met three of the Group W bosses, Larry Fraiberg, George Moynihan, and Tom Goodgame. It had not occurred to me to ask why we were there; I assumed that this was simply another one of those dreary meetings where they were going to bargain with us that if they took some of the 'Late Late', we would, in return, take some of their output. (I subsequently found that Dick Hill did not know why we were there either, that he was simply responding to a message from the Director-General, George Waters, that he had to meet these people, and that I had to be there too.)

We had a nice lunch and a few drinks and easy conversation about the business here and across the water. Around the coffee stage, Larry Fraiberg turned to me and said, 'How do you *feel* about living in America?'

Dick Hill gulped. Niall McCarthy swallowed. I gave what I hoped was an insouciant chuckle and said airily, 'Oh, that'd be lovely—you just make me an offer and I'll be on the next plane.' Fraiberg said very little after that.

We finished lunch, and still there was no mention of bartering or the 'Late Late', and still the penny had not dropped with me. But I gave the other two, Goodgame and Moynihan, a lift back to the Gresham Hotel, and as we were travelling I asked what the lunch had been about. I found it difficult to believe that three busy men would have come all the way to Restaurant na Mara just for lunch, yet there had been no mention of business.

Did I not know? they asked. And I said I did not, that I had just been told today to meet them for lunch on some kind of urgent business.

And then they told me. They had tried to get in touch with me through the Director-General and had been told to get in touch with Dick Hill and Niall McCarthy, and they were mystified, they said, since they had no business with them at all. Their business was with me. They wanted to offer me an opportunity to do a show in America.

And we were all people in the communications business!

It was too late to do any business that day—they were on their way to London. They returned the following week through Dublin, and we met for lunch in the Gresham Hotel. George and Larry were forthright and down-to-earth. Group W had not had a network talk show since Mike Douglas had left them; he'd been on the air five days a week for fifteen years, out of Philadelphia. Group W wanted a replacement, and they thought Gay Byrne was it. The risk was great, and they spelled it out: briefly, I would start with a local show in, say, Boston or Philadelphia; if it went well, then in time it would be bought by the other stations in the Group W chain. Over a period (and always provided that talk shows made Bill Baker's predicted come-back), if the show got established and popular, then it might—repeat *might*—go network.

If that happened, then Gaybo would be up there with Johnny Carson, Merv Griffin, and Donahue. Group W was prepared to take the chance. The question was, was Gay Byrne? The best that could happen was that we'd all make the big time; the worst, that Gaybo would be dropped after a year or two and come creeping back home with his tail between his legs. Like marriage, television shows do not come with a written guarantee.

(It is worth pointing out that against all the trends at that time, Bill Baker's prophecy about the return of talk shows on American television has turned out to be spot-on. Ten out of ten for the crystal-ball man. Now, if the rest of his vision went the same way . . .)

They offered two options as to how it would be worked. The first was that I would move to America—family, lock, stock and barrel—and they would pay all moving expenses and provide an apartment. The second was that I would commute, as David Frost had done, travelling over on a Sunday, doing live shows Monday, Tuesday, Wednesday, and in the meantime recording shows for Thursday and Friday. On Thursday I would travel back to Ireland, arriving back on Friday morning to do the 'Late Late'. (When I outlined that option at home, Kay said, 'Yes—and would they give you a contribution for your gravestone?')

I agreed to go to Philadelphia to do two pilot shows the following January, but still there was no commitment one way or the other. I told the whole story to the 'Late Late' gang but warned them that the information was absolutely confidential. And to give them their due, nothing leaked until the day I actually got home from doing the pilots. And I know that the leak was from America and not from here.

The pilots went very well indeed. One of the guests on one of the shows was Donald O'Connor, of whom I had been a fan since the days of Francis the Talking Mule in the Rialto cinema. We had had him on the 'Late Late', and he was good if not brilliant, one of the more pleasant if not memorable interviews, and I was not expecting anything terrific this time either. But he had always been one of my heroes, and one of my all-time favourite musical numbers is the all-singing, all-dancing 'Make 'Em Laugh', which is indelibly associated with him. So when the chance arose to have him on the American show, I was very pleased.

At the time I had met him in Ireland he was fat and unhealthy and had a serious drink problem. This time he was a different person: lively, fit and well, and having clearly conquered his problem with alcohol. He talked about his early life and his family, Irish and very numerous and all in the circus, all involved in the various disciplines like tight-rope walking and trapeze and juggling. He painted a dreadful picture of being born in a trunk and dragging through this awful itinerant life-style where they chased cheap jobs and were always hungry as they travelled forward and backwards across the United States in the car in which they also ate and slept.

Times were very hard. He told horrendous stores about trekking five hundred miles to get a job, and, having performed with a circus for a week, the proprietor would do a bunk and leave them with no money. There were stories about picking scraps off rubbish dumps or at the side of the road or of begging for food. Then the family would hear of a circus somewhere else and they would sell something or pawn something to get enough money for petrol to get there. They busked and danced in the streets.

It was a wonderful interview, and I knew it. The audience was gripped in that deep, wonderful silence that is so rare in a television studio. I was totally engrossed myself. Even the producer of the show, in which, as in all American television, the commercial break was the prime consideration, realised what was happening and allowed the interview to run over the commercial breaks for a full twenty-five minutes, almost unheard of in commercial television in the United States.

At the end of the interview I asked him to sing. I thought I would get the brush-off—it was a long time since he had performed, and old stars are notoriously vain and touchy—but he looked across at the piano player and said, 'Do you know "A Foggy Day in London Town"?' and the guy did. So he sang a few bars and even ended up with four bars of a little dance. It was exhilarating and moving at the same time.

He tore the place down and me with it. I sat there listening to the audience going bananas, and I knew that I had just done one of the best interviews I was ever likely to do in my life. It was a glorious feeling, but blighted with the agony of frustration that it could not have happened on the 'Late Late' since, if it had, I could have extended the interview almost indefinitely.

RTE

☐ *How do I always end up on the show getting stuck with tall men making me look even smaller than I am? Alan Dukes delving into the middle on one of the first postal quiz draws. And when Richard Keil talks, you listen. A most gentlemanly man, usually cast in the role of a murderous monster, especially in 007 escapades.*

RTE

□

For the other pilot I was told that one of the guests, Christopher Reeves—big, burly Superman—was a bit of a woodener, and that he rarely said much during interviews. I found, when I chatted to him before the show, that, on the contrary, he was charming and articulate and, what was more, we shared a love of flying (geddit?) and an enthusiasm for small planes. We were getting on so well that I decided to chance asking him to play the piano. He did the usual demurring act, but I knew that he was wavering, and, with the encouragement of the audience, I led him over to the piano, which he played, if not brilliantly at least adequately. He was playing a very gentle, soft song, and the lighting director, who was really on the ball, brought down the studio lights to a romantic golden pool that bathed this hunk and his piano. I went for broke. I leaned seductively across the piano, looked out at the audience, and said softly, 'Girls! Just imagine: a fire blazing up a chimney, a white sheepskin rug . . . and just the two of you!' The audience again broke up, and he was pinkly thrilled, and old Gaybo was not too unhappy at his own daring.

There were no guarantees going with this job should I decide to take it, I knew that. The Group W people were very straight with me: they warned me about the chauvinism and conservatism of the American public. Given the best possible scenario, and even if the networks did take up my show, no matter how good it was I would always be a foreigner.

And I also knew, after I got home from doing the pilots, that there was going to be a hiatus of six weeks, and probably more, before I would hear anything at all from them, since the decision-makers were going to India for that period and would be out of touch with everything that might affect me.

That did not stop the newspaper speculation. The story of my American deal broke, and all hell was let loose. I was definitely going, I was definitely not going. They had me damned, ringing me every day to try to find out if I had heard anything. And when I could not help them, they went into print anyway. (Any time I am tempted to take seriously what newspapers write about me, I think of the stories I have heard about Kathleen and me. I have heard on different occasions that (a) we are supposed to be splitting up and returning the girls to 'the orphanage', or that (b) Kathleen is 'above in John o' God's', drying out!) The *Evening Press* published a *definite* story that today, Gay Byrne went to his superiors in RTE and said he would be *definitely* leaving; and Al and Mary rang up, upset and full of concern. The will-he-won't-he speculation dragged on for two-and-a-half months, most of which was taken up with this period of non-communication between myself and Group W.

Kathleen started the period quite optimistic about a future in America,

□

but then, as the time passed, she looked around at 'Onslow' and the quality of our lives here, and her enthusiasm began to fade. Crona was very happy at the notion of going to America—she would go anywhere, I believe; Suzy was reluctant. I was still considering it, but less and less enthusiastically. Prudently, as is my habit, I had my own scouts in the United States, sounding out the situation. I began to get reports from them that my slipping into a groove over there would not be as straightforward as it seemed on first reading. There were small rumblings of discontent from certain quarters, and I began to suspect that I might be letting myself in for another BBC2 situation, in that there was a possibility that I was being imposed on the down-the-line producers, who had no say in my selection. The way for me had not been properly cleared internally by my mentors. I remembered how unhappy I was during the BBC2 period, and began to have grave misgivings about the whole operation.

And I had already seen the internal rivalries in operation, even if from a positive direction. The people at the Philadelphia station were absolutely delighted with the pilots and determined that I should broadcast from there, and made the case that since they had put a lot of effort into the dry runs, they were entitled to it. But it had always been planned that I should do the actual shows from Boston; the pilots were done in Philadelphia only because theirs were the studios available at the time I was able to be in America while those in Boston were not. So a row broke out between Boston and Philadelphia, each trying to have the show originating from its own operation, and appealing to New York. It was flattering, but ominous.

So when the time came for the firm offer, the combination of all of this, and the thought of dragging a half-reluctant family away from 'Onslow' and Howth for big-city noise and an uncertain future, made me say 'no'.

Let me be quite clear on one point. I was quite prepared to take the professional risk. I am now confident enough in my own abilities as a television broadcaster to believe I could have made it within a year, even if the initial period might have been shaky before I was accepted. A television studio is a television studio, no matter where it is. The technology is the same: same lights, four cameras, same angles. There are, of course, some differences. In Ireland, when I walk out to 'warm up' the audience I do not have a personal struggle with them for recognition; I do not have to sell myself. They may love me or hate me, but they *know* me. At the beginning, in Philadelphia, it was difficult to walk out a complete stranger in front of a sceptical audience, but I did win them over (all those years in the Archbishop Byrne Hall!), and as soon as the show proper started, there was never a problem. And in America the commercial breaks come every six minutes; but funnily enough, I never had any difficulty with

□

that. After all, I am used to the same frequency of breaks on the radio show. I adjusted immediately, and the guests were all used to that factor. I also believed, rightly or wrongly, that if I had to come back to Ireland with my tail between my legs, RTE would have me back in some capacity. So the move did not present any professional worries. But in the end, I decided that it would not have been worth the personal problems it brought in its train.

At the risk of being boring about Éamonn Andrews, here was another parallel between our careers. In the fifties, Éamonn was brought to lunch in the 21 Club in New York by the producer of the American version of 'This is Your Life'. 'We are going to change the chairman of the show here,' the producer said. 'It will go out at ten o'clock on a Sunday night, a half hour. You can do anything you like for the rest of the week: fly home to Ireland—anything; the rest of the time is your own.' Then he offered Éamonn a quarter of a million dollars annual salary. In the *fifties*.

Éamonn thought about it, but not for long. He was very, very tempted. But then he thought that to accept was 'only money, stacking up money,' nothing to do with the life he wanted for himself and his family. By the end of the lunch, he had courteously declined the producer's offer.

After I gave them my decision, Group W were very supportive. They came back immediately and said that they would love it if I would come over for a two-week stint that summer, to fill in on 'People Are Talking', a daily talk show from Boston, while its regular presenter was on holidays. I did it, loved it, and was invited back again in 1987 and 1988. But I have a feeling that that will be the end of the connection, because my mentors have all left. George Moynihan and Larry Fraiberg, who have remained very good friends with me, have both now retired, and Bill Baker has gone to public television, where he is in charge coast-to-coast.

The main problem with me in trying to take on anything additional to my RTE work has always been my availability. I work here Monday to Friday on radio, and Friday nights on television. There have been attempts to get me to do weekly shows on British stations: for instance the game shows I did for TVS in Southampton; but if I were in any producer's shoes, I would not go to all the trouble Gay Byrne causes. For instance, on the very first day I was going to TVS, our Aer Lingus 737 suffered a bird strike at Dublin airport, and apart from all of us being damn nearly killed, there were hours of delay. There was a studio and a full staff of crews waiting for this guy Gay Byrne in Southampton, and they couldn't start work for four hours after they were called. Crews don't like that. You could forgive them wondering, 'Is it going to be like this *every* week?' As soon as you are into split-second timing, involving planes and limousines with running

☐

engines, you are in trouble. Whatever about guests, no presenter, no matter how good, is worth the ulcers. In order to do justice to anything in Britain while keeping on the 'Late Late Show', I would have to give up the radio programme. That is not beyond the bounds of possibility, but to go that far I would have to be offered something that I really enjoyed, and the money would have to be good. To give up *everything* in RTE and to move to another country is still not beyond the bounds of possibility either; but that offer would have to be *mega* . . .

I think I would be very reluctant to give up the radio show. In the early seventies I was quite happily producing and presenting the 'Late Late' and presenting, on radio, one of the first 'going-home motoring' programmes, new to RTE, 'Music on the Move'. The schedule was not taxing: I presented it on Mondays, Tuesdays, and Wednesdays, and Joe Linnane took over for Thursdays and Fridays, leaving me free to concentrate on the 'Late Late'. I was enjoying myself.

Billy Wall, a producer in Light Entertainment in radio, came along to me and said he had an idea for a morning radio show. He explained the outline, and asked if I would present it. I was in two minds, because I was not all that keen on trying something completely new; I was not that keen on having to get up so early five days a week; and also, I was really enjoying the even tenor of my work schedule. I did a deal with him, saying I would try it for a month or two: no obligations, no hard feelings; if we all fell out at the end of that time, well and good.

The most extraordinary thing about the 'Gay Byrne Show' is that most radio programmes, no matter what the concept or who the presenter, take time to build and to catch on; but literally from day one, this programme took off. The MORI poll, which appeared just six months after it began, showed, according to John Meagher, who ran the survey, that this programme had caused the biggest shift in radio listenership patterns in Ireland since radio began. It must be remembered that until we came on there was little of interest on Irish radio. Morning radio was pretty dull stuff, and the ground was fertile. The listenership graph shot up immediately, and the amazing thing is that for seventeen years it has remained constant, despite all the additional competition from pirates, Radio 2, and morning television.

We started with bits and pieces of chat and music and acted as a port of last resort in searching for things listeners wanted us to find: books and bits of washing-machines, ancient gramophone records, pieces of china. The response to that was immediate. Usually the criticism of radio programmes that feature music is that there is too much talk. With us, the opposite was the case. The criticisms focused on the fact that there was too much music

□

and that there should be more talk, more interviews, more letters read, more telephone calls. This was unusual.

We were not by any means the first to use the medium of the live telephone call to the programme, but I think we took it a stage further than had been the practice. For instance, we discovered that while certain people with a story to tell or a problem to highlight might have been unwilling to come in to an unfamiliar studio, festooned with technological paraphernalia with strangers around, they were willing to talk to us 'privately' from the security of the bottom of their own stairs or from their own kitchen table, particularly in matters of sex.

I know that all over the world, and not uniquely in Ireland, whenever you go honestly into matters dealing with sex a lot of people become disturbed. I am routinely accused of being prurient, or voyeuristic, or presenting the subject purely for my own titillation and 'to boost flagging ratings', and so on—and I do not yet know how we will get over that. We will get over it, however, because there is a huge minefield of sexual problems out there with which we can possibly help.

The programme changed direction when Billy Wall went on to bigger and better things with Radio 2, and John Caden took over. From the beginning, John was not very keen on collecting money for people or in telling sad stories or in looking for things. He continued our work in the consumer affairs area, but John's approach to this had a lot of 'bite'. (We all found out a lot of things about human nature. We found that people are frequently economical with the truth in their own favour . . .) Having learned the nuts and bolts of how to put any programme together as a researcher on the 'Late Late Show', John was very methodical in his approach. He always had an attitude and point of view about the show as well as the nitty-gritty of the day-to-day running, whereas I have found that a lot of people in this business are dreadfully haphazard about method and detail. A presenter in a studio feels secure when John is outside in the control room. (When he left us to go to 'Morning Ireland', it was that programme's gain and our loss.)

The 'analysts' and hedge-sitters who constantly write and talk about the radio show frequently wondered how John and I worked together so well, when our points of view about the world are so completely different. John is and always has been committed to the politics of the left, very politicised, a supporter of the Workers' Party, active in trade unionism, having been a shop steward. He has a conviction about where the country should be going and what sort of society we should have. I found that he was very good in discussions and arguments, remaining patient and calm, which, I suppose, came from his days as a union negotiator.

☐

I suppose that he saw me as an extremely right-wing person, but we did laugh at one another. I could certainly laugh at him, at the predictability of his attitudes, and he certainly laughed at me and at the predictability of mine. Somewhere in between, we met. I mention this polarity because I believe that the programme was improved by it. I believe that we should have a mix of people who reflect the interests of a wider society.

One thing on which both John and I agreed categorically was our attitude to the Provisional IRA and the perpetration of violence from any side.

Clever people have tended to see a Workers' Party 'grand plan' in the radio show, in the steady drip-drip-drip of negativism about Ireland, which they see as a destabilising function in operation. But that is definitely not John Caden's influence. That is definitely me. And if it was a steady drip, we have definitely projected a steady stream of positive things about Ireland too. But I make no apologies for the drip. I constantly rail about litter and the lack of hygiene in Ireland. I complain vociferously about the decline in general consideration for one's neighbour in this country. I constantly rail about the cost of living in Ireland when I can see, like everyone else, how much cheaper it is to live only sixty miles up the road in Newry. I constantly rail about tax, and I know absolutely that I am expressing a popular point of view.

For ten years, when I was going on and on about the economic pit into which we were inexorably descending, those people saw fit to batter me about my negativism. Some members of the last Fine Gael-Labour coalition were extremely upset at what I had to say daily. It was fed back to me that I was going too far and that the Government resented it. (Well, of course they resented it: they were responsible for it.) Members of that coalition used pressure on RTE people just to get me to shut up. And I would not and I did not.

I know it sounds smug or triumphant, but I was proved to be right, and I think I have a right to say so. In an interview with *Hot Press* magazine— which, in one of its more scurrilous moments, Independent Newspapers stole and reprinted so that it gained wider currency than it would have otherwise had—I opined that the nation was banjaxed. I have not greatly revised my opinion. Although things are definitely improving, at the time of writing, early in 1989, there are still approximately 800,000 people who are working and paying taxes in order to support a population of three-and-a-half million. As well as that, we all pay enormous amounts of money to qualify young people as professionals, and at the same time provide no jobs for them, so that they must, as soon as they qualify, emigrate to bestow the benefit of our money on other countries, leaving us to pay for the next batch.

□

Less than a month before the general election in 1987, Jim Mitchell, the Minister for Communications, made a very specific attack on me about my negative attitudes, and went on to say that there was no reason for this negativism, that everything was under control. But within three weeks there was a general election, fought on the basis of words like 'disaster', 'catastrophe', and 'crisis', used by members of his party, as well as by the other side. Now, of course, there is no-one in the country, up to and including the Taoiseach Charlie Haughey, who does not agree that we are a wretchedly over-taxed people.

Would it be better to sweep these issues under our collective carpet? There are features and articles running constantly in all the newspapers, and items broadcast on other radio and television programmes, confirming what I say. I emphasise that I *know* that things are improving—but tell that to the people who listen to the radio out in Darndale or Neilstown in Dublin, or in Summerhill in Limerick, or Southill in Cork . . .

People think when I go on like this about our taxation system that I'm talking about myself. I'm not. I realise only too well that financially I'm doing better than most people who watch or listen to my programmes. But I feel hugely sorry for so many people around the country who are hard-working, dedicated and talented folk. I see my own colleagues in a place like RTE who work desperately hard to support children and the mortgage and the gas and ESB bills and all the rest of the daily outgoings. I see them take their pay envelope at month's end and open it. The pay-slip shows them the gross, then the deductions, and then the net—and I hear the wails of anguish rising on all sides. And I know that their counterparts in other countries, far less talented and hard-working and dedicated, get paid a great deal more; and, what's more important, are allowed to *keep* a great deal more of what they get.

In most other countries, for doing the work they do and bearing similar responsibilities, they would have a much better life-style, whereas in Ireland they have very little to spare for luxuries. This is the situation that upsets me: it's a horrible little country for sucking its people dry.

I do think the radio show has influence. If you talk about the steady drip, I think that, over the years, television and radio have brought about quite an influence on the freedom of expression of Irish people, which, compared with twenty years ago, is almost breathtaking.

It is not just our radio programme or the 'Late Late Show', it is television and radio in general. On a rather subtle point, I believe that the opening up of radio was caused by television—and radio itself would never have opened up to the degree it has if we had no indigenous television service. When they recruited from outside for the brand-new television service,

RTE

☐ *We could never have estimated beforehand how popular the two Special 25th Anniversary Shows for The Dubliners and The Chieftains would be. They have sold extremely successfully worldwide on video.*

RTE

□

which they had to do because there was no Irish expertise, the people they brought in had a different, fresher cast of mind than the Old Guard in the senior service, with no reverential attitude to hallowed traditions. With their arrival came a relatively fast loosening up of areas for enquiry and discussion. Television led the way, and radio had to follow.

One of the first major talking-points we came across in the programme, and which was indicative of the change in our general direction, arose when someone wrote in out of the blue about the phenomenon of 'the Silence'. In a way that has happened many times subsequently when different issues were concerned, the correspondent wrote out of despair, believing that the experience was unique, only to find that it certainly was not. As in other issues, the original letter was followed by a flood of correspondence that showed that the Silence was by no means uncommon, but that, although most people were aware that it existed, it had never been talked about in the villages, towns and cities of Ireland, out of shame and/or timidity.

Our original correspondent had written to say that the mother and father of the household had not spoken a word to one another for five years but had communicated, even in simple matters like passing the salt at the dinner table, through other members of the family. I read the letter on the air and made some anodyne comment like 'How sad', and assumed that this was the end of it. But we were inundated with letters that outlined similar situations that had gone on for fifteen, twenty, even twenty-five years, with the cause of the original row long forgotten and people tied to one another in totally unworkable relationships. It was clearly a perfectly ordinary and accepted phenomenon of Irish life where there was no divorce possible. Just imagine living for twenty years communicating on the basis of 'Tell your father this' and 'Ask your mother that . . .'

The Silence phenomenon was just the first in a series we have discovered over the years. There have also been heartbreaking individual stories that come in, often anonymously, when people just need to pour their hearts out. In one sense, part of our function has been to turn ourselves into a sort of social welfare bureau, which is a burden, because we do not have the staff to cope with the demands made on us. Just handling the huge volume of mail is a headache, without following up the queries and requests for help. On the other hand, the stories that come in are so harrowing and so genuine that we have to help as best we can. So we find ourselves allocating scarce resources to situations that do not end up on the air, do not improve the radio programme in any way, and should not be our function anyway.

All letters are read—not necessarily on the air, but if you write to the show, your letter receives attention. In fact we made one of our memorable radio programmes entirely out of letters. During the week that immediately followed the dreadful discovery of Ann Lovett's lonely death beside her new-born baby at a Marian grotto in Granard, Co. Longford, the press was full of the story, and the more conservative elements, particularly in the provincial press, were questioning whether the death should have been covered so sensationally. Many people said that capital should not be made of it by 'Dublin 4' or 'anti-Catholic' factions, since it was obviously an isolated incident.

We knew differently. All through that week, the letters came pouring in to us, full of heartbreaking stories of personal experiences. Most were from women who had given birth outside marriage. One, perhaps the most shocking letter I ever received, was from a serving-girl in a big house who had locked herself into a room, had given birth unknown to anyone, and had then murdered the baby.

We edited the letters carefully, then two actresses and I read them out, one by one, with no comment or inflexion, stopping only for commercial breaks. It has been said by commentators, correctly, I believe, that this one programme did a lot to demonstrate the chasm between social reality in this country and a blinkered version of it that is espoused by the kind of people who had been writing to the newspapers condemning their coverage of the Ann Lovett story, which, at least in the more responsible ones, was quite accurate and correctly outraged.

I believe that if the 'Gay Byrne Show' has had influence, this is how it has been done: by doing programmes like this, allowing reality to show through the veils of cant and hypocrisy, because by hearing everyday layers of opinions different from their own, people realise that there are other legitimate points of view, other tolerances, other ways of approach. Twenty-five years ago we were a closed little island, insular and parochial, and we assumed that we all knew what our communal attitudes were, because somebody said so. Maybe it was de Valera, who, in order to know what the Irish people wanted, said he had only to look into his own heart; maybe it was the Pope who knew what we wanted or thought; maybe it was the local teacher. Twenty-eight years after the arrival of television and its knock-on effect on radio, now at least we know that our own leaders and gurus do not always have the only answers. Radio and television have unshackled us. Whether we are happier or not as a result of this freedom is another question.

But I do think that in being set free, we discovered that there are a great many people who do not want the freedom to make up their own minds. When the props of certainty and received opinion fall away, they are at a total loss, and you see them yearning still for a 'safe' society, secure in

217

□

its communal moral values and teachings, where there is no necessity to think.

For myself, it is no secret that I mourn some of the vanished virtues, like respect for law and order. When I was growing up, even among young thugs of my acquaintance, there was always a line beyond which they did not trespass, such as the beating up of old ladies. And whereas a sense of sin did a great deal of damage to a great number of people, it was a useful deterrent in helping society to stay within acceptable codes of behaviour.

On a different level, we have released such tides of generosity within the Irish people that they have certainly overwhelmed me. Two-year-old Colin McStay was a case in point. Mrs Margaret McStay arrived in with Colin, clearly in a desperate state, on a Thursday morning. She told us that without a liver transplant he was going to die. The interview so caught people's imagination that there was a continuous stream of telephone calls to the programme office all throughout that day and the next, asking that Mrs McStay and Colin should appear on the 'Late Late Show' that Saturday night. What followed was amazing. Schoolchildren, housewives, bankers, workers in offices and on building sites all took it upon themselves to raise money. They did not stop until the Colin McStay fund reached one-and-a-half million pounds, which is now in trust and is dispensed to other children in need. We had Colin himself on the 'Late Late' on 25 March 1988, a bouncing, healthy little boy of 5 years old with an engaging, outgoing personality. It is episodes like this that keep the heart going, even when there are set-backs, like the one with little Jamie Marron, whom we also helped but who, sadly, after it seemed he had won, lost the fight.

We always know when the imagination of listeners is being caught during an interview, because the studio telephone lines, which are usually lit up like a Christmas tree throughout the entire programme, go completely dark as people stop dialling and sit to listen. The first time I noticed it particularly was for a full hour while I was interviewing Dr Tiede Herrema, the Dutch kidnap victim of extraordinary courage.

I still get a kick out of the programme after eighteen years, but it is a grind to have to get up every morning at half-past six, five days a week, and beat my way into Montrose. But the habits of a lifetime are hard to break.

I got the chance recently, when the impresario Oliver Barry, boss of Century Communications, asked me to join him when he was setting up his new independent radio station. After a lot of consideration, I turned him down.

Oliver approached me late in 1987, when it was first suggested that commercial radio was on the way. He is a man I have known for many years; I have done business with him in relation to the 'Late Late' on many

☐

occasions, and have done a few concert tours with him. I've always liked him personally. He told me that, in association with the businessman James Stafford, he was putting in an application for the licence to run the independent national radio channel, and advised me very strongly to be associated with it. (As a matter of fact, Oliver was one of the people well to the forefront in advising me to put the CRM affair behind me, and to use in a positive way all that energy I was expending in trying to put things right. He pointed out that if I moved to commercial radio I would, in a relatively short time—and in a much more pleasant manner—not only recoup the money I had lost but add greatly to my present earnings.)

Throughout his negotiations and preparations, Oliver contacted me almost monthly, keeping me informed about what he was doing with his application, all the radio stations he was visiting and so on, and renewing his urgings. When his lengthy written submission was ready, I saw it, although I did not read it in detail. I found it difficult to believe that it could be bettered.

Then the day came when, finally, he made his firm offer. And in fairness both to Oliver and to RTE, I was not required by Oliver to give an answer until after the licence was granted. He was at pains to say that he did not want to use my name as a springboard to get a licence if I did not wish it (although he did say he felt very strongly that it would have been helpful!). Oliver recognised that I was attracted by the challenge of something new, but at the same time he knew that, to move, I would have to overcome a natural laziness on my part and a reluctance to leave a job I still like and an organisation to which I have belonged for thirty years and to which I am loyal.

So he made the offer as attractive as possible. I could write my own ticket. An hour every morning, two hours, three hours—whatever I wanted. Anyone I wanted to move with me? Oliver would do his damnedest to make them an offer they could not refuse. He knew my time off was very valuable: my time off would be maintained. And there would be a share in the equity. By any standards it was an exciting offer.

All along, I had kept my own Director-General informed. Quite early on, I wrote him a note saying, in effect, 'Look, if I don't tell you this you will have one attitude, if I *do* tell you, you will have another . . . But I am putting it on paper that I am in negotiation . . .' He reacted by asking that I do nothing concrete without coming to talk to him. I responded by asking that he should talk to me there and then. And that is what happened. RTE said it would meet whatever Oliver Barry was offering.

So about a week after Century Communications got the licence, I told Oliver that I was staying put (inertia is a critical force!). Despite the niggling

□

'if-onlys', which, I am sure, will never entirely abate, I am very happy where I am. Oliver and I are still the best of friends, I wish him well—and I know that Century is going to be very successful. There will be a rough couple of years for all of us, with all the new stations on the air, and the media will have a wonderful time pitting me against my 'rival' on Century, not to speak about home-grown 'rivals' like Gerry Ryan thrown into the mix as well (this 'rivalry' between myself on Radio 1 and Gerry Ryan on FM2 is entirely a media creation); but, as it did in Britain, everything will eventually settle down and there will be room for all of us.

So I had my chance to change my routine and did not take it. But I still dream that, some time before I die, someone will give me a budget and let me off the studio leash so I can be like Whicker and Murphy and go off to make film-based programmes in the fresh air.

CHAPTER 11
PAUSES FOR THOUGHT
■

hen all is said and done, RTE is my home, and a pleasant one. But I have never seen myself as anything other than a performer—albeit in charge of my own domain on the 'Late Late'. So you could have knocked me down with the customary feather when the last Chairman of the Authority, Fred O'Donovan, invited me to lunch in the National Concert Hall 'for a private, confidential word,' and there asked me if I would be interested in becoming Director-General of RTE. He said that he had been given authorisation by the RTE Authority officially to ask me.

I simply said 'no'. I had never given any indication, or so I thought, that I was at all interested in becoming part of that side of the house. I could not bear to be Number One in an organisation of the size of RTE, whatever about being helpmate to the person so afflicted. I was even more surprised because at the time I had felt that those in the administration block of RTE, commonly referred to as 'the Hilton', believed that they could have a lovely tidy little organisation, well-run and happy, if it were not for all these bloody broadcasters and programme-makers cluttering up the place. (Things in this regard have vastly improved. Perhaps it is competition in the air; perhaps it is just that RTE has at last grown up . . .)

It is not just on 'their' side that there are misconceptions, however. People still go around saying that Fred O'Donovan, as Chairman of the Authority, prevented the 'Late Late Show' from doing a programme on abortion. That is not true. What happened was that Fred got caught up in one of those bouts of mad hysteria that hit this country every now and then. We had Madame Sin and Anna Raeburn on the same programme one night, just at the beginning of the SPUC campaign against abortion. Madame Sin did her thing, and Anna Raeburn revealed that she had had an abortion and spoke movingly of the regret and sadness she felt.

Naturally, SPUC (the Society for the Protection of Unborn Children) manned the barricades and organised their campaign against the 'Late Late' and RTE. The Authority members, used to getting letters at a nice steady trickle, suddenly found themselves buried in the type of avalanche

☐

we are used to; and whereas we take that kind of thing in our stride, I understand how difficult it was for members of the Authority suddenly to find themselves as personal targets, in receipt of threats, anger, and perpetual telephone calls. Fred was one of these targets. His personal view is that he detests abortion, and he let his views be publicly known. But he went further than that, announcing that the 'Late Late' was not a suitable programme for such a discussion.

At that stage we had not even planned one. We had decided to hold our fire and to wait until a date had been set for the referendum, and then to re-create the type of programme we had done on Ireland's entry into the European Community: a courtroom scene, with Europe on trial, prosecuted and defended by real barristers, with a real judge presiding. (We did it again for the divorce referendum). Not having consulted us, or the other members of his Authority, Fred made his public statement.

The Authority was irked that Fred had acted without consulting them, and wrote officially to us asking what our plans were. When they heard what they were, still tentative, they asked us to go ahead with the courtroom programme. As it happened, the date for the referendum was decided while we were on holiday, and it was set for September. None of us would have been back in time to get the programme ready. If the date of the referendum had been late September or early October we most certainly would have done the show. So when people go around saying that Fred O'Donovan, as Chairman of the RTE Authority, prevented us from doing a programme on abortion, it is simply not true. The Authority specifically wanted us to do the programme, we wanted to and intended to, but the timing was wrong, and we simply never got to it. That was our decision, not theirs. Nevertheless, the myth persists.

Fred is Fred, and just unique. I have known him for thirty years. He has a fantastic sense of humour and can make me laugh more than most people I know. He has been a pillar of show business for as long as I can remember. One of the sad days of my life was to learn of the falling out between Fred and Éamonn Andrews, who had been such good partners and so productive together in entrepreneurial show business in this country. (I am reminded of Éamonn's story—nothing to do with Fred, but with Fred's Concert Hall—where Éamonn and the former Taoiseach, Jack Lynch, arrived simultaneously at the doors one afternoon before a run-through of that evening's National Entertainment Awards show. There were the doors, and them locked . . . Éamonn pulled where it said *Pull*, but nothing happened. Himself and Jack were standing there, looking at one another and at the locked doors, when along came the singer Grace Kennedy, one of the stars of the show. 'Meet our former Prime Minister,' says Éamonn.

☐ *God bless those very special people who can always make us laugh - the late Kenneth Williams, John Cleese, Maureen Potter, Rosaleen Linehan.*

☐

'Can't we get in?' asks the singer, plaintively, looking at the locked door. 'No,' says Jack. 'It seems I don't have as much pull as I used to . . .')

I have got along well not only with Fred but with most of the higher-ups, the Authorities and the executive of RE and RTE throughout most of my career. I always believed that Kevin McCourt was the essence of what a Director-General should be: dapper, well-dressed, mannerly, with just the right degree of authority. There was no question but that Kevin was the boss. He was seen a great deal around the campus, engaged in what I now know to be (in the officially sanctioned jargon from the Irish Management Institute) 'management by walking about'. About his term of office we became personal friends. He is the type of man to whom I would go for sound advice, and he told me an anecdote that I feel is worth repeating.

Todd Andrews replaced Éamonn Andrews as Chairman of the RTE Authority, and was Chairman when Kevin took over as Director-General from Ed Roth. I never clapped eyes on Todd Andrews before or during his Chairmanship, although I knew what he looked like: his photograph was frequently in the newspapers. On the second morning of his tenure, Kevin was in his office and received a telephone call from the Chairman. After some chit-chat, welcoming him to his new post and wishing him well and so on, Andrews said that his first order of business as DG should be 'to get rid of that fucker Byrne'. After a suitable pause, Kevin checked which Byrne he meant (or, indeed, which fucker). And when he found out, in the Chairman's graphic detail, he explained that the 'Late Late' was earning a lot of money for RTE and that he didn't really think that Byrne was doing such a bad job—but he would look into it . . . Then he forgot about it. But the instruction from the Chairman was very seriously meant.

As I said, I never personally met Todd Andrews while he was Chairman; but many years after this incident I was having a business lunch in the Goat in Churchtown, and across the room were Todd Andrews and his two fine sons, Niall and David.

As I was leaving, he called me over to their table and shook me warmly by the hand and congratulated me on all the outstanding and terrific work I was doing on radio and television. He said I was the only person of any worth in the place, and went on extolling my virtues to a gratifyingly embarrassing extent, while Niall and David looked on. I accepted his compliments, and omitted to ask him what might have happened if this poor fucker had been fired all those years before by Kevin McCourt, on his, Todd's, instructions!

I have a great regard, too, for John Irvine, the quintessential civil servant but an extremely wise man, considerate and very clever. Tom Hardiman I knew pretty well and liked. I have a good relationship with T. V. Finn, who

☐

I think is a very good Director-General and who has been unfailingly kind, generous and courteous towards me. Apart from Fred O'Donovan, I think it is fair to say that I know the present Chairman of the Authority, Jim Culliton, better than any previous Chairman. He was in school with me, as I have already written, and my relationship with him continues to be a good one. I rejoice in his outstanding business success. Sheila Conroy was a very good Chairman as far as the 'Late Late Show' is concerned. She had a great fondness for the show and a great concern for the 'Late Late' team, and showed it constantly. All of us will always remember her with gratitude.

I believe the station is being well managed at present. In any organisation with a staff of two thousand, in the public or private sector, you will always have a fair proportion of extremely talented, hard-working, dedicated, go-ahead people, and you will also get a good number of passengers: un-talented, dissatisfied or disillusioned people. So it is with RTE. And it has always appeared to be unfair, to say the least, that those who come in at the crack of dawn and work their hearts out until dusk get the same money as those who busk through their allotted hours and then go home.

I am reminded of two lovely stories about two fellow-broadcasters across the water (discretion advises that I keep my mouth shut about some of our own lot!). The first is about that perennial thorn in the side of any broad-casting organisation, journalists' expenses. It appears that for a period in the late 1950s (pre-television) the BBC's Washington correspondent was a doughty man named Douglas Willis; and the story goes that month after month there appeared on his expense account the unpronounceable name of a Polish lunchee, described as 'the Polish Military Attaché'. Doug was quite entitled to entertain this person month after month, of course, since all self-respecting correspondents had to keep their ears to the ground. But some nosy parker in the accounts department of BBC head office in London smelled a rat and began to make enquiries. Of course there was no-one of that name anywhere in the Polish diplomatic service anywhere in the entire world. Doug was informed of London's findings and was invited to explain. 'The man is clearly an impostor,' he said indignantly. 'I shall never trust him again!'

It was the same Doug who went to visit the scene of the tragic loss of the submarine *Truculent* in the Thames Estuary. His expenses came in: '*Item: To hire of tugboat to visit scene of disaster: £100.*' This was duly paid, but unfortunately for Doug, the guy who paid it happened to visit a newsreel cinema in his lunch-hour. He sees a report on the *Truculent* disaster, and there, in the middle of all the river traffic, is the distinct figure of our Doug, pulling mightily on the oars of a rowing-boat. Again, Doug was asked to

□

explain. 'Thanks, mate,' he said chirpily, pulling the expenses sheet towards him. 'I'd forgotten that . . .' And he pencilled in: *'To hire of rowing-boat to get to tugboat: £10.'*

The second story concerns the Franciscan, Fr Agnellus Andrew, who was appointed to the BBC as Religious Affairs Adviser. It came to pass that the Beeb showed a television play that greatly offended the then head man of the Catholic Church in Britain, Cardinal Godfrey. He hauled Fr Agnellus in, explained the depth of his disgust in the strongest possible terms, and then said: 'But you're in the BBC and you'd know better how to express my feelings; so please draft me a letter to the BBC Director-General and I'll sign it.'

Off goes Agnellus, drafts the very strongly worded letter to the BBC, the cardinal signs it, and away it goes.

The DG gets the letter. He hauls Fr Agnellus in. 'I've had this strongly worded complaint from Cardinal Godfrey about a play he didn't like. As our Religious Affairs Adviser, would you draft me a letter in reply, and I'll sign it, because you're so much better at saying these things than I am . . .' So Agnellus drafted that, then drafted the reply, then drafted the riposte . . . Agnellus never said a word to anyone, but spent many happy hours writing and answering strongly worded letters to himself. Everyone was happy. That was the main thing . . . Then everyone lost interest, and the whole thing died a natural death.

Back here at RTE (where such things *never, ever* happen!) it does appear to me at the moment that a great number of people are working very hard and are turning out a great number of programmes with budgets that are paltry by international standards and by the standards by which all the armchair critics judge us. My perception of the place is that our station is sharpening up happily. There is a general air of getting on with the job. We are turning in a profit and are doing well in the ratings generally. We are even going public, hard-selling ourselves, which is a new experience!

I have been asked if I know my own worth to RTE. I probably do not—but which of us does? What my status is within RTE may be a very interesting question for the hedge-sitters and the 'pundits', but very difficult for me to answer. I have no illusions about my irreplaceability (as my father used to say, the graveyards are full of the irreplaceable). Éamonn Andrews was irreplaceable, and within a week of his death they were already on the telephone talking about a replacement for him on 'This is Your Life'. There is no-one, but no-one, who is irreplaceable in broadcasting, or anywhere else.

When people ask me, as they do ad infinitum, if I am aware of the impact I have on people—King Gaybo, Social Worker Gaybo, Taoiseach Gaybo,

☐

Bishop Gaybo, and so on—I can honestly reply that I can see myself in no such role. I am a broadcaster, and that is the beginning and end of it. I say what I mean or what will go down well on the radio. I interview people, and I listen to the answers. So it is a constant source of surprise to me when people fall out of their standing to see me washing my car or mowing the lawn. I get a great giggle when I see the reactions.

For instance, I was walking across the golf course near the house one day, minding my own business as usual, when a woman who was playing golf came up to me. 'It's wonderful to meet you, Gay, oh, I love you, Gay, you really are wonderful, it's a great thrill to meet you . . .'

'Well, thank you, thank you very much . . .'

'Oh, Gay, it's a terrible pity my friend Margaret isn't here to meet you too. Margaret *adores* you! She really thinks the sun, moon and stars shine out of you . . .'

'Well, does she really? Thank you, thank you very much . . .' (Don't know what I was thanking *her* for!)

'I'll tell you now how much she loves you, Gay. We were passing by your house recently and she had to, just *had* to, jump out of her car to kiss your bin!'

Then there was the lady I met who was the proud owner of a former car of mine (she got a good deal: I *mind* my vehicles). Apparently she drove the car into a city-centre car park, and the attendant looked at her accusingly: 'That's Gay Byrne's car!' 'I know,' she answered with a haughty flick of her head— 'I'm his mistress!' And she drove on. I hope he told *everybody*.

So is this what I am 'worth' to RTE: inspirer of bin-kissers, glory of the second-hand car set? What you are 'worth' to RTE is impossible to define. There are financial indicators, I suppose. During the first few years after I came back to Ireland from London I know that I was not being paid what I was worth. I was so anxious to come back, for my own reasons, that I jumped at Gunnar Rugheimer's offer when it was made, without any attempt at bargaining. Sheila O'Donovan, agent to Éamonn and myself at the time, warned me that I was accepting too hastily, selling myself too cheaply. In fact years later, Kevin Roche, who gave me my first real break into radio, always said after we became friends that he knew he had me at bargain-basement rates, and that of all the contract people he had to deal with, I was by far the easiest. I do not believe I ever went to him to complain about money. For each programme, he simply put a figure on a contract, and I signed it.

The ambience is different now and more sophisticated, but in the old days of Radio Éireann in the GPO, the people who ran the station looked on themselves as benefactors. There were queues of writers, budding piano

□

players, announcers, actors, musicians, and hundreds of hopeful Gay Byrnes, who wanted to get on radio so badly that they accepted their opportunities at any price. The powers-that-be, who were very powerful to humble supplicants like me, tried to be 'benign' and 'fair' to everyone. To ask, like Oliver Twist, for more was almost unheard of.

This kind of attitude to performers transferred to Montrose when the station moved to Donnybrook, but only as far as radio artists were concerned. The situation improved dramatically on the television side of things with the opening of RTE television in 1961. Then, in later years, people like Dick Hill came along. Dick, with Muiris Mac Conghail, had a high regard for screen performers. Those in charge of the fledgling RTE television had come from star systems in Britain and America, and for the first time, stars were born in Irish broadcasting. Mind you, because I still worked and lived in Ireland I had to settle for a great deal less by performing for RTE radio and television. I often stood in wonder when I heard of the fees being paid to Terry Wogan and Henry Kelly and Michael Aspel, and even more so to the top performers in America. These were figures that I knew only as telephone numbers (and I doubt if anyone is worth that money). Nevertheless, I was producer and presenter of my own programme in RTE, and this gave me a great deal of freedom, which perhaps was not available to other people.

The financial turning-point for me came when, as I have said, I was considering moving to the United States five years ago. I think that those in charge realised that I was serious and decided to offer me a real incentive to stay here. And the situation improved again when commercial radio came on the scene. I am in no doubt now that RTE cherishes me! (And not alone me: since the advent of the commercial stations, everyone who performs and presents is suddenly seen to be more valuable. Suddenly it has become a seller's market. God bless Oliver Barry!)

I have heard it said that RTE does not accord me the status I am due: no trappings of stardom like a chauffeur-driven car, or even a parking space (I do not need a parking space, because I am in the office before anyone else anyway every morning and have acres of car parking spaces to choose from); no special dressing-room or dresser. Terry Wogan has a chauffeur-driven car and all those perks. Well, first of all I am not Terry Wogan: I do not work for a broadcasting organisation that has either the resources or the audiences that he attracts. Secondly, since I am seen a lot, I am just seen as one of the regular guys—familiarity breeds contempt! Thirdly, because of my producing role I deal with the bosses on a different level than Terry does, which is at one remove, through agents and all the rest of it. And fourthly, I do not *want* any of those trappings.

☐

I am always amused by people who say that television and show business 'stars' are all vain, egotistical, and self-important. It is my experience that the contrary is the case, that they—we—are all insecure. I do not know anyone who has been in the business for twenty, ten, or even a modest five years, getting the regular slammings in the press and the avalanche of mail that we all attract, who could possibly maintain a big head. There is a dreadful need in Irish people to show up the Gay Byrnes, to find the Achilles heel or the weak point. ('We knew him when he was nothing,' or 'Who the hell does he think he is?') The Charlie Haugheys and the Garret FitzGeralds are personally out of reach, but the Gay Byrnes and people like him are not. So the 'fans' write their hate letters and relieve themselves of their grudges.

The odd thing is that nine out of ten times, letters to me start with the phrase, 'I know I speak for the vast majority of people in Ireland when I say . . .' I will get one that starts like that and which is deliriously happy about something I have done or said. Then the very next one out of the pile will say: 'Dear Mr Byrne, I know I speak for the vast majority of people in Ireland when I say that last week's "Late Late Show" was the vilest, the most appalling, the most sinister piece of anti-church' (or anti-Catholic, or anti-family) 'programming it has ever been my misfortune to witness.' The second letter will be referring to precisely the same item as the first.

There are weeks after a particularly controversial 'Late Late Show' during which, if I took the trouble, I could sort the negative and the positive letters into two piles of equal height. And they all know they represent 'the vast majority of people'.

This gives you a certain perspective. You realise that you and the programmes are merely a conduit for what people feel. If they agree with something someone said or I said on the programme, the programme was brilliant, I was brilliant, RTE was quite right to air the subject. If they do not, the programme was heavily loaded and biased. Sifting all of this, it becomes clear that it is not you, the star, but you, the conduit, that is the image to people. There is a side-advantage. It becomes relatively easy to realise what your own opinions are.

The playwright Tom Murphy once said that at the age of 50 he realised that all the opinions he expressed were not his own: that for a great part of his life he was repeating received wisdom. I hit that realisation much earlier; it is something that broadcasting does for you. When you are constantly dealing with controversial topics like sex, religion, hare-coursing, death, abortion, divorce, AIDS, the Irish language, homo-sexuality, unmarried mothers, or the urban-rural divide, and getting avalanches of letters and telephone calls, then unless you are pretty feather-headed, it is impossible not to begin to discern what your own instincts are.

A lot of the pundits who have analysed me and my style over the years say that I have no opinions. A lot of the pundits who have analysed me and my style over the years say my opinions show transparently through my interviewing and presentation style, no matter how I try to conceal them. You can choose which of those opinions suits you best. There cannot be a person in the country who does not know my opinion on divorce, for instance. I voted for divorce and took a pro-divorce stand long before it was a hot issue. I know I am very unpopular with Irish-language enthusiasts. And I am regularly told that I do nothing but encourage people to shop in Northern Ireland and emigrate to Australia.

I try to be open-minded when interviewing people, but the choice and type of questions asked will betray certain feelings. On the other hand, those who analyse me this way are not always right. Remember, all of this performing is *performing*. A lot of my broadcasting style is just that: style. A lot of the indignation and crabbiness and thunderstruck apoplexy is feigned. It comes out of something genuine, but the manner in which it is delivered is a performance. Sometimes I do it to get a reaction, sometimes I do it out of sheer devilment, or the mood I happen to be in that day.

I would be more committed to an opinion now that I am older. It is sometimes still feigned, but I think that there is merit, when doing a daily show, when you get a telephone call or a message of some sort, in saying the first thing that comes into your head, rather than second-guessing. RTE does not officially encourage editorialising or opinionating among presenters on its programmes; in fact the opposite is the case. Under the terms of the Broadcasting Act we are required to be objective and balanced on matters of public controversy. But I think that, more than most, I can get away with sounding off or throwing out an opinion to get a reaction.

People have mentioned that my style has changed sinced the CRM affair; that I have become harder, more intolerant, faster to rise to the bait. I think that a lot of people read a lot into me and my style that is just not there. On the other hand, I have more confidence now in saying, in reaction to something that I think is utter rubbish, 'I think that's utter rubbish.' I feel safer now with my own opinions. I don't think I was ever all that concerned with how people reacted to me; but perhaps the people who think they see a change in my 'style' have noticed that it is my reactions, not me, that are harder than they used to be. I do not honestly know whether the CRM affair was the anvil on which that hardening occurred: I am not that self-analytical. But I think that what a shake-up like that does is make you confront reality. I think that as a people, we Irish are not great at facing reality—our own or our neighbour's. I had to face the truth and just get on with my life.

☐

When, twenty-five years ago, I first began to get crank letters and hate mail, I was far more upset about them than I am now. I remember creeping around the Montrose campus with someone's obscene and hateful, usually anonymous, effluent in my pocket, feeling that those pockets were made of glass and *everybody* could see right through them and knew *exactly* what was in those letters. Now I know that everyone on radio and television gets them. It is the nature of the business. I have been accused, arising out of an airing of a single 'Late Late Show', of being a Fianna Fáil lackey, a Fine Gael hack, an agent of the US imperialist war machine, and a mole for Moscow. I feel, therefore, that I must be doing something right.

The letters continue to come. They can be part of an organised campaign, very easy to spot no matter how the campaign is disguised, with postmarks from all over the country and all the rest of it; or the babblings of single individuals who see in Gay Byrne the personification of all their fears and all the nastiness in the world. They come in floods if there is any current issue of controversy on which I may have expressed an opinion—or even on which I have allowed someone else's opinion to be aired, either on the 'Gay Byrne Show' or the 'Late Late'. Throughout history, the tendency has always been to kill the messenger.

Of course there are genuine letters, from people with genuine grievances. I deal with them in a considered and, I hope, courteous manner, but I deal with those other, vicious correspondents in a saner way now than I used to. First of all, I do not let them upset me. I either consign their trash directly to the wastepaper basket where it belongs and forget about it, or I use it, broadcasting its content. I use it to show ordinary, decent people just what is living in their midst. But sometimes, no matter how hardened I think I am, they hurt.

The following little beauty arrived in the wake of the Enniskillen bombing (let those of delicate sensibilities skip this bit), which, like a lot of people, I had condemned. Naturally it is unsigned and there is no address.

Dear Mr. Smug Fucking Gaybollox,

I have been threatening for some time to write At—not To—you. The reason I delayed so long was that I didn't think you really were worth a postage stamp. Also, I was making allowance for your colossal ignorance—so evident at all times in any programme so handicapped as to include such an objectionable cunt as yourself.

Your performance on radio this morning (18/11/87) in which you saw fit to attack the work of Ireland's best national poet, Thomas Davis and to decry a great tune which was for many years during British occupation, recognised as Ireland's National Anthem, impells me to pen this valedictory protest and no doubt you will notice in the only language which such a half-baked arse-licking West-British, slave-minded, avaracious poor product of the Rialto ghetto of King-lovers and Poppy-wearers and brewery riff-raff could be expected to comprehend. Of course it is well known that your understanding of English is nil—as evinced by your pathetic efforts on radio and TV. It is almost as bad, although not quite, as your inability to chair any discussion on the puerile Late Late fiasco. It is hard to saddle 'Singer' with that—but sure you were only a wet day there after Donore got rid of you. Get wise to yourself, Gaybollox, the days of the glorification of royalty and the British Legion and its hangers-on and their followers is dead in Ireland anyway. No effort however mealy-mouthed on your part to publicise or support a neo-West British clique in this unfortunate country will cut any ice. You may cod the country people who don't know you, but Dublin is a small place, really.

The really serious thing is that you totally misrepresent Ireland to people overseas in a deliberate and diabolical attempt to curry favour with a reactionary and un-Irish element at home.

But you will fail—Oh boy—WON'T you fail.

P.S. Believe me, there are thousands of people in Ireland who feel as I do—and say so!

The writer is obviously male, and obviously went to Synge Street. Maybe he was in my class.

It goes without saying that the long-distance, alcoholic patriots who support the Provo IRA are not terribly keen on my attitude. Like many another, I have condemned violence—on both sides of the divide. Presumably, the UVF don't hear what I say about them, but the Provo supporters regularly write to me. At Christmas 1988 I got a card purporting to be from some regiment or other of 'the Newry IRA'. It said: 'Happy Christmas—it will be your last.'

Another charming missive, which arrived in April of this year, was the following:

Final Warning

Mention the I.R.A. once again and you've had it. We got them in South Armagh so it should be child's play to get you. You'll be bumped off some night between Dollymount and Sutton and dumped in the sea. No excuse even if your ould fella and uncles from the slums of S.C. Road donned the British murderous uniforms. We have monitored you and in 1988 you have—at the taxpayers' expense—slagged the I.R.A. 67 times. Your wife and two adopteds stand in danger too.

Provo I.R.A.

There are several subjects guaranteed to send the letter-writers hurrying to their little cubby-hole desks: sex (of course), violence (sometimes), unmarried mothers, gougers on the dole—all the subjects dear to the hearts of the charitable. But it is on nationalism and the North and associated topics that I get most roastings. The letter above is an extreme example— here is another: more reasoned, but no less bitchy. At least this man had the decency to sign his name and to give his address, but I will spare his blushes by not quoting them here.

21st November, 1987

Gabriel Byrne Esq.,
R.T.E.
Donnybrook,
Dublin 4

Mr. Byrne,

I was listening to your radio programme on Thursday morning last, at that part you devote to reading letters which apparently emanate from various listeners. One lady wrote about the situation in the Six Counties.

It was an entirely reasonable letter, yet it brought forth a tirade from you that was obviously unscripted and therefore could be taken at face value. Quite apart from interrupting your reading of the letter to make way for your own little remarks and quips, you finished by saying that you were fed up with all reference to that 'Cursed Place', the North of Ireland, or Northern Ireland or whatever it was called.

The same 'cursed place', Mr. Byrne, is part of my country. It is beautiful, friendly, courteous, and has produced down the years more than its quota of artists, businessmen and patriots. We remember Henry Joy McCracken, Roger Casement, and indeed Michael Collins who was elected as representative of a Northern constituency; we take it very hard therefore to hear it called by such as you a 'cursed place'. Moreover, I was privileged to serve in the Defence Forces '39–'46 and held the President's Commission. Never in all my time of service did I or any comrade ever apply such a term to our sacred country. It is irksome then to hear it so described by [here it comes, folks] a jumped-up brat from the South Circular Road, whose only god is the fortune he lost to a crook, and whose favorite subject on the air is the femina abdomina.

Please do not read this letter on your programme. I do not welcome the little snide asides you insert for your own amusement. Leave Ireland to the Irish, and wear your Flanders poppy in England—or are you afraid of Terry Wogan? That would be real competition!

I cannot sign myself 'Yours Faithfully' for you are of another faith altogether.

c.c. Director of Broadcasting, R.T.E.

☐

Whatever about the strength of expression in those two letters, I think it is fair to say that neither of them is wild about old Uncle Gaybo. Leaving aside the empty abuse in the first letter, and that the writer of the second letter completely misunderstood what I actually said on the radio programme, I do not for a moment believe that one *single* comment on either a radio or television programme could prompt an outburst of such animosity. I have always believed that such letters stem from a slow and gradual build-up over a long period of hostility to Gay Byrne, his attitudes and opinions, and the manner of their expression. And then there comes some final trigger that prompts the actual writing of the letter. I suppose it is only fair to accept that throughout the years, both on radio and television, I have certainly given my opinions and have allowed my attitudes to be exposed. More importantly, I have facilitated the exposure of the opinions of others, opinions with which a great number of people violently disagree.

There seems to be a more personal involvement with my programmes, both on radio and television, than there is with others; and consequently, people take things they hear or see more personally. So when it is something they do not like, they switch their hostility personally to me. Through the years, in the programmes, we have managed to offend a great many people. Anyone who comes into this business and is on the air as often and for as long as I am—two hours a day, five days a week, for eighteen years, with two hours on television on Fridays for twenty-seven years—and expects to be universally loved is in for a rude awakening.

An old woman wrote to me recently, to placate me in the face of some new outburst of criticism. 'Don't mind what they say about you, Gay,' she wrote, 'the tallest tree catches the wind, and you're the tallest tree in RTE.' I hadn't heard the expression before, and I presume she used it in the *quantitative* sense rather than the *qualitative*. In terms of flying hours on air over the years I guess I'm one of the tallest trees. And because of the nature of the shows I do, which deal with controversial and contentious matters about which people tend to feel strongly, I have managed to offend a great number of people through the years.

Viewers and listeners will always blame the presenter when a programme doesn't work out the way they want. All presenters feel the sharp edge of the public tongue from time to time—a good weekly lash is part of the job, and if you can't take it then the best thing to do is present ballet music and stick to esoterica.

I am not particularly brave—but not particularly faint-hearted either. After all these years it is not too difficult to slough off this kind of thing. Maybe this is why I have been called a cold fish. The endless analyses of me

RTE GUIDE

☐ *Is it possible that Hal Roach and I were ever this young and could do a double act? Is it possible that Hal Roach and I are still alive after all those years?*

REHABILITATION INSTITUTE

☐

that go on in the press, at least the more serious ones that do not concentrate on what I have for my breakfast, seem to conclude that I am some sort of automaton. Wind him up and watch him go. Professionally, I know that I can be quite detached, even in the middle of the most heart-rending interview. It is not that I do not sympathise with the interviewee's plight—I do: but it would hardly be professional if I started to blubber along. I think what people mean is that I can have a lack of empathy. While being sympathetic, I find it difficult to feel along with someone who is suffering or to put myself in his or her place, and maybe that is one of my strengths as an interviewer. I can ask that extra awkward question, push it that extra millimetre, whereas those more sensitive than I would balk, not wanting to appear to be callous.

This does not mean that I cannot be steered towards empathy. The transsexual Jan Morris, for instance, who had had batterings from many interviewers, announced after her appearance that of all the interviews she had done in connection with her book, mine was the only one she had enjoyed, because I had handled her so sensitively. What had happened was that before the show, Pan had battered me over my two thick ears and had warned me how to behave. I do listen.

And I agree that passion is not my strongest attribute; but if I were to become passionate about all the issues that cross my desk daily, I would end up in a mental hospital. I am passionate about some things, such as injustice. But passion means unruliness and disorder. I like order. I like to be tidy in work habits and personally. I work methodically, and my desk is always clear. There are so many calls on me that I must protect something of myself. If I were profligate with my feelings, there would be little of me left. In my own defence I would say that there seems to be space in my heart for only a certain amount of feeling at any given time.

I have said it before, but it is worth repeating, that I am truly amazed at the number of journalists and others who take upon themselves the most tortuous analyses of me. The fact that I know it happens all over the world to other people like me does not stop me being amazed. And there is another difficulty with all this analysis: people are always trying to build me into a more complex man than I really am. I know that there is no such thing, really, as a 'simple' person, but in so far as it is possible, I am very simple. I think that the reason people think I am more complex than I am is those barriers that I have put around the one little piece of me that I keep to myself and through which I will not allow them to see.

I do my best, but people tend to think that if you are on television they own you and all of your time. For instance, I will never, ever go into a pub on my own. I am not really a pub person; but the reason is that I could not

□

be there for more than two minutes without being spotted by some drunk or someone with a chip on his shoulder to whom I am the answer to all dreams. There is a pub tradition whereby the privacy of a man sitting at a bar counter, having a drink and reading a newspaper, is to be respected. This does not apply if you are on television. Even if they have no axe to grind or nothing that they want you to do for them or to find for them and are just being pleasant, I find they look at you expectantly: 'Come on, be Gay Byrne, entertain me,' and you have to make all the running. I get limp. The older I get, the more limp I get, and I find that talking to people I don't have to talk to is more of an effort—particularly small talk, at which I was never brilliant anyway.

I know that in latter years I have offended many people. People who cannot get at me any other way sit in reception in the Radio Centre in the early morning, knowing that this is the only way in to the studios and that I have to pass through there. They make attempts to waylay me, but I have developed a method of coping with it, caring very little about whether their feelings are hurt, because I believe they are being most unfair. My time in the mornings is finite. There are a hundred and one things to be done before the radio show: newspapers to be read and filleted, letters to be sorted out, linking scripts to be written, telephone calls to be organised. I must be on the air on time and I can never get that time back again. Now, when I see those hopeful faces in the reception area, I just hurry on by, saying, 'I'm sorry, I've got to be on the air in time, you'll appreciate that, I'm sure. Talk to so-and-so, I'm afraid I cannot stop now.' And I keep moving.

People have an odd notion that I should go around with a jotter and pencil at the ready, just waiting to log their requests. If they cannot get to me at Montrose, they arrive out to the house and knock at my door.

Even abroad there is no escape. On the occasion when we were doing the 'Late Late' from New York, I went to Mass in St Patrick's Cathedral on Fifth Avenue. Outside the cathedral, there they were, all the smiling faces, all lined up to shake the hand of Gay Byrne and to get autographs. I discovered that day that there are tapes of the 'Late Late Show' in circulation all over the Bronx, Queen's and Manhattan, twenty-four hours after transmission at home. Gay Byrne in the Canaries or in London has a similar experience: there is nowhere on this earth where Irish people do not now live or travel.

I have a very two-faced attitude, I know, because I do enjoy the positive side of all this recognition. People are generally very pleasant. But there are exceptions.

One gorgeous summer afternoon, the sun had caught me, sudden-like. I had been pottering around the garden when it had blazed out from behind the wispy clouds, hot and healing. Everyone else was out of the house, so I just said to myself, 'What the hell,' and took off all my clothes. Mercifully, as it turned out, I left my underpants on.

I was lying blissfully in the back garden, drifting into that floaty, golden, dreamlike state that precedes a doze, when I was covered by a large shadow. I jerked back to reality. There was a big, strapping, strong country-woman looming over me, blocking out the sunlight. An instant chum.

'Well, now, Gay, isn't it great.' (Archly) 'I just *knew* you'd be here and I knew I'd catch you! Now, Gay, here's what I want you to do, and I know you can do this for me, Gay, because I have three children now in Australia and I can't afford to go out there to them.'

During the week, we had announced on the 'Late Late Show' a postal quiz with a prize of a trip to Australia.

'What I want you to do now, Gay, is, I want you to arrange for me and my husband to win that postal quiz, because we want to go to Australia to see our children. Now we don't want that Dunk Island place at all: as long as we get to Australia, we'll look after ourselves. Now you'll do that for us, Gay, won't you now?'

I sat up, trying to look as normal and as charming as possible—as charming as a person can be, clad only in his underpants. 'Sorry, I'd love to be able to do that for you, ma'am, but it's not possible—'

'Now, Gay' (trilling)' —I *know* you can do that for us now, Gay—'

'Look, there will be about half-a-million entries and I can't—'

'Well now, Gay, I have the entry right here in my hand. I can give it to you right now—'

'Ma'am, it is just not possible . . .'

This went on for fully twenty minutes. Finally she got the message, but then changed tack. 'Okay, now, Gay, well now, all you have to do is to go into Budget Travel or Abbey Travel or one of those agencies and use your influence, Gay, and get me and my husband a cheap trip to Australia so we can go and see our three children . . .'

I was losing patience, but was also fully aware of the ludicrousness of my position. Eventually, after almost three-quarters of an hour, I managed to move her up the driveway towards the front gate. She turned belligerent. 'Oh, so we're going now towards the driveway, are we? It's time for me to go, is it? I see. We're being led out, now, are we—we are now being got rid of, is that it?'

'Well, ma'am, I do have a few things to do—'

'Well, as far as *I* could see you had nothing much to do. As far as *I* could see, you were just lying in the garden . . .'

Like David Hanly in one of his more hilarious columns in the *Sunday*

☐

Tribune, I had an uncontrollable urge to lift her skirt and give her an almighty kick in the arse.

I restrained myself. There might have been a large husband waiting out of sight. Coward that I am, I pretended to hear my telephone ringing, and rushed indoors.

My very favourite story about this kind of situation is the one about Mike Murphy, whose joyous attitude to life I envy greatly. No-one, but no-one, is going to get Mike down, and if he sees that anyone might, he changes his job, or his coloration, or whatever it takes to maintain the kick he gets ouf of life. He has somehow managed to organise his life so that he always does exactly as he wants to do. If he is fed up having to get up early in the morning to do a radio programme, he tells the people in charge that he wants to do something else. He insists that he wants to do something else.

I wish I could be the same, but it is difficult to change the ingrained puritanical work-addicted habits of a lifetime, and I am not terribly sure how to go about it. Kathleen Watkins has frequently said to me, 'Mike is doing what he wants to do. He is deciding for himself. Why don't you do likewise?' To my mealy-mouthed reply that there are so many people hanging out of me and depending on me, she simply scoffs that I should go out to Balgriffin cemetery and tell that to Éamonn Andrews, who never got to enjoy the beautiful retirement he had planned.

Mike went for a quiet pint one afternoon with the late Tom McGrath. It was four o'clock in the afternoon, and they chose to go to Gleeson's in Booterstown Avenue. They were sitting at the counter, minding their own business and batting the breeze, when Mike noticed with some trepidation that a drunk farther down the counter had locked on. There is a definite 'lock-on' look that drunks adopt when they are making up their minds to approach someone 'famous'.

With great care, the drunk gets off the bar-stool and walks gingerly down the bar. He stops, wavering, in front of Mike, head forward, eyes at half-mast, lips loose.

'Mike Murphy? You're Mike (*hic*) Murphy?'

Mike knows there is no point in ignoring the guy. 'Yes, I'm Mike Murphy . . .'

(Pause, while the drunk, swaying gently, considers this admission.) 'You're Mike Murphy!'

'Yes, I'm Mike Murphy . . .'

'Mike Murphy! Do you know wha' ir is? Do you know wha' (*hic*) I'm goin' to tell yew now?'

'What?'

'I mean this ver' (*hic*) very *sincerely* now . . .'

□

'Yes?'

'Yew . . .' (he steadies himself) 'yew are fuckin' . . . *brewtal* on television!' He takes a wobbly step backwards to admire the effect of his announcement.

'Really?' says Mike, as noncommittally as he can.

'No jokin' now. No jokin'!' The drunk stabs the air with an unsteady forefinger. 'Yew . . . are the most fuckin' *brewtal* fella I ever seen on the television!'

'Ah, well,' says Mike diplomatically, 'you win a few, you lose a few! Thanks anyway . . .'

But the drunk has not finished. 'Nothin' *pairsonal* now! I just want yew to know you're fuckin' brewtal—roigh?'

'Right!'

'Roigh!'

'Right!'

And the drunk staggers off towards the gents. In mid-stagger, he thinks of something he forgot to say, turns around and comes back. He stops again in front of Mike, leaning forward, until the faces are only inches apart. 'And *furthermore,*' he says, 'even the *wife* thinks you're fuckin' brewtal . . .' (pause) 'and she knows fuck-all!'

Mike still dines out on that story.

If I admire Mike's openness to adventure, at the other end of the scale I admire Tony O'Reilly, in that it seems to me that he is one of the few people who have all the graces. He really is monumental in size, appearance, brainpower, intelligence, wit, charm, good looks, and leadership. By the same token, I have a sneaking regard for the other Tony, Tony Ryan of Guinness Peat Aviation. Because I used to love aircraft, because I still love aviation, I have always kept a watch on his career. Although he is lacking in the personal charm department so filled by Tony O'Reilly, what he has achieved is just stunning by any standards. He is running a fantastic organisation, built from nothing, and is running it all from Ireland. I admire Feargal Quinn hugely, and Ben Dunne, and Gillian Bowler and . . . I'll stop there!

I am sick of the sleeveen begrudgery that one hears in Ireland about successful people. I believe that we will achieve maturity as a nation only when we can recognise and acknowledge that success in business does not automatically equal jackboots and exploitation.

I suppose I would call myself a very right-wing conservative or reactionary. But in one sense I could be classified ideologically as neither one thing nor the other. Right-wing, left-wing, socialist, communist, monetarist—all these labels are only that: labels. I am impatient with labels, and do not

☐

understand the national obsession with classification. I just want to get on with it. I am a pragmatist. I want to do what works. I certainly subscribe to the ideal of social justice for all, but my upbringing and background have geared me to the principle of hard work, well rewarded.

There is a common misconception about me that I hate politicians. It is not so. I find that most individual politicians I meet are ordinary, decent people who work very hard indeed. I think it is appalling that the average minister or leader of a party should have to dash down to Bohola or Claremorris or Fenit every weekend to deal with local issues to do with lamp-standards. The system is wrong, but I cannot understand why they do not change the system. The problem is, of course, that once they get into the system they are in the club, and the club becomes all.

I think that one of our greatest failures as an independent republic is that in sixty or seventy years we have not come up with a better way to run a constituency the size of Manchester or a largish town in America, which can be run by a mayor and a few officials. We have two houses of parliament and 168 TDs and a massive civil service and a presidency, and an army, a navy, and an air force. There must be a more compact and efficient way.

Needless to remark, I would have been an appalling businessman. Apart from the obvious, I do not believe I pay enough attention to detail, and I am far too impatient: it is my besetting sin. I get impatient with windbags on the telephone, the people who go on and on about something that I know in my heart and soul is not going to be productive or of any benefit whatsoever to the 'Late Late Show'. I suppose that is where Maura comes in. Like Kathleen Watkins, she is simply nicer than I am and can appreciate that the person she has on the other end of the line is a human being who probably had to screw up his or her courage to ring the 'Late Late Show' in the first place and who will only make one of those calls ever in a whole lifetime.

And I have got a bad temper, but I do not often lose it. I am more inclined to be grumpy than bad-tempered, and my grumpiness shows. I have been told by friends that I can throw a glance of such ice that it can freeze people on the spot. Some people who know me well, such as the two producers John Williams and John McColgan, would always know from a hundred paces. McColgan has the best approach: 'Oh, God, don't talk to the Star today. Oh, God, wrong day, sorry, talk to you tomorrow, see you tomorrow, tooraloo . . .' I do not like to lose my temper. But I rail and shout and scream at myself a lot in the privacy of my car or on my walks across Howth golf course. I hit myself over the head for some omission or some stupidity. I also fight verbal battles of epic proportions with others. The brilliance of my argument! The wonderful ripostes, the pithy putdowns—all the things I

☐

can never think of to say in real life. I also rail and shout at machinery and technology that breaks down. I have a totally unreasonable attitude to inanimate objects and machinery. They are supposed to work, so why do they not work? Things that give trouble irritate me so much and work me into such a lather of sweat that I know that to onlookers it must be unbearably funny. I empathise completely with Basil Fawlty . . . I can hide it better when I am irritated with people and not with things.

It was a great benefit when the 'Late Late' after twenty-three years went to Friday nights from Saturday, because, although Friday is a long and tiring day, at the end of it I am finished for the week. On Saturdays, when I wake up, there is a lovely jubilant feeling that I am *off! off! off!* I am now very jealous of my Saturdays. I will let nothing, but nothing, interfere with them. Saturdays, Gaybo washes the car or mows the lawn, or just reads and potters about or walks.

In life, there are the lucky ones who work very hard and enjoy every single minute of it. They keep on using the phrase that their job is their hobby and they enjoy it all the time. Although I like it, I think I have passed the stage where my job is my hobby. I am this huge contradiction, in that I resent bitterly not having more time every day to relax on my own and to do the things I want to do. On the other hand, I know that the puritanical streak within me would not allow me to do that.

I am a contented man. If I were to try to think of a moment of pure happiness, what immediately springs to mind is the day in 1958 I stood on the floor of the Guardian Insurance Company, taking a telephone call from Kevin Roche and hearing him ask me to present a music programme on Christmas night. I don't know if it was the happiest moment of my life, but it was certainly a moment of outstanding happiness. I felt excited and vindicated. I knew instinctively that it was the end of one road and the beginning of another. I knew I'd cracked it. It is perhaps a very prosaic definition of what constitutes happiness, but is this not different for everyone?

There was another moment, on Suzy's Confirmation day, when she was so wonderfully happy herself that she took me with her onto her cloud. I remember thinking that if I had made the decision in favour of going to the States, I would have missed this magic . . .

Two other moments I have already mentioned. One was the Conferring Day at Trinity, which was special; and the other was the day I realised I was being headhunted by Westinghouse. Perhaps happiness is too strong for the feeling that day—restoration of hope, or satisfaction, perhaps, after the CRM affair.

Another time of great happiness came this year, when Kathleen and I

☐

celebrated our twenty-fifth wedding anniversary. After seeing so many marriages going on the rocks, and, in the course of so many radio and television programmes, realising that there are so many unhappy people in the world, we know that our marriage has been happier than most. We are growing closer with each passing day—we have to, because we're afraid of the kids! (That's a standard showbiz *joke*—okay?) We are both extremely busy and are interested in each other's doings; we have a lovely home, which we both inordinately enjoy. And we have two smashing daughters, each totally different from the other, and both, like most children, very special to their parents. They've both had to suffer the disadvantages of two famous parents, and I reckon they've come through that with flying colours. (Yes, I know—there were many advantages in that, too.) And, wrapped up in that complete package, Kathleen and I fully appreciate that we have so much more than many people. It's more than enough.

Kathleen derives immense satisfaction not only from her occasional broadcast work but also from her work as a member of the Arts Council, to which she was appointed by Charles Haughey in 1988. She takes her Arts Council duties very seriously indeed and gives time to them.

(I recall that one night many years ago Jim Plunkett Kelly was on the 'Late Late Show', and all the guests that night were asked to define 'happiness'. It was one of those philosophical nights. Jimmy said: 'Happiness is to be able to lie on your death-bed and face the future with confidence.' Maybe that's a bit on the sombre side.)

Not a long list, I agree. We all like to keep our little illusions about ourselves. I do not know what happiness is, really—and I believe that if I found it, I am too much of a pessimist to be happy for long.

I love my work but hate its tyranny, yet they are one and the same thing. At least I know that I have had the privilege of having a go and at the right career for me. Once this bug bites, there is no escape. There are so many hundreds of people in this country who might be talented actors or writers or broadcasters and who have never had the opportunity for one reason or another to stretch their wings but must labour away as frustrated misfits, working to live just to reach retirement, and then to die.

As far as my show business career is concerned, I reckon I've had a charmed existence. I was watching 'This is Your Life' recently; the subject was Engelbert Humperdinck. The story was told that, as a young Jerry Dorsey, he decided on a singing career, but if he had known then what he would have to endure in order to realise his ambition, he might never have bothered to start. There were years spent trudging the streets of London, failed auditions, menial jobs to keep body and soul together, long periods when success seemed completely out of his grasp. There was one bout of a few months when he spent most of

□

every day lying on the floor of his flat, sleeping, because dozing in a prone position cut down on the need for food. He and his young family lived over a furniture store, and he took badly paid musical gigs wherever he could find them, just hanging on to a hope that one day he would be 'discovered'. Then he got TB, which took him off his feet for a year.

After all that, he happened to record a song called 'Release Me'. His agent insisted that he change his name from Jerry Dorsey to the ridiculous Engelbert Humperdinck—and suddenly he had arrived.

As I watched the story unfold on 'This is Your Life', I felt that no-one deserved showbiz success more than he did. I know that the business is littered with such histories of actors, musicians, singers, radio and television people, who have suffered the most extraordinary deprivations as they battled to find a place in the limelight, sustained only by the total conviction that show business was their business and that one day they would make it. Every inch of the way, they had to retain that passion in the gut, that obsessive *need*, that utter refusal to take no for an answer.

You will not get such a story from Gaybo. I wish I could tell you that I starved for my art, but I didn't. From the time I left school, there has not been a week in which I have not earned a wage packet: from insurance, cinemas, insurance again, then car-hire and advertising, and then into television and radio full-time. There was no hiccup along the way. Yes, the conviction was there: that I wanted to be Éamonn Andrews or somebody pretty similar; so was the quiet persistence that in the early days kept me knocking on doors and generally making a nuisance of myself.

Yet all that, at the time, was part of the skit of the thing: there was a lot of fun in it. In so far as I have enjoyed success—albeit within the narrow confines of this little island—I have never had to *suffer* for it, and I have experienced very little rejection. I would have to admit that I got what I wanted fairly easily. Maybe if it had come harder I would appreciate it more. *Sustaining* this success is slightly more troublesome . . . Nor do I believe that what I do is art; nor do I believe that I am talented. I do very much believe that what the late Ray McAnally had, what Rosaleen Linehan has, what Maureen Potter, Brian Friel, John O'Conor, Frank McNamara, Daniel Day-Lewis (this list is a pretty long one, so let's stop there) have is *talent*. What I have is a certain facility that allows me to be my natural self, almost, on radio and television, and it doesn't require any special effort on my part. A facility, no more.

The *preparation* for the radio and television programme is where the effort is required. And I firmly believe that I am a far better producer than I am a performer. Not many people know that, as Michael Caine might say, because I don't mention it much.

☐

I am mindful of this fairly easy success, and not a day passes that I do not remind Gaybo—and those around him—that we are amongst the most fortunate of people. There is a grave danger that we might take what we have for granted, or believe that somehow we deserve what we have been given. I constantly think of the many thousands of others, in show business and outside it, who would give so much for just one chance to do what I do and to have the life that I have. The fact that the job is not quite as glamorous or as exciting as they perceive it is neither here nor there. I have a most agreeable life-style.

When, occasionally, I ask, as we all do, 'What's it all about?' I consciously remember two markers. The first is the letter I received from a woman whose mother had just died after a long, hard illness. It was a simple letter, simply thanking me, on behalf of the woman's mother, for my radio and television work. The letter said that the woman's mother had been a great fan, and that my work had helped her bear her illness, over a long period. The other marker was the little notice kept on his desk by my old Granada boss, David Plowright. I memorised it; and what it said is still totally valid: *When all is said and done, remember that what we're talking about is just a bloody oul' television programme.* When all is said and done, I agree. We in television and radio are not essential, not necessary—and, according to a lot of people, not even desirable . . .

But if Ma and Da had not bribed me all those years ago with that Hercules bike, and if I'd taken that messenger-boy's job with Findlater's . . .

INDEX

A

Adams, Gerry, 154
Ammon, Max, 84
Andrew, Fr Agnellus, 226
Andrews, David, 224
Andrews, Éamonn, 51, 103,
    222–4, 227
  career, 72–6, 80
  Chairman RTE Authority, 30,
    31, 88, 224
  boxing commentator, 50
  BBC, 104
  and Ray Byrne, 22
  and Gay Byrne, 78, 82, 105, 114,
    210, 244
  and Russell Murphy, 124–5
  and 'Late Late Show', 178–9, 195
  death, 105, 138, 226, 239
Andrews, Gráinne, 74–6, 105, 114
Andrews, Niall, 224
Andrews, Todd, 224
Aspel, Michael, 228
Astaire, Adele, 192
Astaire, Ava, 192
Astaire, Fred, 192, 193

B

Baker, Bill, 203–4, 205, 210
Ball, Kenny, 50–51
'Bang-Bang', 69
Banim, Al, 184
Barrington, Dónal, 137
Barror, Cecil, 86
Barry, Michael, 31, 88–9
Barry, Oliver, 218–20, 228
Baskin, Bibi, 202
Baum, Maxie, 52
Bedford, Patrick, 78

Behan, Dominic, 181
Beitz, Joan 118
Bennett, Tony, 18, 48, 58, 69,
    71, 82
  girl-friends, 92–3
Bermingham, Willie, 2
Bernstein, Sidney, 103
Best, Angie, 182
Best, George, 181–2
Blackmore, Lorna, 92
Boland, Tony, 194
Bolster, Sergeant, 20
Boomtown Rats, The, 166, 173
Bourke, Gráinne
  see Andrews, Gráinne
Bourke, Jimmy, 74
Bourke, Lorcan, 74–6
Bourke, Rick, 74
Bowler, Gillian, 240
Bowman, John, 66
Bratman, David, 24
Breathnach, Seán Bán, 177
Brien, Vincent, 181
Brophy, Fr Paddy, 155
Browne, Ivor, 196–8
Browne, Dr Michael, Bp of Galway,
    170–71
Browne, Vincent, 158, 179
Budin, Burt, 170
Burke, Miss, 77
Burns, Mike, 137
Buzan, Tony, 178
Byrne, Al, 18, 19, 22–8, 160, 208
  and Gay Byrne, 1, 4, 92, 99,
    127–8, 146
  youth, 10, 40
  father's death, 11–12
  and mother, 17, 35, 89

☐

and Ray's wedding, 21–2
at Trinity College, 23–5, 55, 76
'number one clerk', 26
and Ernest, 30, 32
school, 44
musicians, 56
acting, 77
Byrne, Alexander, 5
Byrne, Annie (mother), 1, 5–6, 7,
    55–6
and Edward, 8–9
character, 8, 14, 23–4, 40
widowed, 11–14
influence of, 16–18, 42–3, 71
and Ray, 19–22
and Al, 23–8, 35
and Ernest, 29–30
and Mary, 34–5
Bray holidays, 49
and Christian Brothers, 64–5,
    67–8
and Éamonn Andrews, 72, 74
and Kathleen Watkins, 96
death, 89, 99
Byrne, Charlie, 143
Byrne, Crona, 4, 17–18, 70, 113,
    118–19, 120
school, 97–8
adoption, 114–16
and Russell Murphy, 133, 136,
    138
and America, 209
Byrne, Daniel, 5
Byrne, Dorothy, 30, 32
Byrne, Eddie, 86
Byrne, Edward (father), 1, 5, 19,
    20, 30, 55–6
in Guinness's, 6–7
and Annie, 6, 8–9, 35
relations with sons, 9–10
death, 10, 11–12, 76

wartime experience, 10–11, 67
and Al, 26
Bray holidays, 49
Byrne, Ernest, 1, 10, 18, 28–33,
    39, 78, 105
and RTE, 30–31, 88
school, 44
Byrne, Eva, 14, 16
Byrne, Frances, 4, 28, 99, 127–8
Byrne, Gabriel Mary, 28
youth
    health, 8
    relations with father, 9–10,
        16–17, 52
    Rialto St, 18–19, 37–43, 47–8,
        51–4
    apple theft, 42–3
    First Communion, 43–4
    Confirmation, 46–7
    Bray holidays, 49–50
    South Circular Road, 54–8
    Findlater's, 62–3
schooldays
    Rialto national school, 43–4
    Brown Street school, 44–5
    St Teresa's CBS, 45–6
    Synge Street CBS, 59–71
career
    insurance companies, 76, 79,
        80, 84
    broadcasting apprentice,
        76–88
    Granada TV, 87–8, 89, 103
    RTE, 88–9, 106–8, 221–9
    BBC TV, 103–4, 106–8
    abuse received by, 187–9,
        198–200, 231–4
    American prospects, 203–10,
        242
    lack of privacy, 236–9
    honorary degree, 1–4, 242

□

Late Late Show, 84, 106–8, 134, 152–86, 210, 218, 225
  complaints about, 156, 159–65, 221–2
  'Bishop and the Nightie', 159–64
  Trevaskis affair, 164–5
  first show, 168
  Franks v. O'Connor, 168–70
  10th anniversary, 178–9
  R. D. Laing, 196–8
marriage, 120–23
  engagement, 100–102
  wedding, 104–5
  fatherhood, 114–19
  25th anniversary, 242–3
and Russell Murphy, 124–51
  power of attorney, 134, 144
  death, 137–40
  revelation of theft, 140–42
  consequences of theft, 142–6, 148–51, 230, 242
and Éamonn Andrews, 78, 82, 105, 114, 124–5, 210, 244
Howth, 110–11
Dungloe, 111–14, 145
'Gay Byrne Show', 142, 211–20
style of broadcasting, 229–36
character, 240–45
Byrne, Jack Keyes
 see Leonard, Hugh
Byrne, John, 5
Byrne, Joseph, 18
Byrne, Joyce, 21–2, 55
Byrne, Kathleen, 5, 6, 14, 16
Byrne, Louis, 97, 105
Byrne, Mary
 see Orr, Mary
Byrne, Mary, Snr, 5
Byrne, Patrick, 5

Byrne, Ray (Edward), 1, 10, 17, 33, 44, 55, 72, 78, 105
 career, 19–22, 29
Byrne, Richard, 5, 6, 16
Byrne, Robert, 5
Byrne, Suzy, 4, 70, 98, 113, 119, 120
 adoption, 116, 117
 and Russell Murphy, 133, 136, 138
 and America, 209
 Confirmation, 242
Byrne, Thomas, 5
Byrne, William, 5

C
Caden, John, 143, 179, 212–13
Cahill, 48,
Cahn, Sammy, 189–90, 192
Caine, Michael, 244
Callaghan, Maureen, 92
Campbell, Colm, 18, 48–51, 57, 58, 69, 71, 82
 musician, 56
 school, 63–4
 sports grind, 83
 girl-friends, 90, 92–3
Campbell, Noel, 58
Carmichael, Coralie, 77
Carroll, Annie
 see Byrne, Annie
Carroll, Don, 137
Carroll, Kathleen
 see Byrne, Kathleen
Carroll, Lizzie, 5
Carroll, Maggie, 5
Carroll, Tessie, 5
Carroll, Tommy, 5
Carson, Johnny, 203, 205
Cassidy, Larry, 111–12, 138

Cassidy family, 40
Castellaine, George, 102
Chieftains, The, 166
Clancy, Liam, 172
Collins, Kevin, 119–20
Collins, Pan, 117, 119–20, 176,
178–80, 196, 236
Collins, Ronan, 202
Como, Perry, 78
Connolly, Billy, 185–6
Connolly, Maura, 141–2, 145,
150, 155, 197, 241
Conroy, Bronwyn, 131, 132, 147
Conroy, Sheila, 225
Coogan, Tim Pat, 176
Cooney, Mr, 13–14
Copeman, Dina, 57
Copeman, Mr, 57–8
Costello, Declan, 137
Coyle, Mr, 78–9
Cronin, Adrian, 84–5, 88
and 'Late Late Show', 108, 170,
171, 187, 196–7
Crosby, Bing, 68
Crowley, Laurence, 147, 151
Cruise, Jack, 50, 81
Cuddy, Joe, 184
Culliton, Clive, 9
Culliton, Jim, 64, 225
Cummins, Danny, 168
Cusack, Cyril, 137
Cusack, Peter, 83
Cusack, Sinéad, 181–2, 194

D
Dargan, Michael, 137
Davis, Derek, 202
Day-Lewis, Daniel, 244
de Burgh, Chris, 172–3
de Manio, Jack, 129

de Valera, Éamon, 167, 217
Dell, Peggy, 166
Deutsch, George, 105
Deutsch, Julia, 105–6
Devine, Mr, 163
Dignam, Conor, 134, 136, 140, 141
Dillon, James, 109
Din Joe, 98
Doherty, Jim, 193
Donahue, 205
Donnelly, Nuala, 99
Donoghue, Oliver, 179
Dooge, James, 2
Doolan, Dermot, 43, 81
Doolan, Mr, 43, 81
Doonican, Val, 50, 172
Dorsey, Jerry
see Humperdinck, Engelbert
Douglas, Mike, 205
Doyle, Jack, 21
Doyle, Ursula, 99
Dubliners, The, 166
Duffy, Mr, 44
Duignan, Claire, 177
Dunne, Ben, 240
Dunne family, 40

E
Edwards, Hilton, 78
Edwards, Jeanne, 28
Ekland, Britt, 174
Esposito, Michele, 57
Everett, Geoffrey, 68

F
Farmer, Colette, 177
Farrell, Brian, 129, 137, 151, 201
Fawcett, Marie
see Russell Murphy, Marie
Feeney, John, 156–7

Finlay, Tom, 137
Finn, T. Vincent, 150, 224, 225
Finucane, Marian, 159
Fitzpatrick, Harry, 69–70
Fitzpatrick, Val, 81
Flanagan, Oliver, 156
Flavin, Nick, 100
Flood, Finbar, 16
Flood, Jack, 14, 16, 39
Flynn, Deirdre, 94
Foley, Linda, 88
Fonda, Jane, 201
Foster, Dr, 90
Fox, Mr and Mrs, 159
Foyle, Joe, 155
Fraiberg, Larry, 204–5, 210
Franks, Dennis, 168–70
French, Percy, 172
Friel, Brian, 244
Frost, David, 205

G
Gageby, Douglas, 151
Gallagher, Fr Raphael, 188
Gannon, Seán, 137
Geldof, Bob, 173
George, Susan, 200, 201
Giblin, Tommy, 59
Giltrap, Gerald, 1
Glynn, Alan, 80
Godfrey, Cardinal, 226
Gogan, Larry, 81, 143
Goodgame, Tom, 204–5
Goodman, Benny, 70
Graves, Elizabeth, 78
Graves, Robert, 67
Gray, Ken, 168
Greally, Des, 89
Green, Philip, 83
Greevy, Bernadette, 2
Griffin, Merv, 205

Griffin family, 40
Grogan, Vincent, 155, 165
Grundy, Bill, 87, 103–4
Guinness, Arthur,
   Lord Ardilaun, 7
Guinness, Benjamin, 7
Guinness, Edward Cecil, 7

H
Hafner, Mr, 91
Haines, Arthur, 180
Hall, Frank, 106
Hambro, Jocelyn, 132
Hamp, Johnny, 103
Hanly, David, 238
Hardiman, Tom, 224
Harkin, Róisín, 155
Harpur, Bill, 192
Harris, Emmylou, 197
Harvey, Sir Charles, 76
Haughey, Charles, 187, 214, 243
Healy, John, 137
Healy, Shay, 202
Hearne, Dana, 179
Hearne, Mr, 43
Hederman, Carmencita, 2
Heffernan, Fr Brendan, 105, 160
Heffernan, George, 40
Heffernan, Kevin, 2, 40
Heffernan, Tommy, 40, 42
Henchy, Séamus, 129, 151
Hepburn, Audrey, 79–80
Herrema, Dr Tiede, 218
Hewitt, Tim, 77, 87
Hickey, Des, 51
Hickey, Kieran, 51
Higgins, Seán, 48
Hill, Dick, 204, 228
Hilliard, Michael, 88
Hodnett, George, 168
Hoey family, 40

☐

Hollingsworth, John, 40
Hollingsworth, Nick, 40
Hood, David, 102
Hope, Bob, 68
Horgan, Sr Columban, 44
Horgan, Sr Killian, 44
Horne, Kenneth, 68–9
Hothouse Flowers, The, 173–4
Howland, Chris, 87–8
Humperdinck, Engelbert, 243–4
Hutchinson, Coleman, 179–80

I
Illsley, Stanley, 81–2
Incomparable Benzini Brothers,
   The, 173–4
Irvine, John, 224
Ives, Burl, 172

J
Jackson, T. Lesley, 104
James, Harry, 70
'John-Joe', 67–8

K
Kavanagh, John, 60–61
Keane, Marie, 180–81
Kelly, David, 137
Kelly, Dermot, 180–81, 190
Kelly, Henry, 228
Kelly, James Plunkett, 67, 243
Kelly, Seán, 167
Kenna family, 40
Kennedy, Grace, 222–4
Kennelly, Brendan, 4
Kerr, Deborah, 104, 194
Kiel, Richard, 166
Killeen, Florrie, 39
Killeen, Michael, 137
Killeen, Nan, 39
Krupa, Gene, 70

L
Laing, R. D., 196–200
Langan, Tommy, 69
Lanza, Mario, 190
Lavelle, Fr Paul, 136
Layde, Pat, 76, 80
Lemass, Seán, 108
Lennox, Don, 170
Lentin, Louis, 170
Leonard, Hugh, 2, 49, 136, 148,
   151
Levine, June, 154, 155
Leyden, Miss, 43
Linehan, Rosaleen, 244
Linnane, Joe, 86, 88, 110, 211
Logan, Johnny, 143
Longstreet, Joe, 21
Lovett, Ann, 217
Luce, Dr J.V., 1
Lucey, Bro. (Guck), 63–6
Lydon, Jim, 155
Lynch, Fr Bernard, 154
Lynch, Jack, 137, 222–4
Lynch, Joe, 80, 156

M
McAnally, Ray, 244
McCabe, Leo, 81–2
McCann, Dónal, 97
McCann, John, 97
McCarthy, J. A., 77
McCarthy, Niall, 204
McColgan, John, 241
Mac Conghail, Muiris, 238
McCormack, Count Cyril, 168
McCourt, Kevin, 160–62, 165,
   224
McCusker, Patricia, 90
McGahern, John, 164
McGarry, Ian, 143
McGovern, George, 197–8, 200

McGowran, Jack, 195
McGrail, J. A., 62
McGrath, Tom, 84, 167–8, 239
McHugh, John, 154, 179–80
McKay, Dr, 90
McKay, Miss, 90–91
McKenna, Siobhán, 125, 137
McKenna, T.P., 77, 125, 126, 137, 148, 151
McKenzie, Richard, 192
McLean, Don, 172
Mac Liammóir, Mícheál, 61, 78, 166
MacManus, Frank, 66
MacNally, Dónal, 93, 94–5
MacNally, John, 93, 95
MacNally, Tom, 93
McNamara, Frank, 244
McNamara, Michael, 97
McPherson, Stuart, 73
McQuaid, Dr John Charles, Abp of Dublin, 4, 24, 25, 46, 57, 156–7, 165
McStay, Colin, 218
McStay, Margaret, 218
McWeeney, Myles, 179
Madigan, Mr, 52
Magee, Jimmy, 166
Mahoney, Denis (Din Joe), 98
Malagnini, Mario, 172
Malone, Joe, 80, 133
Maloney, Jack, 111, 144
Marron, Jamie, 218
Martin, Linda, 143
Martin, Mary, 143
Mason, James, 104
Maura, Sr, 188
Meagher, John, 211
Meath, Earl of, 5
Meleady, Fr, 24–5

Metcalfe, Ken, 80
Metcalfe, Norman, 80
Miller, Dr Jonathan, 180
Mitchell, Jim, 214
Moloney, Paddy, 2
Monaghan, Christy, 42–3
Monaghan, Mike, 88
Mooney, Seán, 81
Moore, Diarmuid, 155
Moore, Paddy, 51
Morris, Jan, 236
Morris, Stewart, 104
Movita, 21
Moynihan, George, 204–5, 210
Moynihan, Mr, 45–6
Mullen, Verona, 168
Murnane, Mrs, 56
Murphy, Johnny, 50
Murphy, Mike, 121, 201, 220, 239–40
'Murphy, Mrs', 157
Murphy, Tom, 229
Murray, Pete, 68

N
Nash, Cecil, 81
Nelson, Havelock, 57
Nelson, Justin, 122
Newport, Phil, 33
Nicholson, Viv, 197
Niven, David, 193–4
Notaro, Anita, 155
Nulty, Frank, 23, 24

O
Ó Braonáin, Fiachna, 173–4
Ó Briain, Liam, 167
O'Brien, Conor Cruise, 165
O'Brien, Joan, 156
O'Connor, Mr, 52

O'Connor, Des, 190, 192, 200, 201
O'Connor, Donald, 205–6
O'Connor, Fr Fergal, 158
O'Connor, Sinéad, 173
O'Connor, Ulick, 126, 168–70, 197–8
O'Conor, John, 244
O'Dea, Jimmy, 99
O'Donovan, Bill, 74
O'Donovan, Fred, 74, 129, 221, 222, 225
O'Donovan, Sheila, 103, 227
Ó Faracháin, Roibeard, 87
O'Grady, Denis, 170
O'Hagan, Patrick, 31
Ó hAodha, Mícheál, 86, 87
O'Hara, Mary, 94, 172
O'Higgins, Tom, 137
O'Kennedy, Desmond, 80–81, 84
Ó Laoghaire, Bill, 66
O'Leary, Olivia, 151
Olivier, Laurence, 78
Ó Maonlaí, Liam, 173–4
Ó Móráin, Dónal, 156
O'Neill, Frank G., 77
O'Neill, Sergeant, 51
Onjejokwi, Ariwodo Kalunte, 24
O'Reilly, Brendan, 105
O'Reilly, Fr, 56
O'Reilly, Tony, 127, 240
O'Rourke, Tommy, 59–60
Orr, David, 4, 33–4, 89, 96
Orr, Mary, 8, 17, 18, 19, 24, 55, 76, 89, 99, 208
 father's death, 11–12
 marriage, 33–6
 and mother, 34–5
Osborne, Tony, 104
O'Shea, Milo, 67, 180
O'Sullivan, Marie, 99

O'Sullivan, Mary, 196
O'Toole, Laurence, 18

P
Pakenham-Walsh, A. A., 48
Parker, Mrs, 13
Plowright, David, 88, 103
Plowright, Joan, 103
Potter, Maureen, 1, 2, 81, 244
Prestige, Jack, 24, 28, 42
Previn, Dory, 182
Purcell, Noel, 166

Q
Quigley, Godfrey, 137
Quinlan, Derek, 150
Quinn, Feargal, 2, 240
Quinn, Mickey, 17, 24, 25

R
Raeburn, Anna, 221
Reed, Oliver, 200, 201
Reeves, Christopher, 208
Richardson, Eric, 33
Rippon, Angela, 166
Roach, Hal, 81, 166, 184
Roche, Kevin, 83–4, 227, 242
Rogers, Ginger, 192, 193
Ronald, Ronnie, 93
Rosarie, Sr, 44
Roth, Ed, 224
Ruane, Brigid, 154
Rugheimer, Gunnar, 106–8, 160–62, 227,
Russell Murphy, Charles, 89, 124–51, 203, 230, 242
 extravagance, 125–6, 132, 144, 147–8
 drinking, 130–32
 Lourdes visits, 130–32

and Bronwyn Conroy, 131, 132, 147
power of attorney, 134, 144
illness, 135–6
death, 136–40
revelation of embezzlement, 140–42
Russell Murphy, Frank, 126, 128
Russell Murphy, Henry, 126, 128
Russell Murphy, Marie, 126–8, 136, 140, 145, 147
Russell Murphy, Paula, 126, 128
Ryan, Cornelius, 67
Ryan, Dermot, 80
Ryan, Dr Thomas, Bp of Clonfert, 159–64
Ryan, Gerry, 202, 220
Ryan, Tony, 240

S
Sellers, Miranda, 194–5
Sellers, Peter, 194–5
Shaw, Breda, 90
Shaw, George Bernard, 72
Sheehy, Tom, 190–92
Sheeran, Joanie, 158
Silkin, John, 158
Sin, Madame, 221
Sinatra, Frank, 78
Smith, Brendan, 126
Spring, Dick, 137, 187
Stafford, James, 219
Stalker, John, 149, 174
Stanley, Dónal, 87
Stapleton, Jimmy, 51
Streep, Meryl, 201
Strieber, Whitley, 184
Summerfield, Teddy, 103
Sutherland, Peter, 137
Sweeney, Miss, 43
Sweeney, Paddy, 114

Sweeney, Patsy, 112, 113, 143
Synge, John Millington, 72

T
Teidt, Fred, 50
Teresa, Mother, 174
Thompson, Christy, 45
Thorn, Leo, 82
Thornley, David, 155
Thuillier, Harry, 168
Tierney, Gerry, 69–70
Tóibín, Colm, 156
Tolan, Ann, 99–100
Trevaskis, Brian, 164–5
Tutty, Arthur, 84

U
U2, 173
Ustimenko, Irena, 176
Ustimenko, Uri, 176
Ustinov, Peter, 190–92

V
Viney, Michael, 99

W
Wall, Billy, 211, 212
Walsh, Brian, 137
Walshe, Ronnie, 86, 106, 137
Waters, George, 150, 204
Watkins, Clare, 97, 135
Watkins, Dinah, 97
Watkins, Jim, 97, 164
Watkins, Kathleen, 1, 4, 28, 62, 76, 87, 89, 176, 239, 241
career, 94, 98–9
RTE announcer, 99
'Faces and Places', 122
Arts Council, 243
marriage, 93–108, 120–23
engagement, 100–102

wedding 104–5
motherhood, 114–19
privacy, 120–21
rumours, 208
25th anniversary, 242–3
TB, 98, 99, 114
Howth, 110–11
and Russell Murphy, 125, 126,
133, 135, 141–2, 145, 148,
150–51
and Peter Sellers, 194–5
and American prospects, 205,
208, 209
Watkins, Phil, 4, 97
Watkins, Tom, 97
Whelan, Marty, 202
Whelan, Seán, 166
Whicker, Alan, 220
Whiston, 64
White, Olive, 99
Whitty, Mr, 48
Widmark, Richard, 178–9
Williams, Des, 132
Williams, John, 241
Williams, Kenneth, 68–9
Willis, Douglas, 225–6
Wogan, Terry, 73, 143–4, 228
Wynne, Janet, 88

Y
York, Michael, 196
Young, John, 84